The Series in Death, Dying, and Bereavement
Consulting Editor
Robert A. Neimeyer

Beder — Voices of Bereavement: A Casebook for Grief Counselors
Berger — Music of the Soul: Composing Life Out of Loss
Davies — Shadows in the Sun: The Experiences of Sibling Bereavement in Childhood
Jeffreys — Helping Grieving People — When Tears Are Not Enough: A Handbook for Care Providers
Harvey — Perspectives on Loss: A Sourcebook
Katz & Johnson — When Professionals Weep: Emotional and Countertransference Responses in End-of-Life Care
Klass — The Spiritual Lives of Bereaved Parents
Leenaars — Lives and Deaths: Selections from the Works of Edwin S. Shneidman
Lester — Katie's Diary: Unlocking the Mystery of a Suicide
Martin & Doka — Men Don't Cry...Women Do: Transcending Gender Stereotypes of Grief
Nord — Multiple AIDS-Related Loss: A Handbook for Understanding and Surviving a Perpetual Fall
Roos — Chronic Sorrow: A Living Loss
Rosenblatt — Parent Grief: Narratives of Loss and Relationship
Rosenblatt & Wallace — African-American Grief
Silverman — Widow to Widow, Second Edition
Tedeschi & Calhoun — Helping Bereaved Parents: A Clinician's Guide
Werth — Contemporary Perspectives on Rational Suicide

Formerly the Series in Death Education, Aging, and Health Care
Consulting Editor
Hannelore Wass

Bard — Medical Ethics in Practice
Benoliel — Death Education for the Health Professional
Bertman — Facing Death: Images, Insights, and Interventions
Brammer — How to Cope with Life Transitions: The Challenge of Personal Change
Cleiren — Bereavement and Adaptation: A Comparative Study of the Aftermath of Death
Corless & Pittman-Lindeman — AIDS: Principles, Practices, and Politics, Abridged Edition
Corless & Pittman-Lindeman — AIDS: Principles, Practices, and Politics, Reference Edition
Curran — Adolescent Suicidal Behavior
Davidson — The Hospice: Development and Administration. Second Edition
Davidson & Linnolla — Risk Factors in Youth Suicide
Degner & Beaton — Life–Death Decisions in Health Care
Doka — AIDS, Fear, and Society: Challenging the Dreaded Disease
Doty — Communication and Assertion Skills for Older Persons
Epting & Neimeyer — Personal Meanings of Death: Applications for Personal Construct Theory to Clinical Practice
Haber — Health Care for an Aging Society: Cost-Conscious Community Care and Self-Care Approaches
Hughes — Bereavement and Support: Healing in a Group Environment
Irish, Lundquist, & Nelsen — Ethnic Variations in Dying, Death, and Grief: Diversity in Universality
Klass, Silverman, & Nickman — Continuing Bonds: New Understanding of Grief
Lair — Counseling the Terminally Ill: Sharing the Journey
Leenaars, Maltsberger, & Neimeyer — Treatment of Suicidal People
Leenaars & Wenckstern — Suicide Prevention in Schools
Leng — Psychological Care in Old Age
Leviton — Horrendous Death, Health, and Well-Being
Leviton — Horrendous Death and Health: Toward Action
Lindeman, Corby, Downing, & Sanborn — Alzheimer's Day Care: A Basic Guide
Lund — Older Bereaved Spouses: Research with Practical Applications
Neimeyer — Death Anxiety Handbook: Research, Instrumentation, and Application
Papadatou & Papadatos — Children and Death
Prunkl & Berry — Death Week: Exploring the Dying Process
Ricker & Myers — Retirement Counseling: A Practical Guide for Action
Samarel — Caring for Life and Death
Sherron & Lumsden — Introduction to Educational Gerontology. Third Edition
Stillion — Death and Sexes: An Examination of Differential Longevity Attitudes, Behaviors, and Coping Skills
Stillion, McDowell, & May — Suicide Across the Life Span — Premature Exits
Vachon — Occupational Stress in the Care of the Critically Ill, the Dying, and the Bereaved

Wass & Corr — Childhood and Death
Wass & Corr — Helping Children Cope with Death: Guidelines and Resource. Second Edition
Wass, Corr, Pacholski, & Forfar — Death Education II: An Annotated Resource Guide
Wass & Neimeyer — Dying: Facing the Facts. Third Edition
Weenolsen — Transcendence of Loss over the Life Span
Werth — Rational Suicide? Implications for Mental Health Professionals

Music of the Soul

Composing Life Out of Loss

Joy S. Berger

Routledge
Taylor & Francis Group
New York   London

Routledge is an imprint of the
Taylor & Francis Group, an informa business

Published in 2006 by
Routledge
Taylor & Francis Group
270 Madison Avenue
New York, NY 10016

Published in Great Britain by
Routledge
Taylor & Francis Group
2 Park Square
Milton Park, Abingdon
Oxon OX14 4RN

Printed in the United States of America on acid-free paper
10 9 8 7 6 5 4 3 2 1

International Standard Book Number-10: 0-415-95481-9 (Softcover)
International Standard Book Number-13: 978-0-415-95481-5 (Softcover)
Library of Congress Card Number 2006007948

Library of Congress Cataloging-in-Publication Data

Berger, Joy S., 1959-
   Music of the soul : composing life out of loss / Joy S. Berger.
      p. cm.
   Includes bibliographical references (p.   ) and index.
   1. Music therapy. I. Title.

ML3920.B427 2006
615.8'5154--dc22   2006007948

Taylor & Francis Group
is the Academic Division of Informa plc.

Visit the Taylor & Francis Web site at
http://www.taylorandfrancis.com

and the Routledge Web site at
http://www.routledge-ny.com

CONTENTS

SERIES EDITOR'S FOREWORD

Music—as a series of sounds and silences—does not in itself have the power to take people to deep places within, to animate their spirits, or to promote their healing. But as *Music of the Soul* amply illustrates, the inevitable interactions between music and a given individual's memories, emotions, meanings, physical responses and cultural and historical contexts most certainly do. This book is about the power of melding mind and melody, sound and symbol, in the pursuit of profound healing of those facing death and loss.

In these pages, musician, chaplain and healer Joy Berger offers a view of music as both an elastic metaphor and practical method for working with loss in its many forms, ranging from progressive dementia, through the experience of dying, to the challenges of bereavement for those whose lives continue. Berger's writing is musically literate in the best sense, prompting the reader to apply the analogy of themes and counterthemes in a *fugue* or *sonata* to the emotional vicissitudes of unsought transitions, or to follow the development of a symphonic composition and to recognize its parallel to our own development across the lifespan, from our opening *overture* to our final *coda*. Through a felicitous mix of stirring stories, poetic prose, and engaging exercises, Berger draws the reader into a rich trove of musical metaphors for understanding life's progressions, suspensions and resolutions in fresh ways, providing real resources for helping people with the tasks of mourning, memorializing, and moving on.

Part of what makes this book so successful is Berger's total lack of pretentiousness, whether writing for a professional music therapist or a lay reader wholly unfamiliar with music theory. For example, in the face of emotionally difficult material, her penchant for alliteration and word play consistently diminishes defensiveness, inspires insights and creates connections—even for a reader who begins with a sense of uncertainty about his or her own "musicality." Likewise, her effective use of mnemonic devices that help people HEAL (Hear, Explore, Affirm, and Learn) and apply CORE principles (Care, Ownership, Respect, Empowerment) to the helping relationship extend to and through music therapy interventions to illuminate the process of living itself, even in the shadow of loss. No mere cookbook, *Music of the Soul* is a resonant resource manual for coordinating a vast range of creative interventions in the service of helping and healing.

But potential readers would be misled if they understood this to be an abstract book of theory. Instead, these pages contain dozens upon dozens of concrete tools for working with grieving children and teens, bereaved spouses, support groups, the frail elderly and patients with no access to language—at least the language of words. Appendices deepen the learning stimulated by each chapter by fostering further reflection upon and active experimentation with key concepts and methods. Extensive lists of print and web-based sources extend the range of a volume already replete with discussions of the therapeutic potential of musical work of nearly every conceivable genre, from gospel music and popular show tunes to world music and classical compositions. Virtually everything imaginable seems to be covered in practical detail, often formulated as step-by-step "teaching guides" and applications with broad relevance to end-of-life and bereavement care. Linking music therapy concepts and procedures to contemporary theories featuring phases of mourning, tasks of grieving and meaning reconstruction, Berger demonstrates how music articulates with each of these models, ultimately both validating our individuality and building community.

In conclusion, in *Music of the Soul* Berger has orchestrated a major piece of work, one that is in a single stroke both universal and deeply personal in its resonance. I recommend it highly for all of those who seek to reach where words cannot, and join more deeply with those they serve in seeking to compose life out of loss.

Robert A. Neimeyer, Ph.D
Series Editor
April 2006

PREFACE

Music of the Soul: Composing Life Out of Loss was born out of my own loss and grief, over a span of 15 years. Days after completing my doctoral written comprehensive exams in piano performance and psychology of religion, my physician told me, "It's been six months and your hands aren't healing. You have to find a new profession." My music was over? It had been my life, since I was a child. My music professors grasped the horror of my loss. My psychology professors wisely cautioned me against continuing the two years of dissertation research I had already invested in music and grief. They suggested I change my topic to something less personal. I struggled with their words for a week and then voiced, "but the best growth is born in the darkness of the soul." (One of my last piano pieces had been Beethoven's pivotal Sonata Opus 101 in A major, composed in deafness, and marking transformations of his style. It was for a lecture recital on music and grief.) They warned, "You'll get stuck in your own process." I agreed. I probably would. Also, "I'm willing to take that risk. What do you think happens in my practice room everyday? I stretch to learn and do more. I hit limits of what I can't do. I play to find my way through and create artistry from within." Since a teen, I passionately wanted my music "to touch people where they laugh, hurt, and cry." I now added, "and survive."

Thus, I entered my own world of music's memories, pain, comfort, and healing. The same music that had brought joy (and "Joy," my sense of self), now struck pain. Extensive grief and loss literature, notably Colin Parkes' *Bereavement: Studies of Grief in Adult Life* (1987) and William Worden's *Grief Counseling and Grief Therapy* (1991) informed me that what I was experiencing was normal. Hope and healing could be found. My new practice rooms included personal exploration, interdisciplinary research and writing, clinical supervision, and professional accountability (i.e., board certifications in chaplaincy and music therapy). My playing shifted from external piano keyboards to internal emotions, thoughts, and meanings. My ingrained patterns for learning and playing music modulated to learning and playing life: its rhythms, themes, harmonics, styles, and expressions; its essence, creativity, and artistry. More recently, Robert Neimeyer's work on "Meaning Reconstruction" (2001) has validated and enlightened my paths of composing new "music" and creating new meanings, without cutting off the old.

Professionally, I moved faster and further into my pastoral care and music therapy paths. In 1993, hospice became yet another music room. Death and Life became my teachers. As chaplain and music therapist, my new roles were to hear and explore others' "life music," sometimes with literal music, sometimes without. To affirm and learn from and with hospice patients and families. To sustain through life's harsh truths and fragile hopes. To prepare for death. To guide (when wanted). In the midst of loss and brokenness, to heal toward wholeness. This book celebrates the diverse persons I have been privileged to know as a musician, chaplain, music therapist, and now as hospice educator and administrator.

Choosing to not closet myself away in our home study, I created this book on a laptop computer in the living spaces of my home, in cafés, bookstores, and other places where people were milling about. Several vignettes were written in virtual time, illustrating music moments as they occurred. Whether written this year, 10 years ago, or 10 years from now, similar real life sound bytes would exist in any timeframe of writing or reading this book.

Music of the Soul sang out in early mornings with coffee mug nearby and our two dogs greeting the day with me. It grounded me before entering my day's work at hospice. My writing was accompanied by countless CDs and music DVDs, drinking in sounds and sights around. *Music of the Soul* played out its themes in my everyday scores of schedules and improvisations of relating. It was harmonized by my husband's steadfast support. Countless behind-the-scenes daily events were catalysts for portions of this text. John Reed, thank you for do-be-do-being life with artistry and depth, within yourself, and with me (see chapter 5 for "do-be-do-being").

Persons to thank are numerous: family, friends, teachers, colleagues, musicians, ministers, therapists, hospice professionals and volunteers, and oh so many hospice patients and families who have let me know you, and be known by you. Thank you. Our stories are interwoven through this book. Of special note, I thank Jake and Jane Berger, my parents. From an early age on, you empowered me to play my music and explore my paths.

Communities to thank are extensive: hospice, musical, pastoral care, academic, faith, and neighborhood gatherings. No matter how geographically close or scattered we may be, you have given me space to learn, to stretch, and to work out many of the concepts of this book, both musically and metaphorically. Season through season, we experience life and death and everything in between. Of note, the ecumenical faith community of St. Luke's Chapel at The Episcopal Church Home in Louisville gives me a place each Sunday to simultaneously be organist (I can play for short periods), music therapist, and pastoral caregiver through music with our Alzheimer's residents and vital, full-of-life members.

To Bob Neimeyer (editor of this series) and Dana Bliss (Routledge editor), I voice my deep gratitude. You took a risk with this musician's manuscript. You let me keep my style. These hands got to play at a different keyboard, composing life anew.

Now, it is my turn to invite you, readers, to turn the page and enter your own music of the soul. May the sounds stirred within touch you where you laugh, hurt, cry...and survive.

Joy S. Berger, DMA, BCC, MT-BC
Louisville, Kentucky

CHAPTER 1

Music of the Soul — Composing Life Out of Loss

Music of the Soul
What music moves you?
Gets into or comes out of your being?

Music of the Soul
What music expresses your unique essence?
Voices your core self?

Music of the Soul
What is it?

☐ It's About Life
☐ Music of the Soul: Terminology and Metaphors
☐ Readers' Personal Applications
☐ Composing Life in the Midst of Loss

Music of the soul is any music that moves you to your core, innermost part of yourself. Music's animating sound waves join in playful patterns of rhythms, melodies, harmonies, and forms. All civilizations, cultures, and religions give homage to the soul through their unique music. For readers of this book your music may be classical, jazz, gospel, rap, country, new age, ancient chanting, drumming, or something altogether new. Whatever its style, it taps into your core being. Your music of your soul calls forth a new response in the "hear" and now. Imagine:

> You're driving your car, with the radio providing a background pulse as you wind your way through traffic. Opening bars strike a familiar sound, and you're suddenly back in time — and you're in the present — both at the same time. Your heart and mind are thrown into an Oz-like world of chaotic yet connected images, emotions, and "aha" moment meanings of where and who you were back then, and where and who you are now.
>
> Your music weaves together stories of your earliest childhood and most significant life moments. Simultaneously, it can evoke both celebration and sorrow; old meanings interwoven with new; fear and hope. Your music within can provide a *fermata*[1] holding space for memories and meanings, and a gentle release into renewal.

☐ It's About Life

What music sings your emotions and thoughts? What music resonates with your core self, deep within? What music helps you experience and express life more fully? What music shifts you to a different space-place from where you would be had you not experienced the music? What music transforms something within you?

Heads up. A theme of this book is that music of the soul is about *life*. Music sings out lullaby laughter and funeral fears, and every life experience in between. It teaches language ("ABCDEFG...") and woos new love. Music marks time through the ages and for all ages: from cavemen's drumming to today's L.A. Hood raps; and from ancient Egyptian flutes playing homage to pharaohs to today's *American Idol* craze for 15 minutes of fame. This book's music is about one's own life music that communicates an essence of one's "who I am" in the past and future, and especially now in the present.

For centuries, philosophers, musicians, and consumers have debated the age-old question: what music is best? Is it music for art's sake, or music that brings fame and fortune, or music that presents one's religious or political stance, or music that simply endures? Different answers lie in the perceptions of each reader. I ask: what music guides you toward knowing and understanding yourself better — toward expressing and enriching your life? Is it classical music, folk, rock, religious, new age, or something else? Is it a particular style, artist, or title?

While musicologists, critics, and popular music publishers endlessly debate criteria for defining good versus bad music, this author evaluates "music of the soul" using wholly (and "holy") different criteria. Good or bad music of the soul is less about the music and more about the person. The value is not in the music, but in the person's response to the music. It is found when the music shifts from being notes and sounds to stirring meaning within. Such music cannot be forced upon another. Instead, the music sensitively engages and empowers the person.

For you, what music has expressed your grief in the past? What music, today, can take you to places of loss and grief in the present? What music, for you, renews hope?

Music and Mourning

Nearly every civilization, culture, and religion exemplifies the use of music at times of loss and grief. Historical sound bytes from my Western civilization's backyard include:

- Plato (429–347 BCE), who emphasized music education for children, requested that musicians play at his funeral to protect his friends from sorrow and dejection (Hall, 1982, pp. 7–8).
- The nursery song, *"Ring around the rosy, pockets full of posies/Ashes, ashes, we all fall down,"* often is attributed to fear of the bubonic plague in England, in 1665, when "posies" of flowers were carried to ward off the odors of death (which were thought to carry the disease), and "ashes" having referred to either dead bodies or "attishoo" for sneezing, a symptom of the disease.
- Samuel Barber's Adagio for Strings, Opus 11 (1936), familiar to baby boomers from the movie *Platoon*, was played at the funerals of Presidents Franklin D. Roosevelt and John F. Kennedy. On today's news reports, portions of this work are often used to create audio backgrounds for somber photojournalism reflections (Barber, 1989).
- Louis Armstrong's classic "Do You Know What It Means to Miss New Orleans" voiced new meaning on Friday, September 2, 2005 (Armstrong, 2004). For days on end we witnessed flood, famine, and fear. New Orleans's sons, daughters, and adopted residents were leaving on bus after bus. Most could not know whom and what they were leaving, where they were going, or for how long. Harry Connick, Jr. poignantly sang this song to the world for his hometown, his family (his father had been mayor), and his dispersed community. Aaron Neville sang "Louisiana 1927," a ballad about an earlier devastating flood (Newman, 1974). Later in the TV broadcast,

New Orleans musician Wynton Marsalis and others joined Harry in playing Dixieland jazz, calling all to life in the midst of overwhelming sorrow. *The New Yorker* magazine captured New Orleans's musical soul on its cover with art titled, "Requiem" (Jaun, 2005). A solitary sax player plays on from a pier overlooking street signs of a flooded Bourbon Street.

- The list goes on. Many musical forms express grief and loss, flowing from ancient Greek odes through today's rap: the elegy, threnody, nenia, lament, planctus, dirge, troubadour songs, deploration, dumpe, plainte, requiem, spirituals, blues, hymns, folk songs, tragic opera, and ah, yes, country ballads. (More examples are provided in Appendix A, "Through the Ages: A Time Line of Western Grief Music.")

Music written or performed out of the musician's grief, and in turn evoking powerful responses in others can be found in virtually any Western music genre. Consider:

- Beethoven's dark "Tempest" Piano Sonata No. 17 in D minor, Opus 32 was written in the same months as his Heiligenstadter Testament, a suicide note, dated October 6, 1802. He was 32 when he wrote the letter, he had been losing his hearing for six years, a period when he was at the height of his musical career. In the testament he described his void, despair, and isolation from social life. Contrast this music with the joyful triumph of his 1827 "Ode to Joy" from his Symphony No. 9, No. 125 in D minor, Opus 125, composed in complete deafness. Musically, it juxtaposes both "horror" and "joy" themes. Its finale choral text (by Friedrich Schiller) celebrates the union of all mankind. Beethoven's mourning was transformed to the joy of morning.
- The beloved gospel song, "Precious Lord, Take My Hand," was written by Thomas Dorsey in a moment of heartbreak. While performing in St. Louis, his wife Nettie died in childbirth, far away in Chicago, and his newborn son died soon after. Upon learning the news, he penned this text. It was 1932, during the Great Depression. His personal prayer rapidly captured a country's struggles and hopes. He gave voice to those who felt tired, weak, and worn. His vivid imagery of storms and of night portrayed ongoing struggles of the era. He wrote as one who was well-acquainted with death and dying. He prayed to go "home" (Dorsey, 1933/1981). Connecting with countless personal stories, "Precious Lord, Take My Hand" has been recorded by such greats as Mahalia Jackson, Elvis Presley, Nina Simone, and Aretha Franklin. Decades later, it continues to be a favorite for funerals.

- Pink Floyd's popular, psychedelic "Wish You Were Here" (Floyd, 1975/2000a), was an ode to their former band leader Syd Barrett, who had left the band in 1968 due to repeated psychiatric crises. Another musical tribute to Syd, "Shine On You Crazy Diamond," explicitly deals with the aftermath of Syd's breakdown (Floyd, 1975/2000b).
- Eric Clapton's 1992 Grammy-winning "Tears in Heaven" (Clapton, 1992), was written for his 4-year old son, Conor, who died in a tragic fall from a 49th-floor Manhattan apartment in March 1991. Only months earlier, in August 1990, one of Eric's guitarists and two road crew members were killed in a helicopter crash.
- Tim McGraw's 2004 country song "Live Like You Were Dying" was recorded shortly after his father, Tug McGraw, died. It celebrates life anew because of facing death. In an interview, Tim described: "We were rehearsing when Tug was sick, and he died at the beginning of January. We were in the studio at the end of January, and we recorded this around 11:00 or 12:00 at night and everybody just poured a lot of heart and soul into it. I think you can hear that on the record" (Tim McGraw Official Page at GACTV.com, 2004). It became one of the fastest to-the-top singles ever on the market, and was named the 2004 Country Music "Song of the Year" (Nicols & Wiseman, 2004).

The list goes on. Listen further. Beyond your backyard. Over the river and through the woods past grandmother's house to others' homelands. World music examples of funerals and mourning include:

- funeral drums of Ghana;
- *famadihana* rituals in Madagascar;
- Mexico's annual "Day of the Dead" festival;
- the *qawwali* Sufi songs in Pakistan;
- the *kobi* panpipe orchestra of New Guinea;
- the *bajhan* Hindu devotional songs used throughout the mourning period;
- the Chinese Buddhist *sheng-guan*;
- the *bird songs* of the Hualapai Native Americans;
- the *Zari* folk song laments of Georgia;
- the *jazz band* funerals of New Orleans;
- and the Ashkenazic Jewish memorial prayer, Eyl Male Rakhamin. (Many audio examples can be found on *Dancing with the Dead*, Charno, 1998.)

Perhaps, even with our diverse dialects, are we more alike than different? Perhaps, when foreign languages separate us from dialogue, can experiencing each other's music bond us together? (In my head the African-American spiritual sings out, "There is a balm in Gilead to make the wounded whole."

Music for Being In and Moving through Grief

Throughout this book, we will discover music's comfort. We will delve into the stinging sorrow she can evoke. We will venture into the memories and meanings she can stir. We will define ways to use music to help us be in and move through mourning.

Music happens in the moment. Hear. Here. It sounds and moves on. Its sounds form patterns that, like an intricate web, create easy access to emotions, thoughts, memories, physical sensations, and meanings.

While music exists in the "hear" and now, it can call up the past. You are flooded with emotions and long-forgotten memories. You may feel warmed, lost, grateful, and deeply sad, all at the same time. You are reeled into previous experiences of this music, and you are faced with how life is different now.

Music can catapult us into the future. A song's text or context may confront you at undefended, emotional portals. Your silent fears, hopes, or beliefs about your future find voice. You have a powerful moment to be present to yourself. In your inner web of physical, emotional, mental, and spiritual responses, you have a myriad of directions in which you can choose to move.

Our journey through this book is less about an individual piece of music, and more about our experience of music. Too often, well-meaning people "prescribe" a particular piece of music without realizing they are trying to impose their own style and preference on another person. We will examine principles and techniques to focus on empowering the grieving person.

Our explorations will be grounded in contemporary loss–grief theory, music therapy research, music history examples, case studies, and reflective teaching exercises. Case studies represent this author's professional roles as musician, music therapist, and chaplain. Names and identifying facts are changed, except for those stories about Amy, Judy, and Rahul. Concepts remain consistent. Teaching exercises provide tools for you, the reader, to incorporate uses of music within (1) your personal life journey, and (2) your professional role with persons in loss and grief.

☐ Music of the Soul: Terminology and Metaphors

Beethoven proclaimed, "Music should strike fire within" (Crofton & Fraser, 1985, p. 58). I applaud. For persons in grief and loss, I caution: Does that fire warm or burn? Heal or harm? Scorch or fuel? We will explore these dynamics.

The phrase *music of the soul* denotes this ineffable quality of music to strike fire within. Aristotle, Plato, Shakespeare, and Einstein all contemplated music's profound powers (Crofton & Fraser, 1985; Einstein, 1917/1969; Einstein, 1941). Composers and musicologists have theorized about these phenomena for centuries. Words such as *soul*, *transformation*, and *life-changing* hold a spiritual quality. Though music therapy as a discipline has investigated music from an empirical, scientific, behavioral perspective, numerous music therapists demonstrate a shift toward integrating spiritual, transforming, relational, and transcendent qualities of music (Berger, 1993; Bonny, 2001; Bonny & Savary, 1973; Hesser, 2001; Lipe, 2001; Marshman, 2003; Rorke, 2000). For this book's purposes, the phrase *music of the soul* refers to any music that serves as a catalyst to better know and understand oneself, and more specific to this book, enables the individual to be in and move through life's losses and grief.

The term *music of the soul* reflects music's depth, breadth, universality, and individuality. Like Oz's Dorothy opening the door from black and white into a world of color, music of the soul opens a door into one's colorful, artistic self. For our purposes, "music" will be less about prescriptive pieces of music, and more about paths of self-understanding which music can reveal for us. For example, if there is a time, person, or place you would like to revisit, what music would take you there? By simply recalling the music, humming, singing, hearing, or talking about it, most of us easily take that visit, often in a nonthreatening, relationship-building moment of sharing bits of one's life story (see teaching guide 1.1).

Using grief theorists as a basis for grasping grief's processes (Neimeyer, 2001; Parkes, 2001; Worden, 2002), we will venture into our personal "Music of Memories," "Music of Mourning," "Music of Meaning," and "Music of Re-Membering and Moving On" (Berger, 1993). Historical examples, clinical case studies, and questions to readers illuminate these concepts.

Composing life out of loss refers to the phoenix archetype, creating fire and life out of ash. It does not discount the loss. It validates a sense of death within oneself, and a hope for survival and healing. Composing life empowers one to explore what the loss means and then to choose, or even create, one's forever changed life ahead. The phrase *out of loss* does not toss the loss aside, but rather uses the loss to move more freely into life ahead.

Composing life out of loss provides a contemporary phrase for our turn of the 21st century, culturally immersed senses, and humanities/liberal arts trained minds. It provides fresh tools for supporting ourselves and others through easily accessible, well-known modes for personal and community expression. Does any car not have a radio? Any home not have a TV? Do many people not own any music CDs, cassettes, or LPs? Most people have received some type of basic music education in school, or elsewhere. Music of the soul for composing life out of loss identifies those meaningful moments when music intersects with emotions, thoughts, and meanings within.

The theme of composing life is fleshed out in chapter titles that are based on music's core compositional elements: rhythm, melody (themes), harmony, style, and expression. (Check out any music education curriculum. Ask any performer about these elements when learning a new musical piece.) Chapter titles and content apply these basic music metaphors to life and to skills of tending oneself (or another) through loss and grief.

This book's music moves through life's losses into new beginnings. Music for beginning again affirms the risks and creativity inherent both in composing literal music, and in composing life after loss. Beethoven could have stopped paying attention to the music in his head. Eric Clapton could have put away his guitar. They chose to compose.

This book's readers need not be musicians. Chances are, you have already experienced music's powers at funerals, celebrations, religious or cultural gatherings, family moments, in your car, in your memories, or in the spontaneous song that pops into your head. Whether musicians or not, readers can learn simple ways to use everyday music for rich care, especially when loss hits hard. Many music examples represent American popular music, in order to connect with readers' repertoires of easy-to-recognize and easy-to-access music. Most music can be purchased through Internet searches, in either recording or score forms (i.e., http://www.amazon.com, or http://www.musicnotes.com).

Teaching guides for each chapter personalize concepts for readers. A simple cross-reference informs readers that a teaching guide develops the current text further. However, this author cautions: incorporating these principles and techniques into one's professional roles or personal life should not be confused with actually doing music therapy or being a music therapist. Those terms are reserved for trained, board certified professional music therapists. (For more information, see Certification Board for Music Therapists at http://www.cbmt.org and American Music Therapy Association at http://www.musictherapy.org.) Furthermore, because music holds such therapeutic power, without wishing to, or being aware that they are doing so, well-meaning persons can cause harm. This book intends to prevent naïve assumptions about and uses of music, and to provide meaningful ways to experience music when navigating one's way through loss.

Therapist/Healthcare/Hospice Applications and Roles

Teaching exercises encourage the reader to instill these concepts first for oneself, and then with others. "With others" means appropriate applications within one's role, relationship, training, and accountability. For example, interdisciplinary licensed professionals maintain accountability within one's own prescribed roles. A psychotherapist may glean musical tools to use when examining clients' memories, emotions, images, and meanings. A hospice team can learn ways to enhance pain and symptom management, encourage life-review, and engage family and friends in meaningful support. Guidelines are given for using music at vigil support, at the wake/visitation, funerals/memorial services, and through bereavement care. This author's theoretical framework synchronizes musical interventions with the person's grief processes (Parkes, 2001), tasks of mourning (Worden, 2002), and seasons of the soul (Berger, 1993). Music therapists can study loss–grief dynamics in depth, and apply them to their varied populations and settings, such as rehabilitation, special needs children, troubled teens, substance abuse, psychiatry, forensics, long-term care, hospitals, or palliative and hospice care. Throughout, CORE principles and HEALing techniques (acronyms) provide an easy to remember foundation for a wide range of professional and lay roles.

Musicians' Applications and Roles

For musician readers, whatever our roles, we can use music to touch people where they laugh, hurt, cry, and survive. We need musicians who perform with "soul," with musical artistry, and relational connection. We need music lyricists, composers, and publishers who use their skills not just for fame, money, and to entertain, but for expression, interpretation, and to give life to our living. We need music educators in our schools who can sensitively provide musical expression to children and teens who experience divorce, death, community crisis, or other serious losses. We musicians need each others' gifts to create, publish, teach, perform, and value music, with "soul." I hope this book's music examples and concepts will enliven your "aha" moments of music, deepen your own healing, and spark your artistic creativity.

☐ Readers' Personal Applications

Life is a continual flow of changes, endings, and beginnings (see teaching guide 1.2). They can accumulate in any increment and overflow at any time. Life's changes may meet my resistance or my welcome. Life's changes may hold fear or hope. How I deal with life's smaller losses affects how I cope with the large ones. How I face a huge loss will affect how I face my everyday ones. While certain patterns are well-ingrained in me, ultimately, I have many choices as to how I respond to my personal loss (Frankl, 1946/1963). As my previous life settles into ash, can I hear the new rhythms, find my voice, and compose my life ahead? Or can I at least arrange my life for new settings?

We often use the phrase *grief work*. I invite you to add to that *grief play*, not that grief is fun and joyful, but that we can approach it with hope instead of fear. A musician plays an instrument. Feel free to play and explore concepts from this book in your everyday life (see teaching guides 1.3, 1.4). The following questions to you, the reader, introduce the chapters ahead.

Chapter 2. Rhythms of Body and Soul

- Each of us creates rhythmic patterns for our day, for our week. Loss and stress can throw our patterns into chaos. Pull out your calendar. Are you able to keep the beat or do you feel out of synch? Play with musical tempos and terms to create better balance in your schedules.
- Feel the rhythms of your breathing, of your heartbeat. What music energizes you? Calls you to action? Calms you? Moves you into peace? Learn simple techniques to incorporate "3 D's of Music for Pain Management" into simple pain and symptom support.
- An ancient poet penned, "To everything there is a time and a season." How do you know when it is "time" for this season or that? Explore grief's seasons of the soul, reflecting on a major loss in your life (Berger, 1993).
- A huge loss throws your life into chaos. How might you use music for yourself, in synch with your personal timetable of grief? Explore grief's seasons of the soul, paired with (1) music of memories, (2) mourning, (3) meanings, and (4) remembering and moving on.

Chapter 3. Themes and Counterthemes of Life Stories

- Familiar melodies or lyrics can easily evoke memories and emotions that are filled with laughter, warmth, sadness, or deep meanings. The same song can evoke different, deeply personal associations for different persons. This phenomenon lays the groundwork for simple, nonthreatening questions that can open up one's life story, with great emotional and relational impact.
- Explore simple tools for using a musical phrase as a springboard toward dialogue and nonthreatening exploration related to a loss.

- Listen to your own everyday music. For example, what music are you listening to these days? What song or phrase pops into your head and will not leave you alone? What is your unconscious saying to you?
- Any symphony usually has a theme and countertheme that set up a creative tension, or an ongoing juxtaposition. Each of us has recurring themes and counterthemes in ourselves: independence and dependence; self-sufficiency and intimacy; family and career; risk and security; and others. Discover powerful metaphors from classical music forms for hearing the "music" in these creative tensions, versus battling one against the other. When loss occurs, how do these core themes and counterthemes affect your coping?
- Explore simple ways that music might open a window of memory for a loved one with dementia. Even if your loved one shows no response, the music experience may stir important reflections in you. How does your loved one's dementia affect you? What are you learning about your loved one; yourself; about life and living?
- Explore fresh aspects of your own life story:
  - What are your earliest memories of music? Who was there? What details do you remember? What emotions are you feeling, now, as you remember?
  - What music has been there for you in times of celebration? Tragedy and loss?
  - What music takes you to places within of comfort? Of hope?

Chapter 4. Harmonies and Dissonances of Healing

- Life as a repetitive C-major chord (C-E-G) would be boring. Add a B flat to that chord (C-E-G-B flat), and you long to resolve over to an F chord (C-F-A, or C-F-A flat). Like that B flat, what dissonances in your life have disrupted your nice, neat "harmony," and then taken you someplace new?
- What is your tolerance for "dissonance" in music? For dissonance within yourself? For dissonance with others? Whom might you better know and understand by stretching yourself to hear and understand that person's music? (Is there a teen in your house?) What dissonances in your belief system have been stirred by a recent loss?
- Rarely, if ever, does healing after loss imply everything is just fine. More often, one has a mixture of resolved and unresolved emotions, thoughts, and beliefs. Similarly, blues and jazz endings tend to have a just right blend of harmony and dissonance, of beauty and bittersweetness. Remember, blues and jazz were born out of "the blues." What for you, in a major loss, has resolved, and what is portrayed

by that jazz ending? Can you have a sense of completeness, in its incompleteness? A sense of personal wholeness, even with ongoing holes?

Chapter 5. Styles of Doing and Being

- What are your favorite styles of music? Do they correlate with how you "do" life? Consider classical music's structure, jazz's spontaneity, gospel's faith-based texts, folk music's simplicity, or popular music's connections to culture in a geographical area or timeframe in one's life. When loss hits, how does your standard style of doing life work for you? Not work for you?
- How do you feel when someone else tries to impose on you his or her styles of coping with loss?
- Getting through loss means both doing tasks of basic survival and being present to your emotions, thoughts, and evolving meanings. Explore creative tools for pairing the two together in everyday life.
- Definitions for "being" with another through loss and grief are borrowed from pastoral care: sustaining, guiding, healing, reconciling, confronting, and informing. Further, these are paired with music interventions and concepts from previous chapters.

Chapter 6. Expressions of Self and Community

- Identify a moment when music intersected with a significant loss. It gave voice to your silent emotions and thoughts. It may have called forth pain and joy at the same time. You felt cleansed and renewed. What was your own context at that time and what was the music?
- Use a variety of musical symbols and expressions to "score your day," identifying nuances you experience within, or changes you want to make.
- What did you learn as a child about expressing grief and coping with loss? Learn simple music techniques for helping children and teens express their loss and grief.
- Identify a variety of occasions when you experienced music's power at community events to unite persons, empower and transform, comfort, and transcend tragedy.
- What music moments involving loss and grief have occurred in world events in recent months? What do these teach us about our larger world and being in community with each other?

Chapter 7. The Final Cadence

- What music might you want at your funeral, and why?
- Explore what a cadence is, and its rich metaphors for life's endings. Similarly, examine a deceptive cadence, and identify one in your life.
- Explore multiple ways that music can foster intergenerational meaning making.
- Describe CORE Principles for using any music with yourself or another: Care, Ownership, Respect, and Empowerment.
- Discover multiple ways that you can provide physical, emotional, mental, and spiritual care, through simple music interventions. Identify cautions that must be observed, especially if the dying person is no longer able to talk. Discuss the importance of accountability, role, boundaries, and presence.
- If you reach a stage where you can no longer speak clearly, is there music you might want played at that time? Is there music you might want played for specific persons, in your presence? Perhaps a lullaby for an adult child, a love song for a spouse, a song from your teen years to a life-long friend? (Can you hear "Themes and Counterthemes of Life Stories" in a new way?) Are you finding ways to voice those meanings to these persons in your own life, today?

Chapter 8. Composing Life Out of Loss

- Is grief decomposing you, or are you composing life anew?
- "I have loved. I have lost. Who am I, now? Who am I in relationship with others?" What music might help you relate to and redefine your loss and your sense of self?
- Explore further ways music can help you be in and move through grief's seasons of the soul.
- What music has encouraged you through a new beginning, especially during those back-and-forth movements between dwelling in the past and looking toward the future?
- Rhythms, themes and counterthemes, harmonies and dissonances, styles, expressions, and final cadences are synthesized into questions for composing life anew. Any composer or performer maintains characteristics of his or her own style, even when taking on something new. What are your own core, ongoing qualities that move on with you into your new movements and compositions of life?

☐ Composing Life in the Midst of Loss

On this day, in this moment of time, what losses have shaped who you are and where you are in your life journey? What feels healed? What feels raw? What lies yet ahead?

On this day, what music might express any of those feelings or thoughts? If you were to create your own CD or background soundtrack, what music would voice your "you"? Your core essence? As you hear and rehear, and reflect on that music, what do you learn about yourself? What choices do you see more clearly? What doing and being in this world do you embrace more dearly?

Leap ahead in our imagination to our future. You are in the last phases and phrases of your life. Every breath is watched with care. Who might be with you? What melodies might your loved ones spontaneously sing or hum, filling the quiet spaces with emotion, memory, and meaning? Chances are, those future phrases are being instilled in your loved ones' minds today.

I invite you to see your life as a composition in process. Your life experiences create the scores (see teaching guide 1.5). Where are your cadences and endings, those *fine*[2] moments of finishing and completion? Where are your blue note jazz chords, sounding the bittersweet or surprise dissonances of life? What stirrings in your soul call you toward something new? (See teaching guide 1.6.)

I invite you, readers, to hear the core rhythms and themes, harmonies and dissonances of your lives. What elements are seeking resolution? Where is your unique home base? Come on in and roam around.

You need not be a professional musician to find your music of the soul. You do need to be open to those profound moments of "aha" insight or surprise emotions that resonate within. Such awareness of the sounds you hear and the responses they evoke can connect you with yourself and others in rich, transforming ways.

As a clinician and author, I do not attempt to prescribe a formula for defining how anyone's life *should* be. I will, playfully, put out metaphors from music for any takers to explore and create what *can* be.

When I die, what "music" will my life have made and played, or on another note, was it all just work? What joys will I have known and given? What pains will I have endured, relieved, and learned from? Through what endings did I find my way and in what beginnings did I dare to risk anew? In time, over time, and through time, what beauty or expression did my life create?

In my hospice roles, I learn the importance of today. This day. My day. Your day. Our day. I believe in seizing this day. I seek to learn wisdom from our interwoven circles of seasons, years, decades, and centuries. What do I learn from yesterday for today? How does today play into tomorrow?

As a musician, I learn music's powers of expression (expressing outward from oneself) and im-pression (or instilling into oneself) — for the mind, body, emotions, and spirit. In my pastoral care and ministerial roles, I learn relational paths of hearing and traveling through life and death travails with one another, with a sense of what we can know and of the mystical unknown. This book is generated from those experiences.

The most important music is the life well lived, from beginning to end, with all of its notes in between. One's life may resemble a simple folk song, a sophisticated symphony, or a raucous rap. Each is filled with soul. It is yours. It is mine. We are the composers and players. May we tune into our inner rhythms and themes. May we move into life's dissonances and harmonies with personal style and expression.

May we dare life's dance,

sing her songs,

and compose each day with artistic soul.

CHAPTER 2

Rhythms of Body and Soul

The same stream of life that runs through my veins night and day runs through the world and dances in rhythmic measures.

Rabindranath Tagore

Music sets up a certain vibration which unquestionably results in a physical reaction.

George Gershwin

Music reproduces for the most intimate essence, the tempo and the energy of our spiritual being; our tranquility and our restlessness, our animation and our discouragement, our vitality and our weakness— all, in fact, of the fine shades of dynamic variation of our inner life.

Roger Sessions

- ☐ Body Rhythms
- ☐ Soul Rhythms
- ☐ Pausing and Pacing and Pushing On
- ☐ Signals for Action or Rest
- ☐ Music for Pain Relief: Body and Soul
- ☐ Rhythms of the Soul for Being in and Moving through Loss
- ☐ Music for Grief's Seasons of the Soul
- ☐ There Is a Time

Life moves us from rock-a-bye baby cooing to rocking-and-raging teenage cursing, to steadfast-as-a-rock adult responsibilities, to hard-as-rock elderly bones. Each age has characteristic rhythms and tempos. Each day has rhythms of energy and rest. Each person exhibits personal rhythmic patterns of gestures and gait.

Where are you on the life-span continuum? What are the daily rhythms of key persons in your life? What crashes between you because of those conflicting rhythms? What new creativity can flow? Few pieces of music have unison rhythms, rather, they play off of each other by entering in and out, in and out.

Civilizations and cultures have their own rhythms, and much is reflected in their music (Small, 1996). Compare in your mind a medieval Gregorian chant versus a contemporary rap. Today's technology pushes us into complex rhythms of call and immediate response. We expect lightening speed communication and transportation, moving from here to there by car and jet, fax and Internet, cell phone and satellite. Humorously, the two letters IM no longer mean I'm or I am, but rather Instant Message. There is little space or place for solitude or silence. In our complex cross-rhythms and changing meters, we need to carve out time to be. To breathe. To be me. To be we. We need to experience the "I Am" of ourselves, the soul-essence of each other, and the mystical "I Am" of the universe.

☐ Body Rhythms

Find the pulse of your heartbeat. Feel the pace of your breath. Connect with the currents of energy running through you. Are they fast or slow, energized or lethargic, chaotic or focused? Is life pulsing through you or passing you by?

What are the rhythms of your life today? Of your week? Are you able to keep the beat or do you feel out of sync?

Music is a language of time. It pulses with beats and measures, with tempos and movements. It is experienced in the here and now, and then gone. No matter how often a piece of music is repeated, its notes are never again experienced by the musician or listener in exactly the same way. Even with today's digital recordings, the sounds are always experienced in a new moment or context. A piece of music that held meaning yesterday is responded to anew today, and yet again tomorrow.

Life is a language of time. It is experienced in the here and now, then gone. There's a saying, "You can never put your foot in the same stream twice — for it is always flowing and moving on."

□ Soul Rhythms

An ancient poet proclaimed:

> For everything there is a season, and a time to every matter under heaven
>
>> A time to be born, and a time to die,
>> A time to plant, and a time to reap
>> A time to weep, and a time to laugh
>> A time to seek, and a time to lose. (Ecclesiastes 3:1–2, 4a, 5b)

These rhythms hold truth and wisdom today. In *Care of the Soul*, Thomas Moore writes, "Care of the soul is not solving the puzzle of life; quite the opposite, it is an appreciation of the paradoxical mysteries that blend light and darkness into the grandeur of what human life and culture can be" (Moore, 1994, p. xix).

We all experience times when we intuitively know, "it's time!" Invariably, that deep knowing is about some type of movement, action, or risk. It's time to finish my education, get a job, change jobs, ask someone out, end a relationship, get married, get divorced, buy a house, sell a house, have a baby, not have a baby, save money, get a loan, send my kids on into adulthood, become the caregiver for my parent or partner. It's time to call the doctor, get a second opinion, try every treatment possible, to fight for life. It's time to realize medical treatments aren't working, to consider options, to get things in order, to call hospice, to provide comfort and rest, to remember and reflect and prepare for the coming-too-soon future, to gather family and friends, to keep vigil, to say "I love you," to hold on and let go (all at the same time).

We all experience times when we internally scream, "It's not time!" for any of the things listed above. Perhaps, it's *not* time for my marriage to end or for my job to terminate. It's *not* time for my child to deal with adult issues, or for death to come so suddenly and cruelly. Life can ambush us with trauma that throws us into chaos and disarray, disrupting everyday rhythms of who we are and how we do life. "It's not time" reels us into realities of having to begin to accept, to adjust, and survive (see teaching guide 2.1). In the movie *Sleepless in Seattle*, the young widowed father (played by Tom Hanks) describes, "Well, I'm going to get out of bed every morning and breathe in and out, and after awhile, I won't have to remind myself to breathe in and out" (Ephron, 1993). He describes rhythms of body and soul.

FIGURE 2.1

□ Pausing and Pacing and Pushing On

We all need times of silence and pause: the "whew" big breath at the end of a challenging task, the sitting deeply into a favorite chair and zoning out, the day off from work. In music, we have symbols for many kinds of rests. We have longer whole, half, and quarter rests, and shorter 8th, 16th, and 32nd rests. Musical scores have pause, breath, or pedal marks for singers, instrumentalists, and pianists. In orchestral music, players often count their silence for measures on end. For musician-readers, I challenge you to name any piece that does not have either written or assumed rests or releases, however short or long.

Why do we do life different? Too often, you and I fill those spaces with as much multitasking as possible. We cram time off with too much chaos. It is no wonder one of the more popular songs of the turbulent 1960s was "The Sound of Silence" (Simon, 1964). Our word *contemplation* reflects the Greek word *tempo* (for marking a season or time), the Latin word *templum* (a place for observing omens), and *con* (a coming together, a being together) (Pearsall, 1998).

Music Moment: Pause

As I write this on my laptop computer, a thunderstorm has just passed through and knocked out our cable television, Internet broadband, and phone service. Silence. Interruption. Just as I began to write a profound thought on the beauty of silence, my husband (in his living room chair next to me) chimed in, "What are you doing?" I replied, "writing about silence." I read these paragraphs (still in process) to John. We laughed and shared one of those being-together, breathing-together moments after a long workday. Perhaps that chime was my own omen to be, my own "amen" to stop typing and let it be?

Changing Tempos

Musical rhythms can teach us about life: from the short interactions of notes and rests, to the hold-it-together and move-it-along tempos with occasional accelerandos and ritardandos, to the pacing of larger works or concerts. What are the changing tempos of your day? You are both composer and conductor. What is the best tempo for the particular task? What needs to slow down? Speed up? (See Loehr & Schwartz, 2003, for practical principles and interventions for pacing your energies.)

Almost any job has tasks that require top excellence in performance with highly focused energy. Deadlines approach. The moment arrives. Seize the day. Give yourself fully to creating the music. When mistakes occur (for they will), stay with the flow, find the beat and keep playing. Don't let self-doubts defeat you. Past preparations can make or break this moment — this life music.

Calendar Composing

Pull out your calendar for the next several months. What days or weeks will require higher energies? Where do you "score" (write in) rest and renewal, or simply a slower pace? Any opera or Broadway show alternates between the larger, faster pieces and the smaller, slower ones. The pacing keeps both the musicians and audience engaged. Where do you want to insure focused, high energy? Where do you want slower, softer, more fluid rhythms?

In a music therapy class I teach, about three weeks into the semester I have students bring their calendars to class, with all of their assigned exams, papers, and major projects recorded for the semester. After writing these onto a four-month calendar I provide, they pair off with one another to create a rhythmic composition of their anticipated semester. Choosing different percussion instruments, they then "play through" their semester, with accelerandos (at midterm), ritardandos (at fall or spring breaks), and always, always, a vigorous increase of volume, speed, and intensity at the end of the semester. Later in the semester when we repeat this exercise of what had actually happened, students typically report having given more attention and intention to their personal pacing than in prior semesters. They describe an improved awareness of choices they had made regarding time, energy, and values.

I encourage you to try something similar. Pull out your calendar and write in some musical symbols that correspond to what will be needed of you. If you see a presto day (extremely fast) or a *szforzando* meeting (heavily accented), write it in. Score in some rests, or ritardandos (slow down) and fermatas (stretch the moment), and then protect them. Do not give them away. Do you have some type of andante (walking speed) or adagio spaces (even slower) in your day, week, or month? Where is an allegro vivace week (fast and full of life)? Can you create some largo breathing space (very slow) the next week? You are the composer. You are the conductor (see teaching guide 2.2).

Give yourself good pacing. Know when you will need extra reserves of energy, and when you can rest and renew yourself. Oscillations between expending and recovering these energies is a key to building one's capacity to "perform" in the midst of increasing stress (Loehr & Schwartz, 2003). Again, tap into your inner "this is the time" and "this is not the time." You are the musician. This is your life music. Your life.

☐ Signals for Action or Rest

Music that signals a life rhythm change can be found in all cultures. From drums to horns or chants or bells, musical messages communicate "it's time" to stop what you are doing and change your activity. Musical signals for morning and night have existed for centuries, from ancient Tibetan and Gregorian chants and chimes, to preschoolers learning songs for tasks in the morning and lullabies at night. Hear the bugler's Reveille or Taps, or the pre-walkie-talkie drum signals used for military maneuvers. Hear the town hall bells urging all to gather, or the triangle summoning farmhands "come on and eat." In Louisville, Kentucky we know well the Derby bugler's "Call to Post." Around the world, chimes, gongs, singers, buzzers, and beepers mark "it's time" throughout the day.

Five times a day, Muslim *adhans* call people to prayer. Keeping pace with contemporary society, *adhan* computer programs can be downloaded for calls to prayer from one's own computer, for one's own time zone.

Of meaning for me are the Westminster chimes of my childhood doorbell in Savannah, Georgia (announcing "someone's here") and my cell phone's personalized ring tone (announcing "someone's calling"). I'm curious. What is your cell phone's tone, and how did you choose it? What does it say about you? Our musical patterns stem from many cultural, religious, and personal experiences.

On a deeper level, has a piece of music ever resonated so richly within that you were emotionally and spiritually transformed? Or a piece of music confronted you with "it's time" to deal with depths inside? Using music to change one's rhythms of body and soul is easier than you may imagine. Here are but a few examples.

Lethargy to Energy

A report on NBC's *Today* show demonstrated a new musical video game for teens (*Today*, 2004, June 4; http://www.ddrgame.com). A wired mat is placed on the floor in front of the TV and hooked up to video game equipment. The game combines video prompts, a variation on the 1960s Twister game, and aerobics. The person responds to karaoke-like video cues by jumping forward, back, left, right, or center, in synchronization with the music and the video's visual commands. The person combines mental concentration with physical response. Competition can be set up with a partner. The teens moved from couch-potato hypnotic video games to engaged, physical action and interaction. One teen lost 90 pounds. She described at first not even knowing she was losing weight. She was just having fun.

Move ahead in the life cycle to motivating patients in cardiac rehabilitation programs (Metzger, 2004), or to retraining the mind and body after severe trauma or a stroke. Music therapy is often integrated into rehabilitation programs, with amazing results.

Many persons assume that music therapy with hospice patients would only include soft, quiet, soothing music. Not so. While legato, softer styles are often preferred, some patients enjoy music because of its abilities to energize and bring life to life.

For You: What music energizes you? Gets you moving, exercising, or serves as a great backdrop for chores? Use that Walkman. Crank up the speakers. Or, wherever you are, sing.

Steadying Breathing

Linda, a 42-year-old woman, was in dire need of oxygen. She was having great difficulty breathing, suddenly gasping for air in her already weakened condition. Her hospice nurse had just gotten the physician's orders and contacted the equipment agency, but setting up the oxygen tank still required delivery time. Linda had been a professional backup singer for several high profile entertainers. She intuitively knew a few things about music's effects on people. On this afternoon, she gained some control by tuning into her body's erratic breathing and slowly, phrase by phrase, turning it into a steadier breathing in and out, in and out. How? She mentally focused, and quietly began singing a gospel song she had often sung as a child with her grandmother: "I sing because I'm happy/I sing because I'm free/For His eye is on the sparrow/And I know He watches me" (Martin & Gabriel, 1906/1981).

In that moment, Linda found noticeable physical relief, along with spiritual and emotional self-comfort. While this did not replace her need for an oxygen tank, it did give her short-term waiting-staying-steadying power for the process. In what could have been fearful thoughts, she chose to focus not on what she did not have (the oxygen tank), but rather on what she did have, assurance of care.

> **For You:** What music can you readily recall (or sing, or pop in your CD player, or play on an instrument) to help steady and ground your soul? Identify it ahead of time. Create your own re-creative interventions.

Chaos to Serenity

Tara, in her 60s, was determined to live by herself in her downtown home for as long as possible. Feisty and independent, she was not one to show vulnerability. To me as chaplain and music therapist, she described a fearful panic that regularly set in as dusk approached:

- Is this the night I die?
- Will I see another tomorrow?
- How will I die when I die?
- How can I live until I die?
- Will I live on in another form after I die?

She did not want antidepressants to alter her awareness or affect. Her end-stage heart disease held a more unpredictable ending than a disease like cancer. She knew that family, friends, and hospice help were only a phone call away, but she wanted to move into personal reflection without the panic. She had lived her life with intentionality and self-reliance. She wanted the same in her dying. She showed me the CDs labeled "Relaxation" she had bought to calm herself when this panic emerged, but she expressed, "They make me worse. I feel pressure, like I'm not supposed to feel afraid, and I can't get past it."

I explored with Tara the "isoprinciple" of music therapy, that I affectionately call "Match It and Move It." You begin with music that for you, matches what you are feeling, now: mad, sad, glad, or afraid (four basic emotions, or any variation thereof). The style of music also needs to match your preference. Extensive music therapy research confirms the importance of client preference of music (Iwaki, Tanaka, & Hori, 2002). Tara's too-promising CDs were in classical and new age styles. She did not like either. She connected more readily with popular music, Broadway show tunes, and jazz. I played for her a percussive sample from the 1997 *Titanic* movie score, and yes, that matched her anxiety and fear. However, we personalized the intervention when she chose music in a different style, from her *Phantom of the Opera* CD, a favorite story line for her.

Tara chose "Music of the Night" to match, contain, and validate her emotions and interpretations of her day into dusk experiences (Webber, Hart, & Stilgo, 1986). Its text evokes opening oneself to the dark of night with a sense of imagination, tenderness, and surrender. It calls one away from the world one has known. It invites the willing to release one's spirit and let it soar.

A significant theme of this book emerges. Tara had reached a point of readiness within herself for this lyric. It confronted her impending death with heightened sensory, mental, emotional, and spiritual stimuli and meanings. The relevance of "Music of the Night" to the dying process does not make it a right and timely piece of music for all others who are dying (for further exploration, see "Sustaining and Confronting" in chapter 5). Never impose, never assume. Match the music to the person, and where she is within herself. Validate, affirm. Give witness to another's experience.

The person's experience should be validated before **move it** is added, as in "Match It and Move It." The next piece of music helps one shift toward the desired emotional response. Tara and I chose a calmer piece from *Phantom,* and then some smooth jazz. The jazz had a relaxed, easy beat and flow, with a spontaneity for being in the moment, versus a predictable classical score or a free-floating no-rhythm new age style. We sequenced her selections, moving toward a deeper calm of rhythms, mood, and volume.

We burned a CD with Tara's carefully sequenced selections. She created a ritual for herself each evening, as daylight moved into dusk. She intentionally carved out a time and space for her music, emotions, and thoughts. By first hearing the music about the darkness of the night, she validated and granted herself permission to accept her panic feelings as being normal and OK. The jazz music led her into a more relaxed mode, where she then moved her mind and emotions toward serenity.

One more note. We ended the CD with her recording of Frank Sinatra's "My Way." While this song's style may not seem serene, it held for Tara the meanings she was seeking. It led her into those deeper soul-places for reflecting on and learning from her past, present, and future journeys of "My Way" (Anka, recorded by Sinatra, 1969).

> And now, the end is near;
> And so I face the final curtain.
> My friend, I'll say it clear,
> I'll state my case, of which I'm certain.
>
> I've lived a life that's full.
> I've traveled each and ev'ry highway;
> But more, much more than this,
> I did it my way.

In the broader rhythms of dying and grieving, Tara's family read this text at her memorial service. Through her dying, Tara taught us about living.

For You: What situation often triggers panic or another painful response in you? What music would you select for your own "Match It and Move It" CD or IPod? Remember, the purpose is not to escalate the pain, but to provide a safe container to acknowledge and release it (see teaching guide 2.3).

☐ Music for Pain Relief: Body and Soul

Today's scientific research supports what has been known and practiced for centuries: music can ease physical pain. Hebrew scripture tells of young David playing the harp for King Saul to relieve him from an "evil spirit," often interpreted as a severe headache (1 Samuel 16:23). In the famous 1744 text, *The Art of Preserving Health,* John Armstrong (1709–1779), a Scottish-born, Edinburgh-educated, British physician wrote:

"Music exalts each joy, allays each grief,/Expels diseases, softens every pain,/Subdues the rage of poison, and the plague" (cited in Crofton & Fraser, 1985, p. 51).

In *The Healing Drum* (Diallo, 1989), YaYa Diallo opens our Western ears to his African ancestral role of healing through sensitive drumming. For centuries, Tibetan lamas have practiced healing through meditation and musical chanting. These examples but scratch the surface of the worldwide use of music to alleviate pain.

Today's modern music therapy movement largely grew out of tending wounded soldiers after World War II (see http://www.musictherapy. org). Particularly through rehabilitation, music support provided a "something more" of interaction for emotionally and psychologically traumatized soldiers, with additional benefits of relaxing or energizing the body. The international, clinical discipline of music therapy has steadily grown for nearly 60 years (see http://www.voices.no). Recent medical shifts toward interdisciplinary, holistic care integrate music therapy into the patient's clinical care plan, and are implemented by a board certified music therapist (for certification information, see CBMT at www.cbmt.org or AMTA at www.musictherapy.org). In a rightful perspective, music is often called a "complementary" medicine. Music is used in conjunction with a team of interdisciplinary professionals, clinical care plan, and interdisciplinary interventions planned for the patient (Lewis, Vedia, Reuer, Schwan, & Tourin, 2003). Some practical factors regarding pain and the suitability of when might use music for relief include the following:

- intensity, frequency, and duration of pain
- sources of pain (physical, emotional, relational, or spiritual pain; or any combination)
- available resources for the most effective pain relief
- the person's receptivity to music as a therapy agent for comfort.

For readers who do not have access to professional music therapy services, how might you use music to aid you when pain strikes (Magill, 1993)? In synthesizing research articles, applications for patients and families, and teaching hospice professionals, three words often recur: *distract, divert, direct*.

Each concept has a function, from broadly distracting attention away from the pain, to focusing in on emotional or spiritual pain that exacerbates physical pain, in toward a more direct, targeted use of music for calming and quieting the body. No one musical work nor musical style will provide relief for every person. These principles can pave the way (see teaching guide 2.4).

Distract

Any music that distracts attention away from pain can help block the messages of pain to the brain. Basically, the music can be of any type. It just needs to be pleasurable to the person. It can be taped music, but is likely to be more powerful when it is live. Recorded music is more passive, receptive, and mainly involves hearing. Live music involves hearing, seeing, possibly touching (the instrument, the person), and possibly singing or speaking. The purpose of the music is to distract attention away from the negative stimuli, and shift it toward something more positive.

Divert

Using music to release emotional or spiritual pain can, in turn, foster physical relaxation. Anxiety can increase muscle tension, blood pressure, and shallow breathing. Simple questions can lead toward music to use:

- What music energizes you?
- Relaxes you?
- Brings humor?
- Leads to prayer?
- Taps into comforting, supportive memories from the past?
- Brings assurance in the present?
- Provides a sense of hope for the future?

Persons living with chronic pain can create their own "musical menu" by identifying such pieces of music and keeping them nearby, at home, in their car, or at work (see appendix B, "My Music Menu"). When chronic pain cannot be cured, integrating pain management and altering everyday lifestyles is crucial for having a rich quality of life. How does one adjust to the changes? What is ending for the person? What is beginning?

Remembering the dark, shadow side of music's ability to stir painful emotions is crucial. As with lancing a wound, releasing one's sadness, anger, fear, guilt, or whatever else may be an essential way of getting through the pain on the way toward healing. Exploring one's emotions, beliefs, fears, and hopes about one's physical pain can lead to inner transformation and improve the overall quality of life in the midst of ongoing pain. When reframing what the pain and its loss mean to you, purpose and hope can be found in the midst of suffering (Frankl, 1963).

Direct

Music can be used to intentionally direct the body toward a relaxed, calm state of being. As described with Tara, many relaxation recordings exist in different musical styles. First and foremost, the musical style needs to reflect the person's preference. Questions to consider include:

- What style(s) of music do you prefer? Classical? Gospel? Liturgical? Folk? Easy Listening? Pop? Jazz? Rhythm and blues? Nature? Guided imagery? New age?
- Overall, is the music quiet? Smooth? Slow (about 60–72 beats per minute, or less)?
- Is the environment clear of distracting noises? Bright lights? Appliance or other noises?
- Is clothing tight or constricting? Is your chair, sofa, or bed in an optimal position? Get comfortable.
- What type of physical breathing, relaxation exercises are you familiar with so that you can use them initially? (This is called the "induction.")
- Is the music likely to evoke strong negative images for you? If so, be aware, and choose carefully.
- Is the music likely to evoke positive images for the person?

While tending these musical and environmental elements, one must also nurture the inner soul, for tending only the body can be a somewhat superficial intervention. Music can dig much deeper. It can sow seeds of emotion, memory, and meaning (Bonny & Summer, 2002). Images, emotions, and a sense of self can be instilled which later can be recalled when pain recurs, even without the music, and bring calm, peace, and serenity — wholeness within.

☐ Rhythms of the Soul for Being in and Moving through Loss

Through pain and laughter, sorrow and joy, life rocks and rolls and swings us into the dance of life and death itself. Back to our ancient poet, "for everything there is a season and a time." In my hospice ministry and teaching roles, I continue to find universal understandings by putting forth grief as being in and moving through one's seasons of the soul (Berger, 1993).

These are not literal times of three months per season, but rather "seasons" within. Broad "seasons" of fall and winter move into spring and

summer, and then again back into fall. While life's endings and beginnings are not as tidy and predictable as nature's three-month time frames,
such metaphors can hold meaning and wisdom. There is a time to weep,
a time to mourn. There is a time for hibernation and a time for venturing
out. There is a time for planting and a time for harvest. There is a time for
remembering and a time for re-visioning.

Some losses are Arctic, long-winter, no-light griefs. Others are
Florida "the sun'll come out tomorrow" (Strouse & Charnin, 1977) faster
comings through. William Worden identifies "Mediators of mourning"
that affect one's mourning timetable and tasks. These include: (1) the
person who died; (2) the nature of the attachment; (3) circumstances
of death; (4) personality mediators; (5) historical mediators; (6) social
mediators; and (7) concurrent changes (2002, pp. 37–45).

Within these broad seasons of the soul are smaller rhythmic oscillations of night and day, high tides and low tides, waves rolling in and
out, shifts of temperature, of stormy or clear skies. So it is with the soul.
Typically, one experiences broad patterns of rhythmic flow, with more
personalized, spontaneous daily shifts.

Recall a significant loss that you have come through. It may have
been a divorce, the illness and death of a loved one, a job loss, a move,
or something else. Did your being in and coming through loss follow a
path that was something like this? (See teaching guide 2.5.)

Autumn

An autumn or fall season signals that a change is coming. It cannot be
stopped. The days get shorter and nights get longer. Individual colors
come out in those involved. Think about diverse responses within a
family when a major loss occurs. Someone is red, another is yellow or
orange or brown or evergreen. One tree loses its leaves suddenly while
another holds on, loosening its leaves a little at a time. Individuals
each deal with the same loss according to individual personalities and
timetables. Like autumn, the birds — the songs of the soul — fly south.
Nature instinctively prepares itself for more cold ahead. This is a time
for harvesting one's earlier labors, as we do at seasons of retirement,
aging, and life review with the hospice patient and family. Just as leaves
are strewn by the winds, visible reminders of change are everywhere:
clothes that can no longer be worn. Food that can no longer be enjoyed;
daily doing and being together that can no longer be shared as before.
For caregivers this is a time for daily tasks. This autumn of the soul can
also be a time to gather and give thanks.

Winter

A winter season is when the realities of the loss settle in and shift into a cold, darker winter. Insulation from the elements is needed, along with hearth–heart places of warmth and sustenance. Venturing out too far into winter's wilderness can be dangerous, and can lead to slipping, falling, or getting lost. One's well-known, well-worn paths may be covered with ice and snow. The dark is darker. The bright white is brighter. How long, oh God, how long? (Psalm 6:3.) Will this ever end? Will this never end?

Winter into Spring

A spring season does not suddenly bloom. Rather, it is more of winter gradually transforming into spring. As in Frances Hodgson Burnett's story, *The Secret Garden* (1911/1998), in the midst of doom and gloom, one must find the key to enter the hidden garden. One begins to tend the garden day by day. Discern what has died and what still holds life within. Clear away the debris, and prepare for the new. We till the frozen soil, plant seeds from what has been, and risk anew: nurture, tend, and water. We must work with nature's timing, not against it: neither speeding up nor holding back, but in tune with natural processes. The birds — the songs of the soul — return, creating nests for safe waiting and birth. Flowers and weeds begin to sprout. (You may have to give them time to grow to know which is what.) Spring calls forth a risk, a trust, a hope within oneself, without having to cut off the loss, but experiencing its place within one's cycles of life.

Spring into Summer

A summer season is when life regains a new sense of normalcy. It is never exactly the same as any previous year, but it thrives with new verdant, green pastures. Blooms distinguish themselves from weeds. The garden still needs tending, yet it becomes more sturdy. Summer is a time for vacation, when life lends itself to the outdoors and nature. Days are long and filled with sunshine. Occasional summer rains cool down stagnant heat.

After summer, what happens? One's cycles of endings and beginnings begin and end again. And again.

☐ Music for Grief's Seasons of the Soul

In *The Secret Garden*, a singing robin finds the key for Mary to enter the disheveled garden. Similarly, for you and me, music can be a key for entering one's own secret garden to tend the soil of the soul, whatever the season. How? Music can tap into memories, emotions, and meanings. Music can call us to action.

Music can help us be in the moment, in the experience. It can help us be with self and with others in more deeply connected ways. The following chart illustrates this clinician's sense of "Seasons of the Soul," sensitive uses of "Music for Being In and Moving Through Grief's Seasons," and "Care of the Soul." Three grief theorists' concepts are referred to: Colin Parkes's "Processes of Grief" (Parkes, 2001), William Worden's "Tasks of Mourning" (2002), and Robert Neimeyer's "Meaning Reconstruction" (2001). These are explored throughout later portions of this book.

The following chart can be read both horizontally and vertically. The progressive movements in this chart are not rigid, consecutive formulas. Rather, they present fluid, flowing, ever-moving "compositional" patterns. The chart lends itself to highly individualized interventions and outcomes for the mourning person or group.

Starting on the far left, "seasons of the soul" describes what a grieving person or group may be experiencing. Moving across the page, it relates the season to (1) Parkes's processes of grief and Worden's tasks of mourning; (2) basic uses of music for being in and moving through grief, to be adapted within one's role and relationship with the person; and (3) care of the soul dynamics that either the music stirs, or are experienced in relationship between the mourner and the professional.

Moving vertically down the page, these seasons, musical interventions, and relational dynamics flow in progressive time lines. These time lines are not strictly linear, but rather cyclic. They are not measured in prescriptive days, months, or years. Instead, they provide a common language that can apply to most any loss or individual needs. Just as our local weather stations give predictors for any given day, fluctuations and movement constantly occur within any "season." Just as literal seasons have ongoing oscillations between day and night, the grieving person also moves through ongoing cycles of mourning and morning, between loss and restoration (Stroebe & Schut, 2001). Stormy winds or bright sunshine can arise in any season. Turbulence or calm can be in any. So it is, with grief.

Foundations for all of these include Neimeyer's "Meaning Reconstruction," as in continually reconstructing one's life meanings, and this author's "CORE Principles" and HEALing Techniques" for any such uses of music.

TABLE 2.1 Music of the Soul: Composing Life Out of Loss

Seasons of the Soul (Berger, 1993) Processes of Grief (Parkes,1987/2001) Tasks of Mourning (Worden, 1991/2002)		Music for being in and moving through grief's seasons of the soul	Care of the soul An active presence
Fall Rich colors emerge as the potential loss is signaled. The loss begins. Change is here, and cannot be stopped. Individual timetables of letting go. Visible reminders are strewn around. Times for harvest & thanks. Birds fly south. Winter sets in.	**Process:** shock, numbness, denial **Task:** to accept the reality of the loss	**Music for Memories/ Memorializing** At initial loss (i.e., funeral or other ritual), meaningful musical expressions; reality oriented; comfort, hope, strength; affirmation both of faith and that a significant loss has occurred; favorites appropriate when designated as such, not for mere sentimentality; musical styles need to reflect the person.	Primarily **SUSTAINING** the shock and **CONFRONTING** the loss
Winter Cold, dark, empty. The nights are longer and days are shorter. Venturing out can be dangerous, unlike before. Hibernation. Need for hearth–heart places of trust and emotional safety. "How long, oh how long?"	**Process:** longing, yearning, pining, searching for the loss **Task:** to work through the pains of the loss	**Music for Mourning** Memories frequently emerge at sensory, physiological, emotional levels. Invite the person's favorite music & associated memories. Provide a container for intense pain and catharsis. Empowerment, safety, security, and trust are crucial. Respect the person's timetable.	Primarily **GUIDING** to validate and express inner pains Initial **HEALING** (cleansing and bandage of the emotional wounds)
Winter into spring Daily process. Clearing away the dead. Tilling the frozen soil of the soul. Planting with a sense of risk, trust, and nurture. Surprise storms. Gentle growth. New birth.	**Process:** disorganization and despair **Task:** to adjust to an environment in which the loss is missing	**Music for Meanings** More of the same; move toward re-collecting memories and discovering their interwoven meanings. Introduce more music which is new to the person. "Reframe" or reinterpret the past. Meanings guide toward re-formation of self.	Primarily **GUIDING & INFORMING** More **CONFRONTING** than before

(Continued)

TABLE 2.1 Music of the Soul: Composing Life Out of Loss *(Continued)*

Seasons of the Soul (Berger, 1993) Processes of Grief (Parkes,1987/2001) Tasks of Mourning (Worden, 1991/2002)		Music for being in and moving through grief's seasons of the soul	Care of the soul An active present
Spring into summer Fruition of new life. New growth is rooted and sturdy. A time for vacations from the work of mourning; new memory making.	**Process:** reorganization **Task:** to emotionally relocate the loss & move on with life	**Music for** **Remembering &** **Moving into Life** Music at memorials marking losses, or celebrations marking beginnings. Affirm having come through, and what has been learned. Use same music from an earlier catharsis. Use new music that expresses life "now" and ahead.	**HEALING &** **RECONCILING** of the former **GUIDING &** **INFORMING** toward the new

Meaning reconstruction (Neimeyer, 2001): Ongoing exploration of meanings for the present and future

CORE Principles through all Seasons of the Soul: Care, Ownership, Respect, Empowerment (Berger, 1999)

HEALing Techniques through all Seasons of the Soul: Hear, Explore, Affirm, Learn (Berger, 1999)

Sources: Berger, J. S. (1993). *Music as a catalyst for pastoral care within the remembering tasks of grief.* Ann Arbor, Michigan: ProQuest/University Microfilms, Inc., [Pub. #9406295]. Berger, J. S. (1999). *Life music: Rhythms of loss and hope* [VHS]. Cleveland, OH: American Orff-Schulwerk Association. Neimeyer, R. A. (Ed.). (2001). *Meaning reconstruction & the experience of loss.* Washington, DC: American Psychological Association. Parkes, C. M. (1987/2001). *Bereavement: Studies of grief in adult life* (2nd and 3rd American ed.). Madison, CT: International Universities Press. Worden, J. W. (2002). *Grief counseling and grief therapy* (2nd and 3rd ed.). New York: Springer.

Music for Memories and Memorializing

Through the soul's autumn, musical sounds, texts, and expressions can stir an awareness that life is different and changes are set in motion. One's normal present is shifting to a past. Notice it the next time you visit at a funeral home. Everyday language of "is" and "will" suddenly becomes "was," "did," and "used to be."

Usually, a normal shock or numbness protects the person, allowing awareness of the reality to settle in a little at a time. Again and again. And again. Every former attachment is experienced as a change. One realizes the realities of the loss again and again And again.

Music at a funeral or memorial service (do you hear the word *memory*) often confronts such soul-depth places: "These familiar words and sounds hit me harder than ever before. She really has died. My future — forever — is different." The future holds a deep not knowing. It is covered by a dark veil. Winter is approaching. One moves through precarious transitions between past, present, and future. Between knowing and not knowing, grasping at what has been while being thrust into what now is.

Music at a funeral, wake, remembrance, or in those daily spaces, can bring together people, emotions, thoughts, and that "not knowing." Musical reflections can harvest one's life stories and meanings. Music can take persons into their soul-depth gratitude, grief, humor, faith, and much more. It can create a shared experience of being-in and being-with, together. Numerous rituals for remembering can be shared, depending on the nature of the death, and the family's cultural codes, and policies of the funeral home or other setting. Current technology easily empowers family members to create personalized video/ DVD remembrances through pairing photos, videos, music, with text or voice-overs. Or more simply, collections of photos and memorabilia might be displayed, with the person's favorite music playing nearby.

Music at a funeral or memorial service can be deeply sustaining, a comfort for sorrow and a voice of hope. It can call forth expressions from self and community, creating an extraordinary sense of connection between the grieving. Supportive, familiar sounds often cut into the soul with a more profound sense of this new absence. The physical presence of my loved one is now shifting from physical touch, to my memories. Music at a funeral can create a sense of shared sorrow and gratitude for the loved one. This music itself, in the present, can create and store new memories from the funeral itself, for nurture through the long winter ahead.

Music for Mourning

As the normal shock and disbelief at the loss wears off, grief's pains are less numbed. An ongoing season of "winter" settles in. In one's dark, cold silences and crying out of the soul, music can give expression to that which is too deep for words. Caution: music's "fires" of stirring emotion and memories must be handled with care.

You hear the once favorite music. Emotions flood with a fierce "Stop the music!" or "Let me out of here!" The brain suddenly kicks in with a stern "No! We're divorced now!" or "She's dead and I'll never hear her sing that again." After the emotional downpour subsides, a deep, dull melancholy settles in. A pounding pang escalates into irrational irritability.

Beethoven proclaimed, "Music should strike fire within" (quoted in Crofton & Fraser, 1985, p. 58). I applaud and add, for the grieving person, does that fire warm or burn? Scorch or fuel (Berger, 1993)? When music "strikes fire within" it awakens one's emotions, thoughts, physical reactions, and core self. The music becomes a catalyst that causes a change, without itself being consumed. The person's responses heighten when receiving musical stimuli through his or her own filters. The music strikes one's sorrow, fears, hopes, thoughts, or life meanings, often at nonverbal levels.

Such musical stimuli–response experiences can happen with any loss: a divorce, broken relationship, loss of job, change of career, loss of a pet, loss of faith in an institution or belief, changes inherent in raising children and aging parents, and raising-aging ourselves through it all.

Recall a moment in your grief and loss history when music "struck fire" within you. You know, you suddenly brushed away tears and felt overwhelmed with emotion. What intense responses were ignited? Sorrow? Longing? Thankfulness? Relief? Guilt? Hope? Memories? A gut-level realization that the loss was indeed real? Did that experience help move you into and through grief, or stop you from venturing further?

Music can cause more pain than we realize. Too often, musicians not trained in clinical, relational skills (i.e., music therapy, loss-grief therapies) cause harm by "lighting fires" without empowering the grief-stricken person to stop the music. To explore the pain. To honor one's inner timing within a bigger scheme. Too often the focus is on the musical performer versus the grieving person's life-story themes, soul-rhythms, and dissonances stirring around inside. Using music in the soul's "winter" must include empowerment. Through winter's season of the soul, a common coping mechanism is to keep painful stimuli at a distance — buried, put away, silenced. Being a "musician of the soul" requires being comfortable with such silence. It means not imposing music, but rather hearing those places of pain and being a faithful, validating presence.

Anyone using music with another should first and foremost examine one's relationship and role, and use music accordingly. Am I daughter, spouse, friend, hospice nurse, bereavement counselor, music educator, music performer, volunteer, minister? Be the person within the appropriate relationship. Use music accordingly.

Within any relationship, CORE principles for experiencing music for mourning include Care of the person; honoring Ownership of another's timetables and responses; Respect for another's musical tastes; and Empowerment of the person to be in and move through his or her own mourning. Similarly, HEALing techniques include Hear the person; Explore one's emotions and associations with the music; Affirm the person's experience; and continually Learn about grief (these are defined further in appendix E, "CORE Principles and HEALing Techniques").

Music for Meanings

The soul's winter shifts into and out of spring with twists and turns between hope and despair. Memories stirred by music feel less raw, but are more filled with meanings. What do I keep? What do I toss? What from before do I need ahead? Are there any meanings in the meaninglessness of it all? Neimeyer and others describe this as "clearing a space" (Attig, 2001; Hagman, 2001; Neimeyer, 2001; Stroebe & Schut, 2001). Countless musical compositions reflect real-life losses and one's digging around in the soul's soil.

Johannes Brahms composed his *German Requiem* out of deeply personal grief and soul searching. His close friend the composer Robert Schumann had attempted to drown himself in the Rhine River and had been placed in an asylum where he died two years later, in 1856. Brahms began composing his *German Requiem* within months of Schumann's death. He took the strict Latin, Catholic liturgical requiem form and adapted it, changing the requiem's form, structure, contents, and language. He chose texts that voiced his more intimate religious beliefs, not just doctrinal dogmas. He dared to use his native German language, instead of Latin, for personal and community expression and comprehension. While he was composing the work, his mother became seriously ill and died in January 1865. Upon her death, he added into the fifth movement, "As one whom his mother comforteth, so will I comfort you." Musicologists have long noted the impact of these two deaths upon Brahms's compositional processes. Descriptions of our search for meaning from contemporary philosophers and grief scholars add further insight (Frankl, 1963; Neimeyer, 2001).

First performed in 1868, Brahms dedicated his *German Requiem* to Robert Schumann, his mother, and the whole of humanity. Scholars have also noted that this requiem is not for the dead, but for the living. Its impact continues today, as in its 2002 international performances by the Consort Caritatis to raise funds for HIV/AIDS projects in Africa (Dyck, n.d.).

An obscure story about a beloved composer demonstrates how meanings can be worked out through one's music. The young Irving Berlin (age 24) married Dorothy Goetz and took her to Cuba for their honeymoon. She caught typhoid and died five months later. It was 1912. Expressing his grief, he wrote "When I Lost You." It was one of his earliest publications and sold more than six million copies because others, too, found meaning and solace in "When I Lost You" (Benoit, 2003). Later, in 1925, Irving Berlin composed the gentle ballad, "Always," as a wedding gift for his new love, Ellin Mackay. Her father had sent her to Europe to prevent his socialite daughter from marrying the lowly songwriter. Upon her return to New York, Irving and Ellin eloped and were married at New York's City Hall. Irving knew heartbreaking grief from having loved and lost. Still, he voiced love's continuity in this new song, no matter the trials (Berlin, 1925/1984). This love song became a favorite of a quiet couple named Lou and Eleanor Gehrig. Berlin's song, "Always," was woven throughout the 1942 movie of Lou's life, *The Pride of the Yankees* (Reel Classics, 2005). It portrays their love story through his baseball career and crippling disease, Amyotrophic Lateral Sclerosis (ALS), now known as "Lou Gehrig's Disease." Countless persons and families hit with ALS create similar examples of an "Always" commitment to their loved ones (for more information, see http://www.alsa.org).

Irving Berlin's song, "Always," demonstrates: must one be a composer to find meaning through music, through grief's season of winter into spring? Absolutely not. Any radio station, music store, or MP3 download site is loaded with such music, and makes great profit from such purchases. People buy what they are drawn to, whether prompted through marketing or personal connection. Virtually any vocal genre has lyrics from this "season" of trying to find meaning out of loss: blues, jazz, gospel, opera, art songs, Broadway, country, rap, hip hop, rhythm and blues, and the list goes on. Hear but a few: "I Dreamed a Dream," sung by the destitute Fontaine about life's meaninglessness in Broadway's *Les Misérables* (Boubil & Schonberg, 1989); "The Dance" by Garth Brooks (Arato, Miller, & Ball, 1991); or the hauntingly beautiful "Broken Vow," recorded by Josh Grobin (Afanasief, Crokaert, & Foster, 2002).

Christopher Davis, grief researcher, further describes both torment and transformation by questioning what might have been, especially if the death was traumatic (Davis, 2001; Davis & Lehman, 1995; Davis, Lehman, Wortman, Silver, & Thompson, 1995). Much music reveals a rising from the real-life ashes of death and life. For example:

- Reba McEntire's album, *For My Broken Heart*, compiles songs of grief, following the plane-crash deaths of her seven band members and tour manager, in March 1991 (McEntire, 1991).
- Heavy D's hip hop song "Ask Heaven" (Heavy D & the Boys, 1999), voiced his personal coming to terms with the violent deaths of his brothers. "I could've never made this record five years ago. Even three years ago. Being able to address issues like death and drugs and family comes with my maturity" (Hip Online, 2005).
- Bruce Springsteen's "My City of Ruin" introduced the first televised relief concert after 9/11. It voiced sorrow, comfort, and even a call to "rise up" (America: A Tribute to Heroes, 2001; Springsteen, 2002).
- *Our New Orleans 2005* is a poignant, painful and resilient compilation of the music of New Orleans, released December 6, 2005, just three months after the Katrina flood. Its songs include: "Yes We Can," "Cryin' in the Streets," "My Feet Can't Fail Me Now," "Prayer

for New Orleans," "What a Wonderful World," and more (Hurwitz & Bither, 2005).

These few samples became famous because they connected with real life; with similar seasons of the soul within the broader public. Five years, 10 years, and 25 years from now, more life tragedies will have hit, and more music will have emerged.

> **For You:** What music captures a significant loss for you? Moves you from a winter into spring? What music stirs understanding and growth? What "aha" insights have emerged?

Music for Re-membering and Moving Into Life

Coincidentally, summer in the United States begins with Memorial Day weekend. Moving into grief's summer of the soul does not mean cutting the loss off from one's life. It does mean re-membering the dislodged, lost members or parts of the self and working them into a new formation. The broken-off pieces of the puzzle create a new picture that has meaning and purpose for today.

In creating our own "memorial" moments, we revisit and remember previous paths from the loss. Music can be a powerful catalyst, yet again. Reexperiencing the same music from before, at a later season, can affirm the journeys one has traveled through the loss. Where and who was I then? Who am I now? Who am I becoming? What mattered to me before the loss, and what matters differently now? What lies ahead? How have I been challenged and changed, tried and transformed? I share with you Amy's story.

Amy's beautiful baby girl Madison was not expected to live until her own birth, but she did. With great celebration, Amy's favorite lullaby to her daughter began with, "I'm so glad you were born this day" (Jernigan, 2000). Within her first few months, Madison — or "Maddy" — (meaning "strong one") went through open heart surgery. With her valiant life energy and beautiful soul-spirit, Madison became our hospice patient at the tender age of 9 months. Her parents were committed to giving her quality of life for whatever length of time that might be. "I'm so glad you were born" was played and sung by Amy through many late night rockings and holdings and soothings. We were privileged to experience Maddy's first birthday, her second Christmas, and a Valentine's Day. Her smile lit up a room. Madison imprinted her laughter and spirit into everyone's hearts. As Maddy began moving into death, Amy rocked her, with tear-filled eyes and a broken soul, playing her CD and singing "I'm so glad you were born … I'm so glad you came."

At Madison's funeral the song had been transcribed for piano and was sung by a friend at the church. Amy — whom everyone had feared was close to collapsing — began to mouth the words with the singer. In her deepest grief, she found a familiar holding space, and soothing words still affirming, "I'm so glad you were born." The song became a container for raw emotions and gathered community.

The following days, nights, weeks, and months were grief-stricken for Amy, her husband, and their two young sons. They embraced our hospice bereavement services. No matter the care from each other and supportive communities, there were voids that could not be filled. On the one-year anniversary of Madison's death, Amy and I, in their home, pulled out the CD and last videos of Maddy. Amy's family could not bear to hear or see them. They were too painful. Amy chose to experience those images and sounds, in all of their raw pain. She marked a one-year place she needed to honor. More important than *moving past* a one-year marker, was simply *being in* it.

On through more seasons of time and Amy gave birth to a healthy baby boy. A gift to Amy was a new CD, Kenny Loggins's *More Songs from Pooh Corner,* with new sounds and songs for baby Jack, and a song for remembering Maddy in the hearts of their now larger family, "Always, In All Ways" (Loggins, 2000).

Scroll on through time to toddler Jack, who came with his mom Amy to our hospice office one bright Tuesday morning. Amy was now sharing her story with a fresh hospice employee orientation group. In the back of our meeting room, a long-time employee scurried to get the TV working. Something about planes crashing? Attacks? Yes. It was the morning of September 11, 2001. As the tower images broke through the back of the room, in the front a familiar CD sang out "I'm so glad you were born," with Jack moving curiously from person to person. For me and Amy, and perhaps some orientees, a transcendent sense of Madison's spirit once again brought a quiet strength in the midst of fear and horror. For me, a seasoned hospice professional being faced with death in such terrifying scenes, I experienced through the music a sense of Madison's life spirit, guarding and guiding me through the moment at hand.

Out of our own histories and seasons of being in and coming through loss, may we look into the eyes of our loved ones each day with a sense of "I'm so glad you were born." May each of us warmly smile into the mirror with "I'm so glad you were born!" (Do I hear you singing it?)

To everything there is a season and a time. In time, over time, and through time, as hearts pulse and souls search on, may each of us *live* our time — however long or short or somewhere in between.

☐ **There Is a Time**[1]

A Funeral/Memorial Service Reading

For everything there is a season, and a time for every matter,

> A time to be born, and a time to die
> A time to celebrate life, and a time to grieve death
>
> A time for childlike wonder, and a time for adult wisdom
> A time to give care, and a time to need care
>
> A time to laugh, and a time to weep
> A time for community, and a time for solitude

For everything there is a season, and a time for every matter,

> A time to risk love, and a time to learn from love's wounds
> A time to reflect on the past, and a time to re-vision the future
>
> A time to assert "No!" and a time to embrace "Yes!"
> A time to voice fear, and a time to chance trust
>
> A time to give 100% plus, and a time to rest deeply
> A time to fight for a cure, and a time to shift to hospice care

For everything there is a season, and a time for every matter,

> A time to fly like an eagle, and a time to walk yet not faint
> A time to pray for strength that endures, and a time to pray for release from suffering
>
> A time to breathe in, and a time to breathe out
> A time to hold on, and a time to let go
>
> A time to feel a loved one's absence and presence, both at the same time
> Forever transformed by what has been, challenged by what is forever changed

God, grant us wisdom to move into our seasons and seize-the-day moments

Numb us not from the pain, hide us not from the dark
In the midst, grant us comfort, and light, and understanding
For ourselves, and with one another

In the emptiness and the fullness we feel within,

Grant us a renewed commitment to life

For everything there is a season, and a time for every matter.

**Adapted from Ecclesiastes 3 and personalized for
funerals and memorial services
(see teaching guides 2.6 and 2.7)**

Themes and Counterthemes of Life Stories

Music expresses that which cannot be said and in which it is impossible to be silent.

Victor Hugo

We know an age more vividly through its music than its historians.

Rosanne Ambrose-Brown

"I can name that tune in three notes!" How many of us baby boomers tuned in to TV to beat the show's guests at their own game? Patterns of pitch paired with clues brought delight in naming that tune and winning big bucks. Let's play. Since I can't create audible sounds on these pages, let's try, "Finish That Phrase":

- "Twinkle, twinkle ..."
- "Happy birth-..."

- "Amazing ..."
- "You ain't nothing but ..."

How did you do? By suggesting a few paired sounds, you and I just shared a common language. Musically, we could hum, sing, play, or improvise off of any of those phrases, even if only in our minds. A German proverb notes, "Two people can sing together, but not speak together" (Mauk, 1995, p. 50). We sing a tune together and can move into fresh spaces of being with another. With creative sensitivity we can use that togetherness to move into relational qualities of resonance and empathy.

Let's play more. We could springboard off any of the above tunes into a myriad of "getting to know you" directions. Hearing and validating another's life stories creates significant, healing relationships with another, especially through loss and grief (Harvey, 1996). Music can easily take us into our stored stories. Music can easily motion us into our emotions. Why not shift "Name That Tune" and "Finish That Phrase" into "Tell Its Tale"? Here we go.

"Twinkle, twinkle little star, how I wonder what you are." What is the earliest song you remember singing? Who did you sing it with? Who sang it to you? Tell me more.

"Happy birthday to you": When was your happiest birthday? What was going on in your life? When was your unhappiest birthday? What was going on? What could happen between now and your next birthday that would really make you happy? How might you help make that happen? How might you defeat it?

What emotions do you feel as you hear "Amazing Grace"? What stories or times in your life come to mind? Which words or phrases stand out for you, today? Where — within yourself — do you need to find grace and compassion for yourself? To whom, in your everyday world, might you give grace?

When hearing Elvis Presley's "Hound Dog," your mind may jump to fun images on the small screen's *Ed Sullivan Show* or the big screen's *Forrest Gump*. Let's jump in further. Upon hearing that phrase, connect with Elvis's rebellious streak. When you were a teenager, what rockin' and shakin' songs "got it" for you? (No doubt, those songs capture something of your generation, location, and your unique personality.) Or on a darker note, when did someone criticize you and say to you — in essence — "you ain't nothin' but ..." (fill in your own blank). How did that affect you? Did you take it in or challenge it? Or deeper still, to whom might you be communicating that to, through attitude, actions, or words? What impact might that have within him or her? Hearing those themes within and working them out on one's own instrument is the deeper music of the soul.

The questions above are simply samples. Recalling tunes and asking questions to another must be adapted for the person, context, relationships, and roles with each other (see teaching guide 3.1). For example, if a therapist's client mentions a piece of music that stirred a reaction or memory, recognize this potential key for being with another in her or his "secret garden." Enter into the moment through recalling, humming the music with the person, and then take it further into the client's life stories. Invite your client to bring a recording to your next session. Hear. Here.

☐ Life Stories Stirred by Sounds

These simple sounds of music, in and of themselves, do not hold power to go to those deep places within. Rather, it is the individual's complex interaction of memories, emotions, meanings, and physiological responses stored within and retrieved from different parts of the brain (O'Callaghan, 1999).

The same piece of music can stir completely different responses. Likely, the more intense the life event or meaning connected with the musical sounds, the more intense the response is upon hearing it. "Amazing grace, how sweet the sound" provides a prime example. (The mere thought that anyone might find this offensive may horrify others.) The Bill Moyers documentary *Amazing Grace* portrays the multigenerational, multicultural, varied meanings connected with this simple song (Moyers, 2002). What stirs in your mind as you hear "Amazing Grace"?

- A funeral
- A parent, grandparent, or other important person who sang this hymn
- An "aha" moment in your life where this brought comfort or insight
- A dissonance within between religious dogma and life experience
- A sadness or searching for something lost or longed for
- An intense emotional reaction that cannot be explained
- A disdain
- A celebration of the spirit?

As a musician and chaplain, I've witnessed all of these. This is but one melody. As described above, numerous theme and variation[1] responses can arise from this single melody. One of my favorite variations is to replace the word *wretch* with *soul*. While singing this with a hospice patient whose life story was replete with her mother having called her a "wretch" and a "bitch," I spontaneously changed the phrase to "that saved a *soul* like me." Grace was found in that moment. Creative eyes were opened. A new sense of self was seen. A soul-hole was filled becoming a soul-whole.

Tuneful Tales

Musically, a theme is a melody that characterizes the essence of the music composition. It is the main phrase that stands out. It is easily remembered and recognized. A few familiar classical examples include:

- Bach's opening phrase in "Toccata and Fugue in D minor"
- Beethoven's "Ode to Joy," from *Symphony No. 9*
- Tchaikovsky's "Finale" in *Overture to 1812*
- Copeland's "Simple Gifts" motif in *Appalachian Spring.*

In 17th-century Baroque music, certain patterns of sound were assigned to different emotions. Musically, these were known as affections. In later operatic music, Richard Wagner created leitmotifs, or musical themes, to identify key characters in the plot. More contemporary examples include the famous "Tonight" trilogy of songs that weaves together diverse characters in Leonard Bernstein's *West Side Story*, or "One Day More" in Broadway's *Les Misérables*. These musical themes tell stories with a brilliant essence of each character's tale.

A simple musical theme can swing us into our own life stories. Straight from 20th-century American culture, let's take a sentimental journey. Hear these in your head and heart:

- "Take Me Out to the Ballgame"
- "I'll Be Seeing You"
- "I Love Lucy"
- "Rock Around the Clock"
- "Danny Boy"
- "Gilligan's Isle"
- "Let It Be"
- "I Will Survive"
- "New York, New York"
- "Sesame Street"
- "Taps."

For you, what people, places, memories, emotions, and meanings are stirred? (See teaching guide 3.2.)

Each of these tunes evokes tales that are more than the sounds themselves. Some melodies have words while others do not. Each musical pattern has been experienced at both metacommunity and microindividual levels. While many common contexts and interpretations are shared, each reader's memories and meanings are uniquely personal. Consider the different associations with Frank Sinatra's song, "New York, New York" before September 11, 2001, and then after its tragedies. Pair that song with Bruce Springsteen's "My City of Ruin" in the "America: A Tribute to Heroes" benefit concert, late September 2001 (McCarthy-Mill & Gallen, 2001). We could create similar musical "theme" lists for rival nations or for varied national and folk heritages (Chase, 2003), diverse religions and denominations, and contrasting generations of pop music. Each of us can compile our own personalized musical heritage lists, with multilayered keys, which will lead us into better knowing ourselves and each other (see appendix B, "My Music Menu").

Periodically, a colleague and I catch up on life and our friendship at lunch. Anne always turns the table on me and asks, "So what music are you listening to these days?" (See teaching guide 3.3.) The particular song, artist, or style each of us is drawn to at the time consistently connects with where we are in life's stream.

"Row, row, row your boat, gently down the stream. Merrily, merrily, merrily, merrily, life is but a dream." What music most recently popped into your mind and would not let you go? You know, a melody, phrase, or lyric that stirs around again and again, as if it is trying to get your attention? It *is* trying to get your attention. Listen. Hear. Explore the jewels of wisdom it has for you. Much like the unconscious breaking into the conscious through dream images, I firmly believe such pieces of music are bouncing around inside to teach us something more about ourselves and our relating with our world. So, in addition to "what music are you listening to," I ask you, "what music is popping into your thoughts, and what is it saying to you?"

☐ Case Study: "Getting to Know You" When Words Fail

Consider: Suddenly, you have a disease that severely limits your ability to speak or motion to others. Your emotions and thoughts move around inside, but you cannot voice them to your loved ones. Your spirit feels trapped. You experience your family's love and ongoing care for you. You see their concern and compassion etched on their faces. Your smallest facial gestures become a new language of communication with your family. They secure and learn with you the latest communication tools, such as boards with pictures and letters, or even sophisticated computer devices.

Joan's warmth and beauty graced me. Though she could barely sip water, Joan steadfastly squeezed out her genuine Southern hospitality to me, "Tea?" Lou Gehrig's disease (ALS)[2] had crippled her still-young 60-something body, but not her soul. Eager to express pent-up emotions and thoughts, music quickly connected Joan and me. On my portable keyboard I played songs and hymns I thought she might know. Moments of Joan's life unfolded through her nods, smiles and tears, occasional labored words, and a deeply engaged connection.

Joan and her husband had traveled extensively and always loved a good Broadway show. We laughed with the humorous "Getting to Know You" from *The King and I* (Rodgers and Hammerstein, 1999, original 1956). After several more songs to build rapport and trust, I ventured into the lyrics and music from *My Fair Lady* of "Wouldn't It Be Loverly" (Lerner & Lowe, 1998, original 1956). We wept a bit with the poignancy of her overwhelming losses and new senses of "wouldn't it be loverly" to indulge in the simplest of life experiences that she had previously taken for granted. Complete with Joan's elegant hair bun (affectionately coiffed by her daughter), she quickly became to me my own "fair lady."

At future visits, Joan's husband and daughters joined in, adding their favorite stories, and asking for their favorite hymns with Mom. Note the key phrase: *with Mom.* Music gave them space and time to "be." To experience memories and meanings together in the here and now, with the dark future all too near. Tears flowed and hearts were filled with moments of "It Is Well with My Soul" or Joan's all-time gospel favorite, "When We All Get to Heaven."

Between my visits, Joan's family gathered her favorite recordings to keep nearby. We made a menu of music to possibly play when she was feeling sad, glad, fearful, or prayerful (see appendix B, "My Music Menu," and teaching guide 3.4). The music validated what she was feeling. Joan's family heard and gave expression to her soul, held increasingly captive by a ravaging disease. Of note was a CD I had left with "On Eagles' Wings," one of Joan's favorites. The music was from the Oklahoma Bombing Memorial Service, Spring 1995 (*Music from the Oklahoma City Memorial Service,* 1995). The CD's context of suffering, community, and search for hope in such meaninglessness brought into Joan's living room a "communion," or community of faith. Though Joan's abilities to respond decreased through weeks ahead, our life-story repertoire deepened and took on new meanings (you will read more about Joan in "The Final Cadence," chapter 7, pp. 136–137).

☐ Themes and Counterthemes

Hear this musical theme, with no words attached, in your head. (Hint: it has a strong, classical background.)

♪ ♪ ♪

Da- Da- Da

♪----

Du—m

Repeat it. Now, repeat it several times without a pause. If you guessed a reference to Beethoven's Fifth Symphony, you're right. If you are a connoisseur of classical music, you know that a first theme is usually countered by a contrasting second theme, which is played in a different, but related key. In the Baroque fugue,[3] this is called a countertheme. In the fugue, the two contrasting themes interplay with one another throughout the composition.

In the sonata[4] or symphony[5] the theme and countertheme are introduced in the movement's "Exposition" (first section). Often, this "Exposition" repeats, to instill these themes into the listener's recognition. Next, the "Development" section sets in motion a journey of surprise and intrigue. The theme and countertheme fragment and expand, twist and turn, and transpose into various keys. A melody plays in the bass instead of the treble, or overlays upon itself several times in different registers. Previous, predictable harmonies roam into new progressions. The rapt listener is wrapped up in, "Where are we going?" and "How will we get there?"

The symphony or sonata's music comes out of the "Development," and moves into its final "Recapitulation" section, where it recaps the first two themes. Usually, both themes are now played in the tonic, or home key, instead of in different keys. Musically, this all moves toward the final coda ending, with accelerandos and ritardandos and other musical elements that clearly communicate, "This is it! We're at the end, and this has been glorious."

As crazy as it sounds, this most standard form of classical music loosely mirrors our human developmental life span: one's exposition (formative years) moves into one's development (individual paths with twists, turns, modulations, and something altogether new), which moves into one's recapitulation (elder years of life review, with a more stable "home key"), moving toward the coda and final cadence.

Life's Themes and Counterthemes

Life. What themes and counterthemes bounce back and forth in your life again and again? Do they fight against each other, complement one another, or dance in ebb and flow?

How often do people enter counseling at one age and reenter at another age, only to discover they are dealing with similar themes from before? Does the repetition disclose a bad, unconquered demon? Or perhaps, does it reveal themes and counterthemes that have a deeper soul-essence connection with this person's life stories and his or her attempts to survive and cope? Is it a replaying and reworking out of something seeking transformation, or at least a healthier integration into oneself and with others in one's life?

Take a moment to identify some personal themes and counterthemes:

- independence and dependence
- control and vulnerability
- intimacy and solitude
- rigidity and flexibility
- success and failure
- chemical dependency and sobriety
- career and family
- foolishness and wisdom
- holding on and letting go
- risk and security
- avoidance and passive aggressive behaviors
- name your own (see teaching guide 3.5).

When loss and grief hit, we are often thrown into what feels like the development phase of the sonata or symphony. Our core themes and counterthemes emerge here and there in fragments, wandering around in different keys and configurations. A sort of life preservation can kick in to retain the self in the midst of loss. Where am I? Who am I? Where am I going? How will I get there? I'm getting lost in loss. How do I get through? Can I find my way out?

Back to the metaphor from our sonata and symphony. The sonata or symphony's integrity would end if those initial themes were cut off or stopped. Development, growth, and eventually finding one's way home comes from exploring those same themes and counterthemes of one's life. This fragmenting and replaying of previous themes is uniquely individual to the musical piece, and to the person in grief. Patterns are less predictable, but the themes and counterthemes emerge here and there and everywhere.

Back to grief and loss therapy. Psychoanalytic literature of the mid-20th century emphasized decathexis (or cut off) over and against continuity of one's themes with the loss (Hagman, 2001). Emergence of themes could be heard as being pathological, or in lay terms, pathetic. More recent psychoanalytic literature on mourning affirms the significance of maintaining one's connections to and meanings of the loss (Neimeyer, 2001; Hagman, 2001), or using this author's metaphors, one's themes and counterthemes of life story. George Hagman reviews grief–loss literature and points toward new understandings and treatments of mourning, beyond decathexis (Hagman, 2001). Hagman challenges therapists to see that persons' "pathological responses" might be seen instead as "unsuccessful strategies to maintain meaning and preserve the attachment to the lost object" (Hagman, 2001, p. 25). The person may well be trying to survive. Judgments of behaviors from other survivors may miss the mark. The failure may not be in the person, but rather in the "helper" or survivor, for not considering the person's specific personality, relationship to the loss, and familial–cultural background (Hagman, 2001, p. 25). He posits, "mourning is fundamentally an intersubjective process, and many problems arising from bereavement are due to the failure of other survivors to engage the bereaved person in mourning together" (Hagman, 2001, p. 25).

I share with you Earline, who taught me a few things. Picture Whoopi Goldberg, a little younger, and you are on your way to a treat. Listen for themes and counterthemes, and coping.

Case Study: Paradox Meanings

Forty-something Earline was a walking paradox. In the late stages of AIDS, her energy defied what her medical tests indicated. She exuded a childlike charm and streetwise savvy. She was here, there, and everywhere, with her address, phone, and contacts changing so frequently, we sometimes did not know where to find her. As her hospice team, we felt both affection and exasperation. She would swear she did not have money for food, and then be pan-frying thick steaks. She would complain of pain, and then be noncompliant with prescribed medications. Earline was going to do things her way, we learned.

Earline was admitted to our hospice inpatient unit for pain management and caregiving needs. Our inpatient staff stumbled upon a large collection of hospital silverware and tray items wrapped in a hospital pillowcase, in her bedside table drawer. Earline readily explained these were rightfully hers. As chaplain for Earline, part of my role was to address these behaviors with her. We were preparing to discharge her from the acute care unit to a nursing home, with continued hospice care.

In our dialogue, Earline began telling me an elaborate story about having been left by a parent at the local Catholic orphanage when she was age 8 or 9. We all knew Earline could tell a tale. What was I to believe? I retrieved a heavy-duty pre-Vatican II CD from our unit's collection of recordings for patients: "Ave Maria, gratia plena. Maria, gratia plena, Ave Dominus tecum, Benedicta tu in mulie ribus et benedictus." She immediately recognized it and sang along, phrase by phrase. I played a few more familiar and obscure selections, checking for her recognition, and engaging Earline in dialogue. Definitely, she had a Catholic background, sometime, somewhere. The music springboarded us into rich dialogue, where she described the orphanage's strict rules, punishments like cleaning the bathrooms, and also of the ballet classes she loved taking. I was baffled at this newly revealed part of her history; still a little wary, but open to getting to know her more.

Earline living in this white, conservative Catholic setting? Taking ballet? It was quite a picture, with her fiercely free spirit and now ethnically flowing dreadlocks. I began to hear more deeply what she had felt about herself and learned about survival and self in that space and place of her life story, as an African-American child, in white-skinned institution, at that time of our city's history. She had experienced both security and fear, blessing and shame.

The hidden silverware took on a new meaning. Property at the orphanage had been somewhat communal, with little to no personal belongings. Earline's lifelong rebellious streak had sought freedom and worth. She had created a survivor's sense of immunity within the big, punitive systems. Her behavioral methods were poor, but her life meanings were rich. Were we the "parent," once again planning to leave her at an institutional home? In body and spirit, once again, Earline was determined to beat the big, bad systems, both the medical and social systems, and her body's own immune system.

Fast forward several months to Earline being bed bound at a long-term care facility (nursing home), nearing Christmas. She had easily adapted to knowing everyone, and all knowing her. In my ongoing hospice visits to her, we sang a combination of African-American standards ("There Is a Balm" and "Precious Lord, Take My Hand"), "Ave Maria," and Christmas carols. Her favorite? It was the Catholic plainsong "O Come, O Come Emmanual, and ransom captive Israel, that mourns in lonely exile here." We discussed the different times she had felt "captive," with no way out. We celebrated her ways of finding freedom, yes, even here in this nursing home, in her bed. "Rejoice, rejoice, Emannuel shall come to thee O Israel." We talked of God's presence with her, within her, wherever she is, in the core of her life spirit, and through each moment ahead.

We drew from the ballet she had once known. Now unable to move her legs, Earline beautifully moved her arms up and out in graceful, once-trained motions, dancing soulful expression. We sang and I accompanied on my keyboard with a "white" pipe-organ sound, and then a "black" electronic organ sound. Her arm movements spontaneously matched the words — from an upward and outward blossoming at "rejoice" to a hands-in-prayer over her heart at "shall come to thee, O Israel." In that moment, through music and movement, themes and counterthemes of Earline's living and dying transcended time and space.

Knowing Earline affected me deeply. Years later, I hear that "rejoice, rejoice" melody and I give thanks for Earline's freedom-bound life spirit.

☐ Diminishing Dementia: Relating with Memories through Music

Another form of captivity is the slow, stripping of the mind through dementia or Alzheimer's disease. Finding one's way in the world becomes a continual maze. Knowing where and who one is becomes a blank, a hole, a dark fear. Almost any family or professional caregiver for persons with dementia has witnessed music evoking some type of increased alertness or response.

Extensive research studies explore the use of music with dementia patients (Aldridge, 2000; Koger, Chapin, & Brotons, 1998). In my research and clinical practice on music and pastoral care with persons experiencing loss and grief, I have gleaned five progressive processes for relating with another through music and memories (Berger, 2003). For our own memory's sake, I have nicknamed them "5 R's for Relating with Memories" (figure 3.1). This progression is important when engaging the person with dementia. They include: *Respond → Recognize → Recall → Reflect → Re-Vision*. While these focus on dementia care, applications abound for relating through music and memories with highly functioning persons (see teaching guide 3.6).

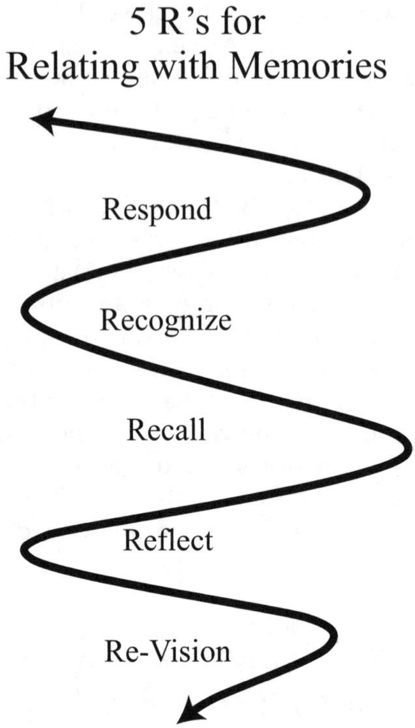

5 R's for
Relating with Memories

Respond

Recognize

Recall

Reflect

Re-Vision

FIGURE 3.1

Respond

The person responds to a musical sound by turning one's head toward the sound, tapping a finger or foot, or nodding one's head to the music, making a sound in response to the music — some kind of physical, observable response to the music stimulus. Does he appear to be calmed and comforted, or irritated and agitated? The focus is less on my music, and more on the person's response to it. Am I making eye contact? Am I in hearing range? Can the person respond by strumming the instrument (i.e., Q-chord)[6] with or without assistance, shaking a maraca or some other instrument, or physically responding in some other way? For the person with advanced dementia, "respond" may be as far as one can go. The goal is to affirm the person. The hope is to support through human interaction. "You are not alone. You are known."

Recognize

The person recognizes the music. Patterns of sound instilled in the brain are engaged. The person hums, sings, or plays the music, matching melody or text from some previous, instilled experience of that music. I find simple questions to family members or friends to be great clues and cues. It also involves them in the process of engaging the patient. For example:

- Do you remember a song your mom or dad often sang, like while doing household chores, in the car, or other everyday moments?
- What was her all-time favorite piece of music? (This may be a specific song or hymn, a recording, an artist, a style.)
- If the person played piano or another instrument, what music scores are stored in the piano bench or music case? What are the most well-worn LPs in her or his personal collection?

Re-creating these pieces of music can provide personalized cues for connecting with the patient's darkened mind. The brightened eyes, nod of the head, smile, or other response to a musical selection can bring a sense of life spirit, awareness, and connection, even if only for a passing moment. Recordings provide actual, re-created sounds of instrumentation, vocal sounds, tempos and textures, instilled in the memory years before. Live music can provide in-the-moment interactions. Whichever is used, encourage connection with the person's life spirit.

A lifelong amateur jazz pianist was losing his fight with a brain disease. Earlier in his diagnosis, he had written a list of his favorite music. He kept it front and center on his piano's music rack. His wife described: "He didn't want to forget. He wanted to remember for as long as he could." Later in his significant deterioration, his elderly wife fell and was seriously injured. With his wife no longer able to take care of him, he was taken to a nursing home, separated from anything and anyone he recognized. His now invalid wife was unable to leave home. Both being hard of hearing, phone conversations were nearly impossible. As I visited his wife in their home, we made cassette tapes of her talking to him. With her permission, I photocopied his hand-written list of music (leaving the original with her), and taped it to the wall by his nursing home bed. With guidance and encouragement to several nursing home staff, they sang those same songs to him while they performed daily tasks, like feeding, bathing, and moving. They played the personalized tape from his wife to him as he was going to sleep at night. Her familiar voice. His familiar songs. Comfort. Care. Presence in the aloneness. Being known, even when you feel you do not know who or where you are.

Recall

The next level of relating is when the person recalls. Recalling may be music or something associated with the music. The recalling from one's memory may be humming, singing, or saying words. Mainly, the person matches responses with the music's patterns. Typically, these songs will be from one's teen or early adulthood years. These tend to be one's years of developing an individual, unique identity. The music may be a song of love, rebellion, home, geographic culture, patriotism, or faith. Mainly, it will be something that had been repeated often and has had some type of emotional expression and meaning for the person.

If you hear the person singing, humming, or whistling, listen. Hear. Listen again. Learn. Affirm. Join in, giving full attention to the person. Do not take away his music and make it your own. Gently give witness to this person's expressions. Hear his world. Be with her in this window moment.

Do not expect the person to generate a favorite song without some type of prompt. For example, begin a phrase, and then prompt the person to join in. Learn from the family what music may be meaningful to the individual. Use the music to engage the person. Closely observe how the person responds with either positive interaction, irritated response, or no response at all.

Lily was sitting in her wheelchair in her nursing home room, with little to no response to me. I did not have much initial information about Lily, and looked around her room for cues about her. Usually, the few items in a long-term care facility are carefully chosen by family members to bring comfort and stir memory. The photo collage on her wall caught my attention. The old photos appeared to be of a family homestead. I asked her about them. She could not recall. Living in Kentucky, I began playing my Q-chord and singing, "The sun shines bright on my old Kentucky home." Her eyes lit up. Lily moved her head. I placed her hand on mine as I strummed and sang. I maintained close eye contact, which she began to return. She recognized the song, especially at the refrain. I stretched out the words of "Weep, no more, my lady," as Lily's face brightened and she slowly recalled and sang bits of phrases. Lily smiled. At the end of the song I asked her again about the photo, and she suddenly recalled, "Oh, that's Brandenburg (KY)," and "that's my Mama and Daddy." As I sang a few more songs, she gradually began to strum the Q-chord with less assistance. She expressed delight (and immediate gratification) in her musical strumming and interaction. She could answer a few more closed questions ("yes," "no," or easy short answers). She was not able to describe or interpret those memories, but our time was good. And it was complete.

Reflect

Reflecting takes "recalling" something from memory and moving it toward meanings of the memory. The interpretations may be quite simple or complex. Reflecting connects the current life moment with past experiences, with an inner wisdom that guides us through. Listen. Hear. Call forth those thoughts in the other, before telling another what to do and how to do and when to do. (How many baby boomers reading this have shifted into caregiving roles for parents? Our generation is known for believing we know it all.)

Elderly adults are in a life stage of finding meaning and making sense of their lives. They repeatedly encounter loss and change: professional roles, health, activities, illnesses and deaths of spouses, friends, and changing support systems. Losing one's own memory and one's own sense of self can be the most devastating of all. Using music for reflecting is not about the music, it is about the person. It is recalling, recollecting, and reflecting on the person's sense of self. Life stories. Relationships. Strengths. Struggles. Fears. Depression. Hopes (Ashida, 1999). It is about affirming one's being in the "hear" and now.

A daughter-in-law and I sang children's songs to her retired schoolteacher mother-in-law, who was having a clearer day in her growing dementia. We affirmed her lifelong gifts living on through many children now grown. She nodded her head. "A,B,C,D,E,F,G ..." "I'm a little teapot ..." She smiled, laughed, and sang a fragment or two as she could, then several more. Then she voiced, "Sometimes I feel so lost." That was the moment. Her voice was far more important than our songs. We moved into validating her realization. We affirmed her in the midst of her loss. We assured her of her physical safety, of being known and taken care of by others, just as she had done for her own parents years before.

The daughter-in-law knew her mother-in-law's history and repertory of music. I was simply facilitator and guide. We shifted to her songs of faith that in earlier years had provided hope while feeling lost: "Great Is Thy Faithfulness," "It Is Well," and "Abide With Me." She sang phrases with us. Tears flowed, paired with nods of feeling heard, supported, and assured. A deep presence with one another was felt. While her verbal language was limited, she readily connected and reflected through her familiar music of the soul.

Reflecting and connecting through music is not limited to the elderly generation. We, the younger generation, can learn from them. We keep, discard, edit, and incorporate aspects from our own reflections on their living and dying. We can learn from their dying about our own living. "On Angel's Wings" is a poignant song written by Karen Taylor-Good, describing her mother's descent into Alzheimer's. Karen celebrates her mother's life, grieves with her life's new losses, and begins to emotionally and spiritually prepare herself for her mother's death (Taylor-Good, 2003).

Alert. Listen, Joy Berger, to the sounds around. While writing this, our recently turned 18-year-old is upstairs with his stereo's volume cranked high. He is playing a CD he had requested for his birthday, the soundtrack songs from *Forrest Gump*. These songs are not his music. (We know those all too well.) These are his dad's music, from the same teenage time frame in his life. Musical expressions and reflections on a controversial war, rebellion, drug culture, search for meaning, and a generation desperately trying to find sense in it all. Perhaps a circle of life? Yes. We can hear each other. We can learn from each other. We can understand it better and stand in it better. Individually. Together.

Re-vision

Recalling and reflecting pulls one's past into the present. Re-visioning imagines one's future into the present. Re-visioning one's future (or revising) validates fears. Strengthens hope. Reframes assumptions. Challenges beliefs that no longer work. Re-visioning finds new ways to hope and cope. For the highly functioning person, Helen Bonny's method of Guided Imagery and Music (GIM) is a psychodynamic mode of music therapy (Bonny & Summer, 2002) for exploring one's past and for re-visioning one's future. On a self-help level, numerous tapes and CDs with music and spoken guided imagery foster meditation, calm, and shifts in thoughts and emotions. Keeping current with technology, music is often paired with biofeedback, computer or video games, and archetypal symbols to teach deep relaxation and imagery.

For the person with dementia, simpler outcomes through music therapy are needed. For example, dealing with tasks in the immediate future can pose great challenges, like shifting attention toward moving in or out of bed, dressing, eating, or bathing. Studies show music therapy in dementia care to be able to reduce agitation and its related behaviors (Vink & Enschede, 2000).

Meaning in the moment can be created in dementia's darkness. It may be simply playing the right song at the right time. It may be changing a word or two, like singing of "my old Indiana home" and "my new Kentucky home, here today" with an alert patient who had recently moved to Louisville, Kentucky to be near her adult children. She "got" it and initiated talking about her transitions.

Whether one is wandering in a darkness of dementia or shadows of grief, music can be a light in the darkness. It can stir that same inner faith, humor, tenacity, or grace that has gotten you thus far.

A song of hope can stir the soul. Hope is not starry, wishful thinking. Hope sees, hears, and feels life's harsh realities. Hope knows fear, sorrow, and loneliness, intimately. Hope hears the many rhythms and themes of who we are, and whispers, "sing, play, dance, compose. This your life. Live it well."

☐ Your Life Story's Tunes and Tales

Enough said about others' music of the soul. This book is of no use if it only talks of others (see teaching guide 3.7). My hope is to join together on a soul-journey. So, to any readers who dare to venture:

- What music taps into your heritage, long before you were born?
- What are your earliest memories of music? Who was there? What details do you remember? What emotions are you feeling now, as you remember?
- What music reminds you of your parents? Your grandparents?
- What music takes you back to grade school? High school?
- As a teen and young adult, what music reflected rebellion for you? Love? Belonging? Separation? Search for meaning?
- What music takes you to years of partnering? Parenting?
- What music has been there for you in times of celebration? Tragedy and loss?
- What music takes you to places within of comfort? Of hope?
- What music might you create, communicating what you want for your future?

Welcome, to your music of the soul.

CHAPTER

Harmonies and Dissonances of Healing

Did you know that our soul is composed of harmony?

Leonardo da Vinci

Music was my refuge. I could crawl into the space between the notes and curl my back to loneliness.

Maya Angelou

Rhythm and harmony penetrate very deeply to the inward places of the soul, and affect it most powerfully, imparting grace.

Plato

☐ Life's Harmonic Progressions
☐ Life's Dissonant Changes
☐ Healing Grief: Hearing Its Dissonances and Harmonies
☐ Harmonies and Dissonances of Healing: Coda or Commencement

Harmony: All is right with the world, love is in the air. Being in the right job with the right people in the right place and making enough money with a huge retirement portfolio. Feeling valued and appreciated. Health and wealth and beauty. Good news. All is right and good?

Dissonance: Something's just not right. Chaos, confusion, and disarray: the broken relationship, the lost job, the unfulfilled dream, unrequited love — shame, blame, guilt, debt, and challenge. Disappointment, sickening news, grief, and loss. Chronic illness, overstretched and stressed caregiving. Impending death, death, living on after death, lost and lonely. Don't know where to go or what to do. All is wrong and bad?

Harmony and dissonance together? Life as a C-major chord would be terribly boring, horribly static. Only a few basic songs can be played with just one chord. For the curious, try "Are You Sleeping, Brother John" (see teaching guide 4.1). In music, dissonances add movement and motion. They add a tension that seeks expansion or eventual resolution. Musicians speak of harmonic movement as progressions, suspensions, and resolutions. If only we could hear life's dissonances as a sense of movement, instead of as roadblocks that keep us from life movement. In life (as in music), perhaps dissonance and harmony are neither all bad nor good, but rather moments for choosing what to create and where to go, now? (See teaching guide 4.2.)

Viktor Frankl wrote of this inner harmony paired with dissonance, and its sense of movement and direction: "What man actually needs is not a tensionless state but rather the striving and struggling for some goal worthy of him. What he needs is not the discharge of tension at any cost, but the call of a potential meaning waiting to be fulfilled by him" (Frankl, 1963, p. 166). I read that quote and hear in my mind Samuel Barber's "Adagio for Strings" (Barber & Slatkin, 1989). It pulses and resonates its artistry through subtle shifts in dissonance and harmony. It creates a musical tension that moves forward, with a capacity for not only holding dissonance and paradox, but also for moving toward a moment of transcendent release.

Paul Minear, emeritus theology professor at Yale, has eloquently described music's abilities to create such powerful moments:

> Music can articulate the rich subtleties experienced in suffering and joy. It is a language native to exiles returning to their native land, the best medium for expressing gratitude so intense as to explode in glorias. It releases a wider spectrum of emotions than can be released by confessional formulas or historical reconstructions. It evokes the sense of mystery that surrounds such homespun words as *death* and *life*. (Minear, 1987, p. 18)

☐ Life's Harmonic Progressions

I marvel at the simple harmonica, the in-your-hand sized instrument which with one breath plays numerous notes together, in harmony with each other. With a mere, gentle movement, the sounds shift with ease to another chord, in harmony with the preceding one, and glide on into the next. The main energy needed is balanced breathing in and out. How I would love to do life like that.

Jump ahead into freshman music theory, often a make-it-or-break-it course for music majors at any university. Its purpose? To instill the rudiments of harmony by hearing, reading, and writing music. A rebel of sorts, my theory professor would play chords at the piano, mischievously taking us down paths which none of us could decipher. He would get to the just-right-before-the-end-waiting-to-resolve chord, and then jovially walk away from the piano and out of the room. Our ears craved that resolution.

I believe we have seasons and times when, like the harmonica, life flows easily from one "chord" to the next. I believe we have seasons and times when life has its unresolved endings, and like the theory class with its nonending, we ache for resolution. What are the harmonic movements between those extremes? In basic harmony courses, we musicians learn of passing tones suspensions, and deceptive cadences (a false ending), and various cadence endings. Do you hear metaphors for how we do life?

More often than not, perhaps real life is more like a rich piece of jazz. The extra notes in those chords, known as "blue notes," or 9ths, 11ths, or even 13ths stretch the standard 1-3-5 chordal sound. Those dissonances add hues and nuances of expression that is just right. Not "all is good" nor "all is bad," but rather a "whether in peace or chaos, I'll find a wellness within." The Alcoholics Anonymous Serenity Prayer affirms, "God grant me the serenity to accept the things I cannot change, the courage to change those I can, and the wisdom to know the difference."

I have never met a hospice patient who had done or said absolutely everything he or she wanted, for whom all of life's frayed endings were tidied up. I have never met a hospice family member for whom everything had been said and done. I have known many who described and radiated a sense of completeness and wholeness. An "it is well" or "all will be well." Who truly (not glibly) voiced a "be at peace" and "goodbye" (which means "God be with you"). Go now in peace. Be at peace. An "amen" kind of "let it be." (For any choral musicians, can you hear the church choir's plagal cadence, "Amen"?)

Starting and Ending Place: My Harmonic Home

Where do you find your "home"? Baseball has a home base. You leave it and circle your way back around to it. Hopes for a home run cheer you to hit the ball as far away as possible, to run faster and smarter than the potential "outs" lurking along the way, and victoriously slide back into home. Cheers. Applause.

Most music has a home key: C major, A-flat major, F minor, E major, C-sharp minor, to name a few. The music then twists and turns within its main structure, and eventually works its way back home. Marie Spoone, my childhood piano teacher, always made sure we knew the "home key" and "tonic" chord of our recital pieces, so that we could find our way "home" if we got lost while playing. (I used it on several occasions.)

In life, where do you find your best sense of "home"? It may be a physical, external place. As I write, I'm sitting on our back porch in the early evening with my husband gardening nearby. This gets it for me. I believe the best, truest sense of "home" is within. It embraces feeling grounded and uplifted, courageous and content.

When significant loss occurs, we can lose that inner sense of home. Thomas Attig describes:

> Our suffering includes "soul pain." I use *soul* to refer to that within us that sinks roots into the world, makes itself at home in our surroundings, finds nourishment and sustenance in the here and now of everyday life. When we suffer soul pain, we feel uprooted. We feel homesick. We feel estranged within and alienated from surroundings transformed by the death and our pain and anguish. We sense that we cannot find our way home to life as it was before the death. (2001, p. 37)

In fact, we cannot "find our way home to life as it was before," because it is no longer as it was before. Loss can severely threaten how we perceive ourselves and how we perceive the world (Davis, 2001). Colin Parkes describes this as a time of "disorganization and despair" (2001, p. 7). William Worden identifies this as a task "to adjust to an environment in which the deceased is missing" (2002, pp. 32–35).

Still, I may need to revisit home to experience what has changed and how I am changing. I may be confronted with the question of where my sense of home is now. Bruce Springsteen's stark ballad, "My Father's House" poignantly describes this (1990).

What literal music helps you move into those "homing" places within? (See teaching guide 4.3.) It may be a lullaby, a love song, a folk tune or hymn. It may be the chiming of a generation to generation grandfather clock that sounds the same tones you have heard through many years of family moments. It may be the sound of your loved one singing or plucking away at a guitar or piano. It may be a memory of a sound. For me, it would be my dad's one-tune whistle, my mom playing piano with the dishwasher swishing in the background, or my husband's spontaneous singing and hearty laugh.

For me, it would be playing from my favorite piano scores or hearing recordings of recitals and concerts in years past. In my car's six-CD player, CD number 1, track 1, is a recording of me playing Debussy's "Reflections in the Water," my signature piano piece years ago. It has more meaning for me than this paragraph allows. It stays in my car's player for those unexpected everyday moments when I need to reconnect with who I am, where I have been, and the yin-yang creative tension of where life is taking me and where I want to go.

In another homeland and an earlier era, Victor Hugo (1802–1885) asked, "Who among us has not found peace in a song?" (quoted in Exley, 1992). Hugo, a French poet and novelist, rather than a composer, knew this sense of finding peace, rest, and "home." Throughout his 1862 novel *Les Misérables,* he explores themes of being outcast, homeless, and on the run. The 1987 Broadway musical adaptation poignantly captures this search for an inner home in its songs, "Castle on a Cloud," "I Dreamed a Dream," and "Javert's Suicide" (Boubil & Schonberg, 1989). The story's threads also weave loss into life, and grit into grace. These are experienced in its songs, "What Have I Done," "Bring Him Home," and the gentle "Finale" between Jean Valjean and Fontine. Grief researchers explore this profound ability of life's losses to grow us and transform us (Calhoun & Tedeschi, 2001; Davis, 2001; Tedeschi & Calhoun, 1995).

Venturing Out from Home

How far do I venture out from "home"? What is my range of harmonic movement in this world? Am I comfortable only when living life like a basic I-IV-V chord structure, in keys like C, F, and G? Or, can I find my way through "the music" of a wider variety of life situations, settings, and relationships?

At another extreme, do I always have to stir up an atonal dissonance with little cohesiveness or meaning? The music I choose to hear or create often reflects my preference. (Try it. Check it out.) I need to know my parameters for exploring and finding my way back, or for creating my way on ahead. What are my parameters for being able to hear others' home keys, especially when loss and grief are present (Goss & Klass, 2005)? Is it focused in my own cultural rules? Political stances? Religious dogmas? Family clan?

A Need for Order and Safety

Gretchen could barely stand the noises her 8- and 10-year-old grandchildren brought into the house. Yes, she wanted them to visit her husband, who was dying, but their active childhood sounds were too much for her. Gretchen avoided words about her husband's impending death. They were too dissonant, too painful. I learned from their hospice team that Gretchen grew up in World War II Germany. The little girl Gretchen was warned, "Be quiet! Don't make noise!" Realities of attack or death were too close. Stoicism was demanded.

I was called to provide music therapy support for Gretchen, for hospice supports both the patient and the family. Music therapy is used in many clinical settings to calm anxiety and stress (e.g., Burns, Labbé, Arke et al., 2001; Knights & Rickard, 2000; Walworth, 2000).

Though verbal engagement with Gretchen was limited, she was receptive to me playing classical music for her on her spinet piano. I chose music that was not too dissonant, not too loud or too personal. I played safe, contained, gentle German sounds, like minuets from Anna Magdalena Bach's Notebook (Bach, 1960), Schumann's "Träumerei" ("Dreaming") (Schumann, 1990), or Brahms' "Intermezzo in A Major, Op. 118, No. 2" (Brahms, 1971). The classical music played for Gretchen, in her home, provided a space to safely "be" with the dissonances of her husband's illness, and to build bridges with her hospice team. Her guarded emotional safety zone was not to be shamed. It had been her childhood survival. Our response abilities required us to hear her life more deeply. We needed to understand and support Gretchen within her sense of "harmonic home."

Others' Harmonic Homes

Let's push it further. Is *my* comfort range limited to Western musical sounds? While I claim my sense of "home base," can I emotionally allow another to value something altogether different? With music, we all become critics.

Can I at least listen to others' sounds, even if I don't "get" them? Can I intentionally listen to another's homeland modes of expression, with hopes of better understanding the other? Replaying a theme from chapter 1, who might you or I get to know and understand better by really hearing his or her music? A friend? A family member? Another religion? Or another region? Might another's prayers for survival be held safely and voiced soulfully in one's music (Amir, 2004; Heitzman, 2005)?

Find an artist whose music is terribly offensive to you. For example, if you hate rap music, try Kanye West's "Jesus Walks" (West, 2004) or Eminem's "Lose Yourself" (Mathers, 2002). Listen, really listen to texts with filters that tune into emotions, thoughts, and another's search for meaning. What is the musician voicing? Pain? Sorrow? Fear? Jealousy? Determination? Is he or she searching for intimacy? Expressing feelings of rage or revenge? To what do you relate? May we stretch our hearing, knowing, and understanding of ourselves and each other.

☐ Life's Dissonant Changes

You hear a familiar melody, but the harmonies supporting it have all changed. Try Joni Mitchell's 2000 recording of "Both Sides Now" (Mitchell, 2000; original recording 1968). They push and pull you at surprise tension points. You don't know where or when or even *if* the dissonances will resolve. You wonder if the familiar homelike harmonic structures will return. (Does that sound like living with a teenager or a family member with dementia?) Let's move it from literal music to life metaphor. A challenge exists.

- Can I hear the new chords, with whatever pain or discord they bring to me?
- What are they telling me? Teaching me?
- Can I move into the new phase?
- Or do I insist on a rigid formula that hopes to insure my former security? No doubt, the dissonance can get more painful.

Do the new underlying harmonies harm or harmonize your sense of self in your changing life setting? Is your home key always C major, or can you have a wider range of modulations and explorations? When life gets really uncomfortable, like playing a piano piece in G-flat major or F-sharp minor, can you settle in and find your way?

Beethoven and the Beatles: Beyond Their Hair

In Western music, any major shift in musical style has been characterized largely by its new use of dissonance. Ironically, the now common "third" interval used when harmonizing was once considered by the Roman Catholic church to have been a sound of the devil, or evil itself. It was forbidden. Jump ahead several centuries. Both Beethoven and the Beatles were revolutionary in their musical genres for having introduced new dissonances and shifting them toward a new, normal sense of harmony. Is it any wonder that both Beethoven and the Beatles contextually were at pivotal points in history? Is it no wonder that both had survived childhood traumas filled with great dissonance?

Ludwig van Beethoven heralded the freedom of the common man, through the French Revolution and its impact through Europe. (Hear his "Finale" from Symphony No. 9, and read its texts.) He rebelled against being a conventional court musician and dedicated himself to being a musician of the people. More personally, his loss of hearing was a catalyst for his musical expressions of darker emotions, and explorations of increased dissonances and instrumental effects, wider musical ranges, and brighter celebrations. These are evidenced in pieces like his "Tempest" Piano Sonata No. 17 in D minor, Opus 32, written in 1802 as his hearing was leaving, and his last Piano Sonata, No. 32 in C minor, Opus 111, written in 1827 in total deafness.

Similarly, the Beatles were born between 1940 and 1943, in Liverpool, England. Their formative years of sound and sensory stimulation were wrought with war, bombings, sirens, and terror. Their music connected with and catapulted the 1960s Western youth culture into sounds of war protests, the search for love and peace, and an escape from unrelieved pain through drugs. John Winston Lennon was given up at birth (1940) by his parents to relatives (Kane, 2005). He wrote his famous "Strawberry Fields" (Lennon & McCartney, 1967) about his own childhood refuge, a Salvation Army orphanage in a field near his home, where young John played with his boyhood friends, Pete Shotton and Ivan Vaughn. Recall from your memory another familiar Beatles' text, "Let It Be" (McCartney & Lennon, 1970). "Mother Mary," in this song, was Paul McCartney's own mother, who had died when he was 13 years old.

Musically, both Beethoven and the Beatles expanded their harmonic vocabularies to create truer expressions of their soul dissonances. Historically, both created music that connected with the people, or in Jungian terms, the larger "collective unconscious," which then birthed new harmonic norms (Jung & Adler, 1981; Jung & Adler, 1981/1991; Marshman, 2003).

In your life-harmonics lingo, where have your personal, pivotal points occurred? What dissonances or complete key changes have revolutionized your life? (See teaching guide 4.4.)

Chaos Clusters

I was visiting 37-year-old Pacho in his small, downtown, immaculate apartment. As chief dishwasher for a nearby restaurant, he lived a humble, loyal work ethic. Pacho was coping with horrific stomach pains, due to his metastasized cancer. Ethnically marginalized and financially poor, he had struggled to find adequate medical care. Help was too little, too late. Even then, Pacho described his doctor's hesitancy at telling him how advanced his tumors were, with little room for allowing Pacho's questions.

At each visit, Pacho and I used my portable keyboard as a visual/aural/tactile tool for him to select keyboard notes and describe his "high's" and "low's" of pain, of the week, or whatever we were describing (see appendix C, "Keyboard Quality of Life: Highs and Lows"). As was our ritual, Pacho played some "high" and "low" keyboard sounds and related them to moments of his past week: "highs" of his girl friend being there for him and of medicines reducing the physical pain. "Lows" included "getting weaker," "knowing I won't get better," and friends and family "not hearing me," "not understanding." A cousin had told him to just get up and go outside to play some ball, "and you'll feel better." Pacho asserted, "They don't realize how sick I am. They tell me to just pray and God'll take care of it. Yeah, right. Where was God when the doctors pushed me aside?"

Pacho's distress today was deep, and overwhelming. Realities of his shortened life span were hitting. His family and friends kept discounting how badly he felt, and his sense of shortened time. No words could ease his pain. The dissonances he felt were right on target. He needed to feel heard, to be validated.

Today, like my college theory teacher, I played different chords with dissonances that urged a sense of movement. Our interspersed music and dialogue continued. "Yes. That's what I feel." He felt the dissonances and wanted life movement from others, not stagnation. He talked about his too-little-too-late medical treatment, and kind hearted, gentle Pacho displayed anger and despair. My music shifted.

I played several clusters on the keyboard, crashing my whole hand down and randomly hitting whatever was in its path (see teaching guide 4.5). Low. High. He played them too. "Yeah. That's it." Hard and loud. No gentleness with this. No nice, sweet harmonies. Crashing dissonance.

There was a moment, a time, a being with, a connection. The discomfort was heard and was not evaded. There was no shift to something more pleasant. No shoulds or discounts allowed.

Again, Pacho quietly said, "That's it." I affirmed, through keyboard sound and emotional, spiritual presence.

We stayed with "it" for awhile. We gave dissonant sounds space and time to be heard.

To be felt.
To be validated.
To be.
(How I wish I could write in a reader's fermata.)
To be with.
Hear.
There is God.

Here is God.
Hear is God — with us — in the chaos clusters of pain and fear and
distress.
Nothing is too ugly.
Nothing is too profane.
(Can I write in another fermata?)

☐ Healing Grief: Hearing Its Dissonances and Harmonies

Any piece of music consists of various patterns. The variables of those patterns provide musical understanding, and also distinguish it from any other musical composition. The musical experience is never again repeated (even with a digital recording), for the person creating the music or listening is in a different time frame and context from before.

Similarities exist with loss and grief. Theorists from various civilizations and disciplines have identified grief's key patterns. Those patterns provide understanding for being in and moving through one's grief toward healing. Grief theorists affirm the highly individual experiences of the person, due to one's context, timeframe, and meanings of the loss for the person (Neimeyer, 2001; Worden, 2002).

For example, in 1900 life expectancy in the United States was 47 years old. One of every two babies under one year old died. Losing a child to death was an expected rite of passage for young mothers (Parkes, 2002, p. 368). Curative medical treatments did not exist. Grief, loss, and survival held different assumptions and meanings than they do today.

Through the 20th century's advances in medicine, psychology, sociology, counseling, and so forth, key grief theorist John Bowlby researched attachment and loss (1980), and Elizabeth Kübler-Ross examined stages of grief not for surviving loss (as often attributed), but rather for preparing to move toward death and cope with its numerous losses (Kübler-Ross, 1969).

In more recent years, hospice and its bereavement care have brought grief counseling and support to our grassroots population. Grief and loss support is provided from interdisciplinary professionals — in our homes, hospitals, long-term care centers, ecumenical memorial services, community support groups, schools, and so forth. Three contemporary key grief–loss theorists' concepts are examined: Parkes (2001), Worden (2002), both of which are now being examined in a creative tension by Neimeyer (2001).

Processes of Grief and Tasks of Mourning

Parkes's book *Bereavement: Studies of grief in adult life* was the first empirical, scientific study of bereavement loss (Parkes, 1972/1987/2001). He summarizes, "grief is a process and not a state. Grief is not a set of symptoms which start after a loss and then eventually fade away. It involves a succession of clinical pictures which blend into and replace one another" (p. 7). Parkes describes those pictures of what is happening to the person. While the British Parkes describes "what is happening," the American psychologist William Worden puts forth "what I can do" with his "Tasks of Mourning" (2002, pp. 26–37). These tasks are proactive. They occur in cycles, in both micro and macro time frames. (Parkes's phrases, "disorganization and despair" and "reorganization" are from his second edition, 1987, p. 27.)

I experience these processes and tasks in an oscillation with each other, much like the well-known Serenity Prayer.[1] Loosely, and my own interpretation, Parkes's processes describe what is happening to me that I cannot change. I seek a serenity to face and accept these. Worden's tasks affirm what I can do and in time (not to be prematurely rushed), prays for courage to be in and move through these. Affirming the rest of the prayer, we seek wisdom to discern the difference and timing between the two.

1. Numbness and Accepting the Reality of the Loss. Initially, the person experiences a numbness (Parkes, 2001, p. 7), shock, and denial (Parkes, 1983, p. 27). These serve as an emotional airbag to protect the person from the full impact of what is happening. Worden defines the first task of mourning as being, "to accept the reality of the loss" (2002, pp. 27–30). Accepting reality is not a one-time occurrence, but rather an ongoing task

---

TABLE 4.1 Parkes's processes of grief and Worden's tasks of mourning

Processes of grief	Tasks of mourning
1. Numbness, shock, and denial	1. To accept the reality of the loss
2. Searching, longing, pining for the loss	2. To work through the pains of the loss
3. Disorganization and despair	3. To adjust to an environment in which the deceased [attachment] is missing –External adjustments –Internal adjustments –Spiritual adjustments
4. Reorganization	4. To emotionally relocate the loss and move on with life

Sources: Parkes, C. M. (1987). *Bereavement: Studies of grief in adult life* (2nd ed.). Madison, CT: International Universities Press.
Worden, J. W. (2002). *Grief counseling and grief therapy* (3rd ed.). New York: Springer.

again and again as the person is confronted with realities of the loss. "I have cancer." "My marriage is in danger." "He's dying." "She's dead. She died. I won't see her again."

With a typical hospice journey, these pieces of acceptance can come with hearing the diagnosis and prognosis, viewing test results and gathering information, deciding it's time for hospice care, experiencing changes, keeping vigil, being present at and after death, watching the body being moved from the home, being involved in funeral plans and rituals, and experiencing ongoing life moments without the other's physical presence. Taking it in all at once is too much. Too crippling and crushing. The body, mind, emotions, and soul have a grand wisdom for self-care, for finding an equilibrium to get through, even in one's wretched reeling. Your inner wisdom of life themes and rhythms and dissonances is different from anyone else's — even others experiencing the same loss. *There is a time for numbness … There is a dissonance in accepting the loss …*

2. Searching, Longing and Working Through the Pains. These realizations lead to a natural searching, longing, and pining for the loss (Parkes, 2001, pp. 43–59). The numbness and shock wear off. Continued realities of the loss expose countless pains. Consciously or unconsciously, one often searches for connection with the loss to relieve the pain. Much like phantom pains after an amputation, each nerve ending or attachment is awakened to go find the loss and reconnect it to the self. The harsh reality hits again: "He's not here," "I'm dying," "My job is gone," "We are no longer married." In this time, the task of mourning is "to work through the pains of grief" (Worden, 2002, pp. 30–32). Such pains may be profound sorrow, sadness, anger, guilt, loneliness, fear, and perhaps even relief.

Research on emotional intelligence (EI) teaches us that physiologically, the brain directs fight–flight stimuli to the emotional centers of the brain thousands of times faster than to its thinking counterparts (Goleman, 1995). Sudden rage or sorrow floods the brain and one's physical responses. Panic, anger, or sorrow suddenly supersede all else. "Let me out of here!" "Oh, God, this can't be happening!" "How can I live without her?"

As the pains kick in, this is a particularly vulnerable time for the person to seek numbing through substance abuse or other ways to avoid the pain. Marker events like birthdays, anniversaries, and holidays can be difficult because they evoke specific memories, emotions, and a new awareness that life has changed so dramatically. One may long for what was and fear what lies ahead. One may claim a deep gratitude for what was, or a relief and hope for what has changed, and will change more. The two opposites may be in creative tension, together. *There is a time for searching … There is a dissonance in experiencing the pain …*

3. Disorganization and Adjusting to Life. Life is no longer as it was. The loss can vacate roles, tasks, and places of meaning that must be tended.

Former ways of doing and being no longer work. An ongoing state of chaos, uncertainty, or desires to get everything back in place can ensue. Much like moving into a new house, this can be an important time of gleaning — not just material items, but also meanings. What do I keep? What do I toss? What do I pass on to another? What has this person (or attachment) meant to me in the past, and in the here and now? Where do I go with this in my future?

Worden identifies these as external adjustments, internal adjustments, and spiritual adjustments (2002, pp. 32–35). Research on gender differences with loss and grief demonstrates that typically, women deal with grief at more verbal and emotional levels, while men deal with grief in more doing, action modes. Both modes are needed: yin and yang, doing and being. Adjusting to a past no longer here and a future not yet defined. Getting grounded in the new present. *There is a time for disorganization ... There is dissonance and new harmony in adjusting ...*

4. Reorganization and Emotionally Relocating the Loss. The loss is not cut off. Discarded. Thrown away. Forgotten. The once present significant part of oneself is reintegrated, "re-membered" back into one's dis-membered self, in a new and different way. It is reorganized, relocated within one's emotions, thoughts, and focus of energy. Life moves to a new place of attachment and investment, largely shaped by what has been learned from the loss. This does not happen in one moment. Rather, it has been a clearing, tilling, planting, and nurturing of the soul's soil, throughout one's seasons of grief. There is a time for reorganizing and emotionally relocating the loss. It is a culmination of countless dissonances and harmonies supporting and moving one's personal themes along the stream of life music, life composition. *There is a time for reorganizing and emotionally relocating the loss ... It is a culmination of countless dissonances and harmonies and supporting and moving one's personal themes along the stream of life music, life composition ...*

Mediators of Mourning

Both Parkes and Worden identify common patterns of moving through grief, while asserting the individual's particular timing, meanings, coping skills, and impact of the loss. Worden further identifies these personal factors that affect one's coping and healing as "Mediators of Mourning." These include: (1) the person who died; (2) nature of attachment; (3) circumstances of death; (4) personality mediators; (5) historical mediators; (6) social mediators; and (7) concurrent changes (2002, pp. 37–45).

Meaning Reconstruction, Robert Neimeyer

Anniversaries and other marker moments continue to resurrect the loss. Some meanings cannot be grasped until they are experienced within one's continuum of time. Consider, for example, that at age 5 a child loses a parent. That loss takes on different meanings at ages 5, 10, 15, 25, 45, 65, and even 95. The loss and its "emotional relocation" take on varied forms through experiencing realities and emotions of the parent's death, integrating a new parent into the home, moving through teen years, leaving home, experiencing partnering and birthing of children, through learning how to parent, letting one's own children move into adulthood, experiencing grandparenting, and perhaps even as an elderly person in dementia calling and searching out again for "Mama" or "Daddy," and being comforted and cradled into death's release. *There is a time ...*

My life experiences resonate profoundly with these descriptions of ongoing "reconstructing meaning" (Neimeyer, 2001). While my hospice experiences both affirm this, they also teach me that not everyone wants to go to deep meaning levels. Some people simply want to function without much reflection or re-visioning. I voice that not with judgment, but with honesty. Still, wisdom and new meaning can emerge even in simple moments. A simple, strophic song can have much beauty and richness.

Healing and Wellness

In this age of everything from vaccinations to transplants, we too often equate "healing" only with the disappearance or remission of a disease or malady. The word *healing* is much richer, defined in numerous dictionaries as becoming healthy, sound, or whole. I hear that to be less of a prescribed checklist (like when I get my car serviced), and more of an ongoing process for creating soundness and wholeness. I understand "healing" to be a guide toward knowledge, understanding, and wisdom — towards finding my way. Not a magical pill, but a seeking and finding, a searching and learning, a dissonance resolving into a harmony, even with its blue notes. Such healing goes into one's depths of being, whether they are physically sculpted like an Olympian, or physically fragile and dying, or somewhere in between. Healing can be for the wounded body, mind, emotions, or spirit. The African-American spiritual comforts with, "There is a balm in Gilead, to make the wounded whole."

Wellness in the midst of disease? Yes. Wholeness in the midst of limitations? Yes. Completeness in the midst of imperfection? Yes. Peace and trust in the midst of not knowing, but still having to choose which risky road to ride? Yes. When a hospice patient or bereaved family member tells me she or he is "fine," I often affirm with, "Yes, and 'fine' has a wide range of feelings and meanings."

Similarly, a gospel song expresses:

> When peace like a river attendeth my way
>
> When sorrows like sea billows roll
>
> Whatever my lot, thou hast taught me to say
>
> It is well, it is well with my soul.
>
> It is well, with my soul, It is well, it is well, with my soul.

"It is Well" was written by Horatio Spafford in 1874. Its context is well-known among gospel musicians. Horatio's four daughters had recently drowned at sea. While traveling from the United States to join his grief-stricken wife in Wales, the ship's captain called Horatio to the deck as they neared the site of his daughters' deaths. Reportedly, he wrote the text right then and there. The story behind the phrase "whatever my lot" is less known. Three years earlier Horatio had lost large real estate holdings in the great Chicago fire of 1871. Shortly thereafter, his 4-year-old son died.

"It is well" is not a glib denial, repression, or cover-up. "It is well" is a source of meaning and hope that abides with us through the pain. "It is well" believes in being in and moving through grief (see teaching guide 4.6).

It is well: wellness. The word *well* also comes from the word *whole*. However, give it a "double entendre." Think of a well from which you draw water. Water for daily sustenance. Nurture drawn from the very ground itself. Healing requires drawing waters from the wells within, digging deeply into the soils of the soul. Give it another meaning. Think of the verb *well*, as in to well up and overflow; or the adverb *well* that relates to intimacy or closeness, as in "you know me well." Hear again: "It is well, it is well, with my soul."

A Healing Technique: Hear, Explore, Affirm, Learn

What balms can salve the bombed soul? What music might make the wounded whole? (See teaching guide 4.7.) Some HEALing techniques involve literal uses of music. Others employ musical metaphors for insight and understanding. Various tools and techniques are provided throughout this book, particularly at appendix E, "CORE Principles (Being) and HEALing Techniques (Doing)." Hear, explore, affirm, and learn these tools. You can find exercises for further self-reflection (See chapter 4 teaching guides.)

As I write this section, the Shaker hymn "'Tis a gift to be simple ..." has emerged in my thoughts. Let us simplify these seemingly complex tools. Try this technique with any potential use of music, with any person.

Choose a verb from the acronym, HEAL: Hear. Explore. Affirm. Learn.

Add the person's music.

- Hear _____'s music.
- Explore _____'s music.
- Affirm _____'s music.
- Learn from _____'s music.

You have just had easy access into knowing yourself or someone else, better. Drop the word *music* and add the name of the person. Yourself. Your partner or spouse. Your parent or child. Your friend or colleague. Your client or student.

- Hear _____.
- Explore _____.
- Affirm _____.
- Learn _____.

Herein can lie healing and wellness in the midst of sorrow and grief, in the ever changing harmonies and dissonances of life. Hear. Be present to the sounds around you and within.

☐ Harmonies and Dissonances of Healing: Coda or Commencement

Many age-old conflicts never fully resolve: war, disease, hatred, injustice, inhumanity. Closer in, those dissonances may be our own family differences or self-destructive patterns. Many personal life themes and counterthemes reemerge again and again throughout the life journey. In the midst of such discord, can I find harmony within myself? With another? Can I use my personal dissonances to create harmonic movement in my world? Thomas Moore writes in *Care of the Soul*: "Often care of the soul means not taking sides when there is a conflict at a deep level. It may be necessary to stretch the heart wide enough to embrace contradiction and paradox" (1994, p. 14).

A coda is a musical ending. A commencement is a beginning, graduating out of the old and into the new. Most fairy tales end with the nice, tidy, closed ending of *"and they all lived happily ever after."* I cannot close this chapter with a prescribed "do this" and "you will be healed," for your sense of "wholeness" and "wellness" cannot be defined by me. That is your life task to discern. To Hear. Explore. Affirm. Learn.

To compose, I can, like my college music theory teacher, open the door or score for you with "and they all lived...?" Where do you take it? When and how and with whom will you move? "And we all lived...?" "And I will live...?"

CHAPTER 5

Styles of Doing and Being

Reportedly on a subway wall:

To do is to be.

Socrates

To be is to do.

Descartes

Do-be-do-be-do-be.

Frank Sinatra

☐ Know Your Styles for Doing Life
☐ Music as a Catalyst for Being in Loss More Fully
☐ Music Moment: A Doing and Being Commemoration

Getting though loss requires *doing* tasks of ongoing, everyday living and *being* present to oneself and significant others. Do-be-do-be-do-be. Your basic lifestyles of doing life and being with others anchor you while so much else is in chaos.

Typically, your loss does not just affect you, but also others in your spheres of daily life. Others' styles of relating with you often intensify, revealing more of who they are and how they cope with loss. Others too often give advice and try to get you to incorporate their styles of doing and being into your life: different styles, different strokes. To whom do

I listen? With whom do I set boundaries? Whose loss is it, anyway? All of these different messages can become gibberish. I may feel I lose my own voice, not knowing what to say or where to go. Perhaps, can I create my own "do-be-do-be" scat improvisation until my own thoughts become clearer? Let's play a game.

Name one of your favorite songs. Anything. Now, imagine a kaleidoscope of musicians individually playing or singing that same song: Aretha Franklin, Placido Domingo, Usher, Celine Dion, Louis Armstrong, Bob Dylan, Norah Jones, Stevie Wonder, Dolly Parton, Bobby McFerrin, the Vienna Boys Choir, Elton John, John Williams, George Winston, Eminem, or even ol' Kermit the Frog. Style. Essence. One's unique personality and core essence shines through. Now, pretend that several of these musicians who have honed a personal style insist that for your song to be valid and good, you must sing it in his or her style. Others freely assume they have the answers to your personal struggles.

Welcome to the world of dealing with your loss. Everyday life continues. Your *doing* everyday tasks and *being* in multiple roles keep you improvising your own *do-be-do-be-do-being.*

How might you claim your own style in the midst of so much calamity and unasked for counsel? Let's see if musical styles might have anything to teach us.

What are your favorite styles of music? Classical? Country? Jazz? Gospel or rap? Maybe R&B? What about big band or hip-hop? Salsa or reggae? Opera? New Age? Alternative or international? What musical characteristics do you especially enjoy?

Of those musical characteristics you identify, which ones reflect your personal style, your ways of doing and being in the world? For example, do you prefer to live life in a classical style of everything being organized, well-scored, orchestrated, and a predictable sense of what will happen next? Or, do you live life in a jazz, improvisational, go-with-the-flow, playing off of patterns of whatever is happening in the moment? Do you live life like a country ballad's unfolding and ongoing life story? Do you live out oppressed emotions rapped around your insides and exploding to come out? Note: one style is not good while another is bad. One is not right while another is wrong. They are simply different. They express an essence of the person.

Take it further. What musical styles describe how you cope with your loss? (See teaching guide 5.1.) Let's add in a few more styles to those listed above: religious roots, gospel faith, grassroots folk, a driving rock beat, dramatic opera, easy listening, new age flow, rhythmic reggae, or something else. Let's add in one more: silence. Calm in the core of calamity. Claim your own essence, your own styles of doing and being that work for you. Become aware of those styles that do not work.

Let's play another game. Think of your loss. Pretend your favorite "song" has been taken from you. You are forced to sing another song that you do not know, in a style you have never tried, and with little coaching along the way (see teaching guide 5.2). Welcome to doing grief work and being in mourning. No one said this game was fun. How might it shift if someone came over to sit with you, be with you, and hum your music with you?

☐ Know Your Styles for Doing Life

Socrates had it right, "Know thyself." Loss tosses around your knowing, doing, and being. "But I don't know" may feel more accurate as you attempt to redo daily life. As introduced in chapter 4, research on emotional intelligence (EI) teaches us how intense emotions trigger physiological reactions. These triggers temporarily hijack the brain's thought processes (Goleman, 1995). Grief and loss can be an ongoing hijacking. We alternate between numbed out defenses and overwhelming, on edge emotions. We react without thinking. We do and say things that later we ask ourselves, "Why did I ..."; "If only I had ...." Still, your deeper "knowing" can pull together emotions and intelligence, heart and mind, body and soul. Still, sometimes we need to quiet our doing and tune into being. In one's stillness and quiet, being and doing can join in a powerful partnership. EI research scientifically confirms the importance of calming oneself and choosing one's responses (Goleman, 1995), or to use our music metaphors, choosing one's "style."

Both the ancient Socrates and current EI affirm, "first, know thyself." Indeed, loss threatens to take away your sense of who you are and what you do and how you feel about yourself in your world. Still, you are the only you that has been or will be. On Nina Simone's *Saga of the Good Life and Hard Times* compilation, she sings a litany of "I ain't got no ..." (mother, job, ...). Musically and joyfully, Nina switches into a humorous, full heart and soul, "... but I got myself!" (Simone, 1997).

If you were to burn your own *Saga of the Good Life and Hard Times* CD with music from or about your life experiences, what would your music reveal about you, about your growth and evolution? Note different styles you were drawn to at various times in your life. Describe those styles. Pull out your timeline from teaching guide 1.2. What patterns do you see?

Look beyond yourself. Whose style(s) for dealing with loss do you admire? Who mentors you, by your choice, from near or afar? (See teaching guide 5.3.) What new style do you want to infuse into your everyday coping?

To Do or To Be: Is That the Question?

Experiencing a loss does not grant us long-term license to stop doing and being. Most cultures and religions set aside a period of time considered acceptable for grieving, and then one's world moves on. An especially relevant song is "Without You," from *Rent* (Larson, 1996/2005). In today's business world, human resource departments typically allow two to five days for funeral leave, and carefully define relationships that are or are not included. Though grief continues, the employee must continue to do the work. He is expected to function, mentally and emotionally. Like Worden's task of adjusting to one's environment, "Without You" sings of life going on in one's outer world, yet of dying inside.

The loss shifts one's normal "doing." Early on, a life-threatening illness might interrupt your routines with hospitalizations, complex treatments, and time-consuming care. It may mean taking on another person's tasks, roles, and functions or having to give away ones that hold meaning for you. Just after a death, it may mean *doing* tasks like making funeral arrangements and going through the motions of a wake or visitation, all the while *being* in an emotional space that is surreal. Depending on the severity of loss, or mediators of mourning (Worden, 2002), one's sense of being in this world can be thrown all around. "I just don't feel like myself." We might immerse ourselves in extreme "doing," to cover up or cut off the painful "being" within.

Musicians know: *Do* the technical skills required to make the music; *be* into the music. Don't be tied down by it, but take it into yourself. Be connected to it and give it your own style. Sing or play from your core self, your core soul. Be fully engaged. Quality music making calls for both doing and being.

How might we play with that in our daily lives, especially when loss threatens to destroy us, too? Let's play with our own do-be-do-be impromptu scats and planned scores: *do* the tasks, and *be* engaged with life, now (see teaching guide 5.4).

How often do we use daily "To Do" lists, either written or mental? Like, today I need to do: errands, phone calls, bills, groceries, etcetera ad infinitum. How often do we use daily "To Be" lists? Like, today I want to be: peaceful, present, humorous, calm, productive, patient, engaged, guarded, strong, wise, supportive, open, reflective, or understanding. Of the two, which might have more lasting significance?

With the following exercise, common "To Do's" are listed in the left column (add your own). In the right column, a variety of "To Be's" are listed (add your own). Now for the swing. Select a "doing" task on the left, and pair it with a "being" quality on the right. For example, you will carpool children. What do you want your style or your presence to

FIGURE 5.1

be with them? Irritable? (We all have those negative energies that we choose or that sneak in.) Something else? Try warm and open. A simple swing of attitude intent can completely change the experience, either beforehand, or in the immediate moment.

Play with the do-be list some more (see appendix D, "My Do-Be-Do-Be-Do-Be's" for a blank list). Just as unplanned tasks interrupt my day, so do unwanted emotions and unintended attitudes. A key component of EI is to choose my responses, to regulate or manage my responses to the given stimuli (Goleman, 1995).

A musical musician (versus simply a skilled musician) knows when and how to shift a style here and there. A musical musician intuitively infuses emotions and soulful essence in the just-right times and places. Likewise, you and I have response abilities to choose who we want to be and how we want to do life. With fun, fervor, and a bit of foolishness, I challenge: be and do, do and be. Intend your attitude. Choose or lose. Do-Be-Do-Be-Do-Be.

Doing Life Creatively

"What do you do that's creative?" For years, Dr. Leah Dickstein routinely has posed this question to her psychiatry patients, medical school students, and physician colleagues. She describes "What do you do that's creative?" as being a nonthreatening, life-affirming entry into another's self-worth, daily life, social interactions, and places of meaning. People's answers reveal multiple layers of insight and possible intervention. She has encouraged countless patients and former medical students to get to know and renew themselves through the art of doing something creative: drawing, painting, sculpting, writing, journaling, composing, playing a musical instrument, baking, sewing, designing and constructing a room, gardening, photography, even simply enjoying nature through hiking or sky diving. Her one criterion for residents in her arts–medicine elective course was to try something they had never done before. Creativity requires risk, choice, and life spirit. (Do I hear an interface with our seasons of the soul?) She knows that giving life and care to others requires first nurturing life in oneself (L. S. Goldman, Myers, & Dickstein, 2002).

The question, "What do you do that's creative?" can be applied more specifically to loss and grief (Berger, 1993; Bertman, 1999; see teaching guide 5.5). We need to focus not just on our pain and pathology, but on our strengths and resources for coping. The grief–loss therapist can be acquainted with a wealth of artistic outlets and encourage clients to use their own talents to explore one's grief. Honor and respect the person's modality and styles. Ask questions. Be the learner. Let your client teach you about his or her journey, from artistry created from within.

We, musicians, talk of "playing" an instrument. For musician readers, do you play or work your music? For all of us, musicians or not, do we play or work our lives? Do we create our "music" with a sense of drudgery or "re-creation"? What if we moved into our "music" to re-create both the music and oneself? To strengthen one's physical, emotional, mental, and spiritual being in the midst of increased stress? (For practical, nonmusical principles and interventions for such self-care, see Loehr & Schwartz, 2003.)

☐ Music as a Catalyst for Being in Loss More Fully

Let's revisit literal music. In chapter 2 we examined ways in which music can be a catalyst for memorializing, mourning, for exploring meanings, and for moving on. The *doing* of music can lead to *being* more present to life itself (see appendix E, "CORE Principles and HEALing Techniques").

Such *doing* of music and *being* in loss more fully was experienced on January 26, 1996 by the cast of *Rent* at their opening performance. Jonathan Larson, the show's creator and composer had unexpectedly died the night before, just hours after the cast had finished their final dress rehearsal. He was 35. Would the show go on that night or not? Jonathan's parents insisted, "yes." *Rent*'s songs created containers and catalysts for cast members, family, and friends to be in the loss more fully, individually and together. Paradoxes of lyrics and life collided. They sang their pain, with passion and transformed meanings: "One Song Glory," "Will I," "Another Day," "Without You," and "Seasons of Love" (Columbus & Larson, 2005).

For yourself, recall a previous life-ending or life-beginning moment when music grabbed hold of you. Suddenly, you tuned into yourself, you connected deeply with others. Music engaged you physically (i.e., tears, laughter, changed heart rate, breathing); emotionally (mad, sad, glad, afraid); mentally (associations, imagery, thoughts); spiritually (meanings, core essence, what matters to you); and relationally (connecting with others). How do you describe that soul-depth interaction? What happened that made it matter to you now, months or years later? How might we understand and navigate those musical catalyst moments with skill and sensitivity?

Care of the Soul, an Active Presence

I understand such care of the soul to begin with presence, an openness, a "being with" self or other through sounds or silence — fully hearing the here and now. I offer several functions from pastoral care (i.e., care of the soul) to describe this active presence: *sustaining* and *confronting, healing* and *reconciling*, and *guiding* and *informing* (Berger, 1993; Hiltner, 1958; Rowatt, 1989). They can be experienced in any combination with each other. They connect you to your core, to your essence, to your life. Throughout such catalytic moments, these elements focus on an active presence within the self or in relationship with another. The music and musician are simply tools. Doing the music leads to being more present to loss and living. Do-be-do-be. Play with the following kinds of active presence, both (1) without literal music to grasp the "being" concepts, and (2) with literal music, to play with "doing" music to strike those fires within (see teaching guide 5.6).

FIGURE 5.2

Sustaining and Confronting

Sustaining and confronting go hand in hand. To sustain means to stand with another person. Sustaining oneself is what keeps one alive when all hope feels lost. Sustaining is longer, broader, and deeper than comfort. It is not about sympathetically rescuing another. Rather, it affirms our common humanity with one another, with a humility and empathic compassion. It encourages self-acceptance while seeking to preserve hope. To sustain respects another's ownership of experience. It does not transfer one's own assumptions onto another. It cares enough to learn the other's experience. Sustaining sees life as a whole. To sustain is to assure abiding care, no matter what.

Although sustaining and confronting appear to be in opposition to each other, they actually function together in a creative tension (Rowatt, 1989). One without the other can be harmful, even dangerous.

Confronting is not an in-your-face blasting of another. Rather, confronting faces truth with another. Confronting takes in larger truths, with hope for getting through, whatever the outcome. It is an empathic, "I'm with you as we see what's really going on." Much like the Serenity prayer, confronting asks, "What can I change, what can I not change? What do I hold onto and what do I let go?"

Confronting can be, "He really has died, and isn't coming back." It may be the gut feeling that "it's time" to change or move on from a relationship, job, or conflict. Confronting can be within oneself, or in relationship with another. It may be a slow realization, or a sudden "I get it" moment. It can spur an intense fight or flight reaction. Confronting, too, honors ownership of personal choice and of one's own experiences. It discerns what one can and cannot take on. Confronting, paired with a sustaining presence, can lead to deeper knowledge, understanding, and wisdom.

In our "Seasons of the Soul" paradigm, sustaining and confronting are inherent through the processes and tasks of being in and moving through grief (Berger, 1993). At the onset of a loss, sustaining protects one from the shock and confronting accepts the realities that the loss has occurred (Berger, 1993). Confronting during one's "winter" happens frequently, and with deep pain. Healing and reconciling are needed. At any season when grief's processes and tasks become stuck, confronting sensitively stimulates awareness of choice. It meets rather than avoids one's many struggles along the grief journey. Sustaining provides hope for being in and moving through the pains.

Confronting another without sustaining can be cruel. Sustaining another without appropriate confronting can lead to gangrenous harm.

With music of the soul, the terms *sustaining* and *confronting* can articulate one's profound experiences of hope, support, insight, and truthfulness stirred by a musical experience. It may be a sudden engulfing of grief or inspiration of hope stirred by a piece of music. Crucial to this musician's understanding is that these uses of music are not just about the music. They are about the person's experience through the music. These being–doing qualities can bring soul care within oneself.

CORE principles apply again: Care, Ownership, Respect, and Empowerment. Start with yourself. Honor and explore your soul in your music making, whoever you are. Wherever you are in your life's losses and paths toward healing.

Healing and Reconciling

Healing and reconciling transform brokenness into wholeness. Healing restores an individual's sense of self in this world. Reconciling reforms relationships with others. When loss strikes the soul, healing takes time. Time after time after time. Just as the body physically heals cell by cell, the soul heals memory by memory, meaning by meaning, experience and experience again. Again and again and again.

Healing deep grief parallels phantom pains after amputation of a limb. After an amputation, the brain continues to send neurosignals to the missing limb. Parkes describes this grief process as pining, yearning, and searching for the loss (2001). It is normal; common. It may be picking up the phone to call your mother, and realizing she's not there. It may be automatically reaching for your spouse's favorite food in the grocery store, and being confronted with "he's too sick to eat." It may be hearing that familiar song in an all-too-new-too-painful context. Its sounds and words dig deeply within, with grave truths.

Healing the soul can be like lancing one's raw, burned emotions, and tenderly bandaging them for quiet healing. The term *denial* is overused too often. All broken connections to the loss cannot be felt, nor healed at one time.

Reconciling moves healing to relationships with others. During this winter of the soul, others' words and actions can be especially painful, wounding again and again, as they "don't get" the realities of the loss for the person. Job cried out: "My spirit is broken, my days are extinguished,/The grave is ready for me/Surely mockers are with me,/And my eye gazes on their provocation" (Job 17:1, NRSV).

The loss itself may confront earlier brokenness: a brother who shames his brother for being gay and contracting AIDS; an adult child who provides final days of care to an abusive parent; the disenfranchised grief when a former spouse dies. The term *disenfranchised grief* validates loss and grief that is not openly acknowledged, mourned, or ritualized. The mourner's relationship to the loss and subsequent impact of the loss are not recognized, thus cutting one off from social support (Doka, 2002).

Reconciling creates space for openness and understanding to begin. It honors vulnerability and needs for protection. Reconciling rebuilds broken trust, with new understandings and expectations. Reconciling redefines broken hopes into present realities, with a new paradigm of hope for the future. Consider the chemically dependent family member, the estranged parent and adult child relationship, or the dissolved business partnership.

Tune into your own CORE: Care for, Own, Respect, and Empower your own life experiences. What wound needs healing? What relationship needs reconciling? What music takes you to places of mind-emotion-soul expression and exploration? Actively mourning acknowledges one's loss and releases one's pain: emotionally, physically, mentally, relationally, and spiritually. Each person's doing and being is different from another's. Our styles of tending loss usually reflect what we learned about coping through earlier losses. This can be a powerful time to heal and reconcile poor lessons from before:

"Don't talk about it, especially with children."
"Be the victim, and I'll get a lot of sympathy."
"I caused this. I'm to blame. I'm totally worthless."
"Just ignore it, and the pain will go away."
"Don't trust. Don't risk relationship. I'll just get hurt."
"Just pray and God will fix it. If not, I don't have enough faith."

Healing and reconciling live in places of endings and beginnings. One's private pangs gradually heal. One accepts the loss and begins to find one's way through everyday living again. One is forever changed. New meanings begin to break through. Winter's mourning gradually blooms into spring's morning.

Guiding and Informing

Guiding evokes. *Informing* teaches. Much of this book has been written in a guiding style to ask questions and stir your own reflections. Guiding calls forth memories, emotions, and understandings from within the person. It connects with one's internal life and brings it out. Informing introduces new information or interpretations. It connects a broader external world with one's internal mind and emotions.

Too often, when someone initially experiences a loss we hastily inform them what they should do. (Whose discomfort are we easing, theirs or ours?) Unknowingly, we kill off opportunities to sustain by jumping into informing. Hear yourself saying: "You should ...," "You need to ...," "Just ...." How has that felt for you when others, no doubt, have said the same to you? We arrogantly make ourselves the master and commander over another's life and loss and their efforts to live through it.

There is a time to guide and a time to inform. Guiding and informing seek not to control, but to lend a new lens for seeing and facing truth (confronting and sustaining), and to provide tools for healing and reconciling life's wounds. Through this book we have explored countless ways that music can be a powerful tool for evoking emotions, memories, and meaning and for instilling new ones. New meanings can be caught and taught through music. Let's add a few more to those listed in this book thus far:

- "Wanting Memories," by Sweet Honey in the Rock
- "Wyck," from Broadway's *The Secret Garden*
- "How Can I Help You Say Goodbye," recorded by Patti Lovelace
- "Where've You Been," recorded by Kathy Mattea
- "My Father's House," by Bruce Springsteen
- "Seasons of Love," from *Rent*, by Jonathan Larson, a rock-stage version of the opera *La Bohème* (Larson, 1996/2005).

What would you add? What music has evoked or instilled new knowledge, new understanding, or new wisdom?

Care for the soul — for the person's essence — can be stirred by countless musicians: through music therapists, composers, performers, producers, educators, ministers, and amateurs. However, anyone's *doing* of music must be integrated with sensitively *being* tuned into (1) one's own motives, roles, skills, parameters, and limitations, and (2) the other's seasons of the soul and receptivity or not to your music. An offering of music is just that, an offer. Its function is to serve, not to impose. It begins with knowing and understanding one's own music of the soul.

Putting it Together

Hear Stephen Sondheim's song, "Putting It Together," one piece at a time, time after time to create one's masterpiece of art (Sondheim, 1984/2005). Here. You are the work of art.

Where are you in your seasons of the soul? What processes of grief are you experiencing, and what tasks of mourning can you tend? How might music help you be in and move through your seasons of the soul? (See teaching guide 5.7.) Moving beyond the music itself, what care of the soul might you seek or give through different seasons and times? Let's view a summary from the paradigm chart from chapter 2, this time focusing on the far right column, "Care of the Soul."

TABLE 5.1 Focus on Care of the Soul

Seasons of the Soul (Berger, 1993) Processes of Grief (Parkes, 1987/2001) Tasks of Mourning (Worden, 1991/2002)		Music for being in and moving through grief's seasons of the soul	Care of the soul An active presence
Fall	**Process:** shock, numbness, denial	**Music for Memories/ Memorializing**	Primarily **SUSTAINING** the shock and **CONFRONTING** the loss
	Task: To accept the reality of the loss		
Winter	**Process:** longing, yearning, pining, searching for the loss	**Music for Mourning**	Primarily **GUIDING** to validate and express inner pains Initial **HEALING** (cleansing and bandage of the emotional wounds)
	Task: to work through the pains of the loss		
Winter into spring	**Process:** disorganization and despair	**Music for Meanings**	Primarily **GUIDING** & **INFORMING** More *confronting* than before
	Task: to adjust to an environment in which the loss is missing		
Spring into summer	**Process:** reorganization	**Music for Remembering & Moving into Life**	**HEALING** & **RECONCILING** of the former **GUIDING** & **INFORMING** toward the new
	Task: to emotionally relocate the loss & move on with life		

Meaning reconstruction (Neimeyer, 2001): Ongoing exploration of meanings for the present and future

CORE Principles through all Seasons of the Soul: Care, Ownership, Respect, Empowerment (Berger, 1999)

HEALing Techniques through all Seasons of the Soul: Hear, Explore, Affirm, Learn (Berger, 1999)

Sources: Berger, J. S. (1993). *Music as a catalyst for pastoral care within the remembering tasks of grief.* Ann Arbor, Michigan: ProQuest /University Microfilms, Inc., [Pub. #9406295]. Berger, J. S. (1999). *Life music: Rhythms of loss and hope* [VHS]. Cleveland, OH: American Orff-Schulwerk Association. Neimeyer, R. A. (Ed.). (2001). *Meaning reconstruction and the experience of loss.* Washington, D.C.: American Psychological Association. Parkes, C. M. (1987). *Bereavement: Studies of grief in adult life* (2nd ed.). Madison, CT: International Universities Press. Worden, J. W. (2002). *Grief counseling and grief therapy: A handbook for the mental health practitioner* (2nd and 3rd ed.). New York: Springer.

☐ Music Moment: A Doing and Being Commemoration

This morning is September 11, 2004, the third anniversary. Families, friends, and larger communities are gathered at Ground Zero in New York City. Bells ring to mark the moments the planes hit. Silence.

Family members read poems. Weep. Hold up high photos of lost loved ones. Write remembrances on boards. Three years later is different from one year later, different from 30 years later. This morning marks an important mourning. Gentle string music accompanies the readers. Multicolored roses are strewn into a pool of water. Young children gather at the small pool's edge, crying. While only 3 or 4 years old, their young lives already have been forever formed and shaped by the enormous grief they have experienced in their families.

Parents and grandparents of World Trade Center victims are reading names. Again and again, they complete their lists of names with "My son," "Our daughter," "Our grandson," "My granddaughter," and "We love you very much." Loss does not stop love. Love is not cut off, but continues, often more valued than before. It can change how one sees life and lives on.

I am struck by these families' hugely personal, active, "doing" roles throughout this memorial, in contrast with their one-year memorial service, at this same site. Of course, the first anniversary was so raw, so painful. The sorrow continues. Still, family members are able to stand with strength in ways that would have been too huge two years before. Their being and doing shines a light of hope in the midst of their ongoing loss.

Television viewers witness live scenes from this service interwoven with still photos from the tragedies. The background music, supporting the reading of names, honors a culturally diverse community. The earlier string music has shifted to a Native American flute paired with an oboe, now a bassoon. Now a flute and French horn. Diverse sounds. Nationalities of names. Emotions, images, and meanings. A husband and wife just ended their list with "and our two sons." The background music is now quietly playing "Going Home."

The setting moves to the Courthouse Plaza in Arlington, Virginia, where a bell is rung 184 times for the victims from the Pentagon. Later still, families gather in Shanksville, Pennsylvania. Bells toll across the state. A news commentator reflects, "We all remember where we were. None of us knew how it would affect us. When I heard the news about my home city, New York, I had no idea it would mean my son would end up being sent off to war in Iraq."

Bells mark a moment of silence, commemorating when each tower fell. Other church bells are heard in the distance.

Another commentator voices, "I'm struck by the outpouring of sorrow, and the support felt by all by coming together in their grief." Sustaining is happening. Confronting. Healing. Reconciling. Guiding. Even bits of informing. Back and forth between different sites. Back and forth between communities and individuals. Outpourings of sorrow, meaning, and love. This is not a time to feed hate or revenge. This is a time for remembering, for love, for hope.

This musical moment strikes a chord in me. The Young People's Chorus of New York City, a multicultural chorus for international music styles and education is singing:

There's a place for us

Somewhere a place for us …

We'll find a new way of living

We'll find a way of forgiving …

Hold my hand and we're halfway there …

Somehow. Someday. Somewhere. (Bernstein & Sondheim, 1957)

CHAPTER 6

Expressions of Self and Community

Harmony of spirit springs forth from the soul and finds expression or blossoms forth in the form of music.

Confucius

Joy is more joyful, given a tune.

Jane Swan

If I were not a physicist, I would probably be a musician. I often think in music. I live my daydreams in music. I see my life in terms of music.

Albert Einstein

To me, music is the original human language. We didn't say words to each other when we were in a primordial state. We made sounds and noises. Music is essentially the manipulation of sound. It has the power to arouse, it has the power to frighten. It has the power to elevate, it has the power to make people feel sacred. It also has the power to make people feel profane.

Billy Joel

☐ Ricky's Rhyme for This Time
☐ Music's Expressive Powers
☐ Personal Expressions: Children and Teens
☐ Community Expressions
☐ Global Expressions
☐ Ode to Expressions of the Soul

Ricky's words were golden. Each was chosen well. Ricky persevered through his severe speech impediment, painfully aware that others often lost patience. He selected each word with care, shaping sounds to express his core self. His words came one at a time, or in short phrases. He mastered nonverbal communication. He exhibited a rich presence, less dependent on words, and more on human connection. For myself, a lively talker, I needed to not fill the spaces nor complete his sentences. Our dialogue was easier and more engaged when I voiced questions to Ricky in ways that fostered short, personalized answers. He was eager to voice his thoughts, and hungry to be heard.

Regularly, we used "highs" and "lows" on my portable keyboard to explore multiple needs (see appendix C; teaching guide 6.1). We experimented with rhythmic patterns programmed into the keyboard. We found Ricky could put several words together more easily when they were stimulated by a background beat. I asked, "Through your illness, what are you learning?" Two mantras emerged. We put them to a beat:

1. I want to **LIVE** my **LIFE** — the **WAY I WANT!** [Repeat]

2. I **DON'T** — **WANT** — **PEO**-ple to feel sor-**RY** - for **ME!** [Repeat]

I asked, "What do you want to teach your family and friends?" With paper and pen, keyboard and creativity, we honed out strings of words and phrases, and wove them into this poem. On Ricky's behalf and with his permission to share this with others, I invite you to hear and learn Ricky's expression of the soul.

☐ Ricky's Rhyme for This Time

I want to **LIVE** my **LIFE** — the **WAY I WANT!** [Repeat]

I **DON'T** — **WANT** — **PEO**-ple to feel sor-**RY** - for **ME!** [Repeat]

I want my friends to learn what I have and what I'm doing about it.

I've got a small tumor with big, BIG, **B-I-G** problems!

Seizures …

Headaches …

Nausea …

Pain, PAIN, **P-A-I-N!**

Can't **EAT**

Can't **WORK**

Can't **RUN**

Can't **WALK**

[Snap the beat …]

I can **KEEP** on — lovin' my fam'ly

I can **KEEP** on — lovin' my neighbors

I can **KEEP** on — lovin' my friends

I can **KEEP** on — lovin' **MY SELF!**

[Snaps fade out …]

Can you? Can you?

Can you love yourself no matter what?

I WANT

I want **YOU**

I want you to **LOVE YOURSELF** … no matter what!

No matter what! No matter what!

I WANT YOU TO LOVE YOURSELF NO MATTER WHAT!

[Snap the beat]

No matter what … No matter what … No matter what …

Epilogue

Ricky's words proclaim wisdom for us all. As a music therapist, I simply provided tools for meaningful communication. The truths and life passion were Ricky's. What a privilege to listen and learn.

☐ Music's Expressive Powers

Aristotle wrote of music's powers to affect the moral character of the soul (quoted in Crofton & Fraser, 1985). In 1749 a London physician, Richard Brocklesby, wrote *Reflection on the Power of Music*, describing music's abilities to calm fear and sadness with persons experiencing delirium and melancholia. He also discussed music as aiding pregnant women and the elderly (Rorke, 2000).

At the 1997 international broadcast of the Grammy Awards, Michael Greene, President and CEO of the National Academy of Recording Arts and Sciences (NARAS) voiced: "When we look at the body of evidence that the arts contribute to our society, it is absolutely astounding. Music therapists are breaking down the walls of silence and affliction of autism, Alzheimer's and Parkinson's disease" (Greene, 1997).

Many research articles discuss music's powers to heal through facilitating personal expressions at physical, mental, emotional, and spiritual levels (Brookes, 2002; Wheeler, 2005). A sampling of recent music therapy articles include, but are not limited to, improving dementia patients' language (Brotons & Koger, 1999); effecting self-disclosure (Jensen, 2000); working through grief and finding a personal identity (Smeijster & van den Hurk, 1998); improving mood and quality of life for persons with cancer (Burns, 2000; Waldon, 2000); and improving quality of life for palliative care and hospice patients (Aldridge, 1999; Hilliard, 2002; Rykov & Salmon, 1998).

More personally, identify a time when music powerfully expressed your grief. What was your loss and context? How did the music affect you, then? What music might powerfully impact you in your contexts, today?

Your Choice — Your Voice

Thus far, we have explored music as a tool for coping with loss and grief through rhythms of body and soul, themes and counterthemes of life stories, harmonies and dissonances of healing, and styles of doing and being. We have delved into past meanings evoked by music. We have played with "calendar composing" for the future. Let us be more present in the present.

The *present*. The present is a here-and-now moment in time's stream of past — present — future. Another double entendre awaits: the present as a gift, a treasure, an offering. This gift of time. This present: my time, your time, our time. There is a time. *This is the time.*

If you had a choice of speaking to only one person today, who would that person be and what would you say? This day is your day. This time is your time. Carpe diem. Seize your day. If today, you could play, sing, or experience only one piece of music, what would it be? Why? What does that selection say about you, today? (See teaching guide 6.2.)

Let's move the music into metaphor. Are you living today out of a digitally remastered remake of someone else's script? Or is your life alive and well in this present moment, never before experienced exactly as now, and never again to be repeated? *This is the time for... what?* In this moment and time, what is your music of life?

Score Your Day

"Score your day?" I do not mean with grades like A, B, C, D, or F, nor with passing or failing, I mean, with meaning. How might you score your day? (See teaching guide 6.3.)

Which musical symbols of expression could describe your day, today?[1]

Volume: ppp, pp, p, mp, mf, f, ff, fff
Graduations in volume: crescendo < > diminuendo
Tempos: largo, adagio, andante, allegro, presto
Gradations in tempo: accelerando, ritardando
Articulation: legato, staccato
Moods or Special Effects: dolce, furioso, sforzando
Solo, or With Others: soli, tutti[1]
Which of the above symbols describe where you are in your loss?
Which symbols describe where you want to be in your future?
What timetable would you want for those changes to occur?
Which meaning words could describe you, today? (add your own)

Being with yourself: chaotic, fearful, anxious, calm, peaceful, centered
Being with others: critical, controlling, respectful, empowering
Guiding forces: rebellion, rules, dogmas, beliefs, intuition, spirituality
Sense of self: false, in process, authentic, soulful
Sense of relationships: conflicted, fake, social, friendship, soul mate
Sense of purpose in your world: destructive, empty, functional, destiny

Which of the above words express where you are in your current loss? What difference(s) do you want to create, for yourself or with others? Herein lies your music. Hear your inner music within. Play it, sing it out. Do-be-do-be-do-be it with passion and ownership of your day.

Whom would you want to hear your music? Whose music do you want to hear better?

Privatized versus Collective Grief

Too often, our Western psychology and culture has privatized the individual's grief (Goss & Klass, 2005). One's private world is opened, analyzed, and closed back up, with too little ongoing conversation and exploration about the loss within one's broader systems of family, friends, and community. One's loss is quietly absent wherever one goes. Being present with others can intensify the loss. Others often ignore or gloss over the loss with clichés. Out of their own discomfort with expressing grief, others can reinforce the mourner's stark awareness of absence and aloneness in the world. In truth, each person is probably mourning in his or her own individual style, with little knowledge or skill to enter another's pain, or openness to letting others into one's own.

To lock oneself or another into a hushed world of memories and pain is to cut off opportunities for healing and growth. "Hush little baby, don't you cry, Papa's gonna buy you a mockingbird. If that mockingbird don't sing, Papa's gonna buy you a diamond ring. If that diamond ring don't shine, Papa's gonna buy you a ...." Let's not be too hard on Papa, for the models and experiences he had may have taught him to hush, or to buy and provide things when faced with fear or sadness.

Yes, there is a time for comforting presence. There is a time for solitude, and a time for broader community. Its key is the person's right and ability to choose which she needs, and when. I am reminded of the spiritual, "Sometimes I feel like a motherless child, a long way from home." Usually, I hear this focused on "motherless child" or "a long way from home." This time I hear, "sometimes." "*Sometimes.*" "*Sometimes* I feel like a motherless child." Stroebe and Schut affirm our need for "sometimes." Not all of the time, but sometimes. We need varied times to move back and forth and in and out between loss and restoration (Stroebe & Schut, 2001). I grieve that home is no longer as it was before. I ask, where is home? How can I find it? Can I create it anew? Will I have to go it alone or is there room enough at the table for more?

Open up new meaning making for a family or larger group of friends and community (Goss & Klass, 2005; Nadeau, 1998, 2001). Expand potentials for deeper, broader healing.

"Shall we gather at the river, where bright angel feet have trod" (Lowry, 1864/1990, written during the Civil War by this pastor and poet). For example, at holidays the family may light a candle or have a moment of remembrance before the meal. At more formal ceremonies, like weddings or birth blessings, both the absence and presence of the deceased loved one — however one defines that (Goss & Klass, 2005) — can be acknowledged and honored, like with a candle and words in a printed program, or from the officiant. The ceremony might include a piece of music that holds meaning related to the deceased loved one or other loss. An example was "Always, In All Ways," for Amy, at the birth of Jack, with poignant memories of her baby Madison (chapter 2; Loggins, 2000). Deeper expression and meaning can be added when a family member or friend sings or plays the music. However, in formal or public gatherings like a wedding, insure that key persons know about and want the music. Lyrics might be adjusted for the new context. Do not set up someone for a surprise, because painful emotions can overwhelm and take over emotions and meanings of the moment (see teaching guide 6.4). Empower.

Changing Western Attitudes toward Grief

One's family, community of support (or not), cultural context, and religious beliefs profoundly affect one's attitude toward grief (Goss & Klass, 2005). Many cultural beliefs about loss and grief can be traced through the arts: literature, visual arts, and music (Berger, 1993; Minear, 1987; Pacholski, 1986).

For example, Robert Schumann's 1830 art song cycle, *Frauenliebe und Leben*, Opus 42 (A Woman's Love and Life*)*, darkly depicts a woman's life as being empty and forever over after her husband dies. Gloria Gaynor's 1979 "I Will Survive" heralded an age of a woman's independence and ability to thrive after losing a love, as did Celine Dion's 1997 *Titanic*-sized "My Heart Will Go On" (Horner & Jennings, 1997). Countless examples exist in various genres.

A little known gospel song titled "Go Bury Thy Sorrow" in a 1940 hymnal depicts common religious and cultural beliefs about grief at that time in our American history. This meager song powerfully validated a woman's 1940s wartime stillbirth. She never saw or held her baby. She had been hospitalized and anesthetized through the birth. Well-meaning family and friends discarded all baby furniture, clothes, and other infant items before she returned home. Her son's name was never voiced. Surgery at the stillbirth left her infertile. Just after the Depression and now during World War II, her family, culture, and faith community admonished her with words and actions similar to the gospel song: "Go bury thy sorrow, the world hath its share; Go bury it deeply, go hide it with care" (Bachelor & Bliss, 1941, no. 293).

This stillbirth, still-buried, unresolved loss broke through her consciousness and demanded attention some 50 years later when her adopted daughter died. In struggling with her overwhelming grief, the gospel song "Go Bury Thy Sorrow" validated her earlier experience, without shame or blame.

Western, 20th-century theorists pioneered influential descriptions of grief: Sigmund Freud, John Bowlby, Elizabeth Kübler-Ross, and Dame Cicely Saunders. Contemporary grief theorists further define evolving theories and therapies for healing grief: reorganization (Parkes, 2001), emotional relocations of the loss (Worden, 2002), complicated grief (Rando, 1993), disenfranchised grief (Doka, 2002), and meaning reconstruction (Neimeyer, 2001), to name but a few.

Since the mid-1990s there has been a turn away from the 20th-century, Western psychological focus on decathexis, or cutting off the loss, toward a redefining of self through an open, evolving continuity with the loss (Hagman, 2001). Healing comes not from cutting off, but from oscillating between grieving the loss and restoring oneself (Stroebe & Schut, 2001), and reweaving the fabric of one's life into a new wholeness (Attig, 1996, 2001). We are forever different because of this person's presence in our lives. We are forever different because of the loss. What do we learn? What do we hope for now? How do we live today?

A continuum of beliefs exists. Countless religions and cultures believe that the deceased person continues to live in another form and can directly affect our lives on earth (Goss & Klass, 2005). Simultaneously, countless others believe that death "is it," nothing more exists after death. As professionals, we need to stretch our necks up and down and around to see beliefs beyond our own.

Whatever one believes about loss and grief, this author's loss and grief credos embrace mystery, curiosity, and a faith that much more exists than any one of us can fully know. Whatever this author's tenets regarding loss and grief, what are yours, the readers', and how do they affect your choices and paths in the present?

☐ Personal Expressions: Children and Teens

Many of our responses to today's losses come directly from what we learned about loss and grief when we were children. Which of these feel familiar?

- It's OK honey, you can tell me what you're feeling.
- Stop that! Quit being a cry-baby.

- It's like she's asleep.
- She's gone to be with Jesus.
- God needed him more than we do.
- How can you even ask that?
- You feel angry. Grandpa's not here. Can you tell me about it?
- Just be quiet. I can't take anymore from you.
- What are some favorite times we can always remember about Granny?
- It's all my fault.
- It's OK for me to be sad. It's not OK to be mad. I'm bad when I'm mad.
- If only I _____, then Mama won't be so sad.
- If only I _____, then Daddy won't be so mad.
- Where's _____ ? He'll be back soon. I'll keep watching for him. If I_____, he'll be back.
- Don't hope. Don't trust. Don't believe.

As children, we absorb the grief responses of those closest to us. We learn to express, repress, ignore, store, or act out our feelings and thoughts. As children, we often feel responsible for the responses of those around us, and for the loss itself. We might question, or not question. The meanings we learn and the roles we take on as children play themselves out in our adult worlds in how we cope with trauma and loss. These can lead to poor, ineffective coping. In Paul Valent's work with people experiencing compassion fatigue, he examines the long-term effects of such survival messages. Preface each of the following with, "I must":

- "Save others"
- "Be saved by others"
- "Achieve goal"
- "Surrender goal"
- "Remove danger"
- "Remove oneself from danger"
- "Obtain scarce essentials"
- "Create more essentials" (Valent, 1995, p. 32).

Rhythms reemerge of "there is a time." There is a time to feel or think just about any of the above. What do we do with those responses? A child's curiosity may be answered negatively with shame, or positively with openness, truthfulness, and age-appropriate understanding. Children will feel and think and interpret their grief experiences. Children deserve healthy ways to express and explore their questions, fears, and curiosities (Stokes, 2004). They are worth our time and care. In your own childhood, what losses did you experience and what did you learn? As an adult, and in your professional roles, how do you relate with children experiencing loss? What are you teaching them, and what are you learning from them?

Extensive resources about children's grief exist (Altilio, 2002; Corr, 2004; Doka, 1995, 2003; Worden, 1996). Additional resources focus on music (Aasgarrd, 1999; Berger, 1999; Dunn, 1999; Gaffney, 2002). Especially with children, CORE principles and HEALing techniques apply, within one's professional role or personal relationship with the child.

Care. Ownership. Respect. Empowerment.
Hear. Explore. Affirm. Learn.

Tools for Professionals who Work with Children

First, explore and familiarize yourself with children's developmental ways of coping with loss (Corr, 2004; Worden, 1996). They correlate closely with developmental psychology, such as the importance of trust, being the center of one's universe, imaginary thinking, skill development, shifts from concrete to abstract thinking, and shifts from parents to peers in forming one's identity. Such foundations for getting to know and understand the child or teen are crucial. Building on that, the following music tools can be added (see teaching guide 6.5).

1. Have a variety of sound-making instruments nearby. Children learn aurally, visually, and tactilely. Basic, easy to use instruments can stimulate all three. Just as child therapists keep toys, art materials, puppets and dolls nearby, have a variety of sound-makers as well. For example: a beautiful sounding bell (like a Zen chime), a grating sound (like a gyro), maracas, a gong, a soft sound (like sand blocks), a fun sound (like jingle bells), a sharp sound (like a woodblock), and others. Create variety. You can simply ask, "Which instrument fits what you feel today? Why?"

A teenager who used to play football chose a gyro and grated it with all of the energy and coordination he could muster. I asked him, "Do you feel angry that your body doesn't do what your mind tells it to?" He responded with a full-body nod, "Yes!"

Or, the variety of instruments may give expression to a more focused question. For example, a 6-year-old had been asking, "What will heaven be like?" Upon putting the question back to him, he explored sounds on different instruments, and he chose a beautiful Zen chime. Its high pitched, clear sound resonated on and on and on. We gave the chime to his parents when he died.

A wide drum can provide a great, contained physical space for interactive play. Sit on opposite sides of the drum. "Let's talk to each other on this drum. I'll start." Play a short rhythm. Encourage the child to play back. The child might simply repeat your rhythm or express the child's own rhythm. There is no right or wrong. Add words to sounds, or keep the dialogue wordless, and then talk about what you were "saying." Fun and laughter can create trust and interaction.

2. Do not assume to know what the child is expressing. Ask, explore, affirm, learn, validate, join in. When you suggest an interpretation, based on your knowledge of the child, check it out with the child. Give ownership of the expression and experience to the child.

3. Learn the child's music. Interact. What music reminds him of the loss? What music helps her feel better? Why? Sing and play it together.

4. Compose or rewrite a song. For the more expressive child, put his words to music, or take a familiar song and guide her in changing or rewriting the words. If the child has written any thoughts or poetry, an easy way to sing it is to use the three sounds in the familiar childhood chant, "Na-na-na-na-na-na." In the do-re-mi system, these notes are sol-mi-la. On a piano, they are G-E-A, starting on G, and then moving in any order. To add another pitch, try a lower or higher C. Any current music education teachers are certain to be familiar with additional improvisational patterns, from both the Kodaly and Orff music education systems (see the American Orff-Schulwerk Association, http://www. aosa.org).

5. Create a rainstorm on the piano. This is fun, easy, powerful, and interactive. Hold the piano's right pedal to the floor through this whole activity. Strum the black keys with both hands (not individual fingers), starting softly up high and working your way down low. Hit some low, black key clusters for thunder. Create your own volume, speed, intensity, and variations, again just by strumming the black keys with the sustaining pedal kept down. Work your way back up the keyboard, ending with a gentle strumming. The child can be part of any of these tasks, like strumming the black keys with you, adding in the thunder, holding the pedal, or telling you when to make the storm grow bigger or get smaller. Use this to dialogue with the child about how the loss is like a storm. Let the child create and control the thunder or other portions again.

This works well because it uses a pentatonic, five-note scale. Any notes can be played together in any combination. These patterns create a resonance, versus dissonance. Many folk songs and early American hymns are built on these five notes. Countless other improvisational activities are available through Orff-Schulwerk music education techniques and resources.

6. Mad — Sad — Glad — Afraid. This exercise has multiple variations, depending on the age and makeup of the group. Simply, it is a four-note song: Mad (F), Sad (lower C), Afraid (G), Glad (A). Teach it one note and word at a time. Have the group sing the word with inflections and facial expressions that match the words. If possible, have a pitched instrument (like a resonator bell or choir chime) for each emotion. Ask "who's feeling ____?" (for each emotion), and let that person(s) play the instrument while the group sings. Relationally, this provides personal expression with community accompaniment and validation.

Lead group dialogues about each word. Talk in age-appropriate language. Be sensitive to individuals' responses. To instill it into members' memory banks, put them together, adding only one word at a time: Mad; Mad — Sad; Mad — Sad — Afraid; Mad — Sad — Afraid — Glad.

7. Use these tools to reconnect with your own childhood losses. Today, identify something you would have liked to have expressed as a child. Pick an occasion when you wish you had been heard and understood and write it down. If possible, use the same medium you would have used then. For example, try writing with a big, thick crayon or marker on white paper. Or, use a lined writing pad, designed for first-graders. Take your time, be with it, with yourself. Use those sol-mi-la pitches to sing it. For men, use your falsetto voice (high, light). What would you like to have heard said back to you? Write it. Sing it, using your adult voice. Give yourself the care you did not receive earlier. Open yourself to hearing and voicing those same things to others, whatever age or life stage they may be.

8. Be open to your own healing. See your own strengths and challenges with grief today. Be open to your own in-the-moment balms. Look and hear within. Look and hear around.

Case Study: How Do We Learn to Say Goodbye?

Katy and Tom's mom was admitted to hospice. The hospital's discharge planner told us the caregiver was their grandmother. Visiting their home, we soon learned that Grandma's mental illness left her with bare coping skills. Katy and Tom, ages 13 and 11, had been doing most of the family caregiving for over a year. Katy, especially, saw us as intruders who were going to take away her relationship with her Mama. Through the next months our hospice nurse, social worker, and additional team members focused on getting undue responsibilities off of the kids, while coaching and affirming them with more age-appropriate tasks for being involved and expressing their care.

Mama's illness, dying, death, and funeral planning were filled with turmoil, family conflict, and extreme challenges. Complex histories of family loss and broken coping emerged and occurred again. When needs exceeded what could be provided at home, Mama was taken to our inpatient unit. While in her final hours (a stage we call "actively dying"), Tom crawled under her bed and refused to come out. Relatives yelled at him, "Git outta there, right now! Don't you know your Mama's gonna die right on top o' you!" Our team took the upset adults to another room. Our child therapist placed a pillow under the bed with the words, "Here — this is for you." In a short time, Tom emerged. Validation, presence, dialogue, and interaction with Tom led to him picking out a "#1 Mom" pin at the hospital's gift shop. He gently pinned it to his Mama's nightgown, and kissed her cheek.

Conflicts between family members erupted throughout the death, funeral planning, and at the funeral home. Per Mama's earlier instructions, Katy emptied their bank account with a debit card and brought the cash, stuffed in her girl-sized purse, to the funeral home to pay for the funeral. The funeral director worked out other arrangements. One family member demanded a large cash payment for having driven the children back and forth to the hospital, about three miles distance.

As their hospice chaplain, I was asked to lead the funeral. They were Christian and the kids had previously attended Sunday School, but currently they had no church community. As the funeral director and I guided them in planning the visitation and funeral, adults verbally cut down any desires or emotions expressed by Tom or Katy.

Katy requested Wynona Judd's song, "It's Never Easy to Ever Say Goodbye," because "me and Mama used to listen to it." I assured her we would use it. Grandma wanted "Peace in the Valley" by Elvis. Yes. Through the following visitation, I gathered more life stories from family members and spent time getting to know as many as I could. Pieces of family puzzles were now fitting together, explaining their voids of peace.

I found Katy's song and listened to it closely (Shamblin & Nelson, 1992). While preparing the funeral homily, I was haunted by several phrases and nuances in the song about it "ain't" being easy, but letting go, going our separate ways, and then meeting again up in heaven. An intuitive dissonance stuck in me. I had to hear it. From recent conversations, our social worker feared Katy might use the money to leave town on a Greyhound bus. She and our child therapist followed up with Katy. From my interactions with Katy, I had a sense of "It ain't easy, but I'm tough, and I can cut off what I feel, and I'm supposed to do hard things." In this context, this music felt congruent with, and reinforcing of a cut-off from her grief, either physically by leaving or even through suicidal ideation for a reunion somewhere above. This is in no way a generalization or criticism of this song, it is an interpretation, within this specific context. I reflected on the dissonance I was feeling. Was it just me, or might it hold a truth to explore further? I felt compelled both to use this song and to take it deeper.

I recalled another song, similar in contemporary country style and sound, titled "How Can I Help You Say Goodbye" (Taylor-Good & Collins, 1993). It is a three-stanza ballad about a girl's grief as a child, young woman, and later at "Mama's" bed as she is dying (see teaching guide 6.6). The refrain sings:

Mama whispered softly, "Time will ease your pain

Life's about changing, nothin' ever stays the same,"

And she said,

"How can I help you to say goodbye?

It's ok to hurt, and it's ok to cry

Come let me hold you and I will try.

How can I help you to say goodbye?" (Taylor-Good & Collins, 1993)

I found the CD, and wove it into my homily, tying the two songs together. Reflecting on the two texts and musical nuances, I felt the image of Mama, whispering, holding, and comforting added a softer, connected, and nurturing meaning to "it ain't easy, but I can do it." Was this text denying death? Perhaps. More importantly, it could affirm an ongoing nurture versus a cutoff and shutdown. Katy and Tom were only beginning to shift their relationships with their mother from her physical presence to their personal, lifelong, inner meanings. Using the pastoral language from chapter 5, "it ain't easy" *confronted* death and *guided* (evoked) earlier memories. "How can I help you say goodbye" *sustained* nurture and *informed* (instilled) new ways to experience their loss.

The morning of the funeral, Katy proudly arrived wearing the exact same dress and hat that Mama was wearing, in her casket. "Isn't it pretty? Just like Mama. We picked em out together at the store." Moments later in the funeral home's chapel, I was testing the Wynona Judd CD on my boom box. Tom chimed in, "Oh, can you play my favorite? It's on there, too." He didn't know the song's name, but we started up different tracks. "That's it! That's the one." I, who believe in music's soul-depth power, was astounded. In my thoughts, I worked the refrain of "No One Else On Earth" into my homily (Lorber, Harris, & Colucci, 1992). For Tom, losing his mother was a hurt like none other, now, nor at any other time in his future. Loving and being loved by his mother was like no other love, especially at 11 years of age. I made note of the CD's track and location of the song's refrain. Tom's voice would be expressed and heard.

This funeral was a time to firmly stand and move and relate in my ministerial role, with both children and extended family. Sustaining. Confronting. Healing. Reconciling. Guiding. Informing. As Grandma and the family sat down and settled in, they heard, "There will be peace in the valley for me." Grandma and I connected. I remember her eyes and the "thanks" she mouthed to me. I included in my opening words of welcome and readings, "Nothing can separate us from the love of God" (Romans 8:38–39). I adapted my "There Is a Time" reading (in chapter 2) for the needs present in this time, this place, and with this family. Later, in the homily, I talked about Katy and Tom having been like the Old Testament's David. Like the young David, they too had fought a big, ol' Goliath. Their Goliath had been cancer. Even though Mama had died, they had courageously loved her and taken care of her. In their own way, they had beaten cancer, because nothing and no one — not even death — can separate them from their Mama's love for them, or their love for her. I publicly affirmed Katy and Tom to their extended family.

This same boy David, later became a king. Way back then as a boy, he was strong enough to take on Goliath, and "lions and tigers and bears." Still, he was gentle enough to take care of sheep. This same David really liked to write poetry and sing songs to express what was going on inside. "Yea, though I walk through the valley of the shadow of death, I will fear no evil, for You are with me," (Psalm 23:4). Like David's expressions way back then, the music today, had been chosen by Katy and Tom to voice what they wanted to say.

I wove together the recordings of "It's Never Easy to Say Goodbye" and later, "How Can I Help You Say Goodbye" with spoken interpretations. I affirmed that Katy and Tom had done incredible things that "ain't easy," and this is a time to tell them what a great job they did, and to thank them. There are times they have been all grown up, and doing adult tasks, and dealing with adult decisions. It ain't easy, and they've done it. There are times to take care of others, and times to let them be 13 and 11 years old. These are times they need and deserve our care and support.

I validated how this death affected each person in this room in deeply personal ways.

We are reminded of earlier funerals in this same funeral chapel, when saying goodbye to other family and friends. This is a time to look around, and see each other's tears, hear each other's fears, and to feel each other's sadness. This is a time to give and find support and hope. There are a lot of things you'll probably always see different or disagree on. Still, this time of death is a time to come together in how much you do mean to each other. I've heard it and seen it in your stories these past days, and in you being here, today. This is a time to set aside grievances, and to grieve.

From the faces, glances, and energy in the room, many of those gathered got it. The moments of music provided containers for experiencing something together, especially sounds and words they had heard and sung in everyday life. The music provided punctuation within the homily. It was not about the music. It was about their loss and grief, individually and collectively.

I advocated that the legal will (which family members were disputing) was yet another way "Mama" personally said to Katy and Tom, "How can I help you say goodbye?" I added that "goodbye" means "God be with you," and although "your Mama is no longer physically here, she'll always be with you, in new and different ways." After the funeral, I gave my CDs to Katy and Tom. I encouraged them to play and sing those songs when they missed her.

I had my own goodbyes to say as Katy and Tom's hospice care transferred to bereavement counselors. As professionals, we absorb pain and struggles from others' tragedies. Compassion fatigue can set in (Figley, 1995; 2002). This was a time for me. Spiritual fullness and exhaustion; profound sadness; unnamed stirrings and searchings. For my self-care, I burned a CD with those four songs: "It's Never Easy to Say Goodbye," "No One Else on Earth," "How Can I Help You Say Goodbye," and "There Will Be Peace in the Valley." I played them in my car between new hospice visits, searching through what I was learning from it all. Katy and Tom's guardians did not respond to calls from our hospice bereavement care. Questions haunted me. Professionally, I had to let it be and let it go.

In my mind I changed the last song to "*Will there* be peace in the valley for *you*?" Years later, I do not know. I wonder. Whatever Katy and Tom's loss and grief experiences are today, I hope those moments mattered.

Teens' Musical Expressions: A Personal Story

Typically, Western teenagers' music changes course from their parents' music. If in doubt, trace it from about 1920 onwards. It is a normal, cultural way of becoming differentiated. Our baby boomer LPs, 8-tracks, cassettes, and even CDs are now replaced with MTV, MP3, cell phone ring tones, IPods, and more.

Is this a time for adult judgment? Maybe, maybe not. That is a personal decision based on one's values. Wherever one is on that continuum, I encourage, these teen years can be a time to listen and to learn. Is it possible that teens' music may actually be some type of gift, signaling to them and to us parents that a childhood age of innocence is shifting? Developmental changes, losses, and growth are in motion, and like our teens' music, these changes will not and cannot be stopped. Is it possible, that the music pounding away (why is it always so loud and so percussive?) can give us space and place to work through our own thoughts and emotions in the changes taking place throughout the household? When and how did yesterday's lullabies and rocking chairs rock and lock you into this adolescent roller coaster ride?

Think about it.

From about age 13 on, our teenager knew that because of my job, one of his teenage jobs was to teach me about his music. My car's left three radio buttons were mine, and the right three were his. His music was his, just as mine was mine. Through these teen years, I have been tested by this "pro" on identifying performers, titles, or what the singer was saying. While recoiling at some lyrics, I've turned the table with, "help me get it" and "what do you think?" It has been an easy access into some tough subjects, through his language. He often would tell me some kind of real-life story about the performer. Such dialogue engages values, differences of opinion, and calls for respect in the midst of differences.

Additionally, in the car and at home, he learned that he does not own everyone else's sound space: in the car, at home, nor in everyday interactions. It is about both generations and multigenerations hearing and respecting each other. Now as he moves into adulthood, those moments still exist of, "Hey, here's a new song you need to hear." The song always has a personalized, relevant meaning. I'm eager to hear, here.

☐ Community Expressions

We shift again from the personal to the communal experiences of music and grief. From the West African griot and jali musical story-tellers to our Nashville country ballad composers, from Vatican choir prayers to Moroccan gnawa music for healing ceremonies, communities gather and move through life's journey to the beats of their own drums, and the sounds of their own music. Most cultures and religions have rituals that involve music for developmental events of birth, adolescence, marriage, and death. Most cultures have musical rituals for religious and national holidays, celebrations, military occasions, and somber grief.

Consider, what would a wedding be without music? A graduation? An inauguration? What would Christmas be without "Silent Night" or Yom Kippur without "Kol Nidre"? What would the Derby be without "My Old

Kentucky Home" or the Super Bowl without "The Star Spangled Banner"? For a moment, opposing athletes and teams come together in community. "Com" means joining together. "Unity" means as a unit, oneness, wholeness, in harmony. Music creates a moment for communities to come together.

Music Moment: The Olympics, Summer 2004

Imagine the Olympic Games without music. Bleak. Recall moments of the Olympic Games with music — competition is transcended, common humanity and achievements are celebrated. I captured the following moment while watching the 2004 Olympic Opening Ceremonies, televised from Greece.

It begins with music — of course. A multitude of drummers are walking into the stadium, playing a solemn march. They stop playing. Silence. A solitary drummer plays from the site of the original Olympic games (shown on a big screen via electronic video and the marvels of taped and real time). In response, another drummer responds from the 21st-century stadium. An enthusiastic drumming debate takes over between the drummer of old and the drummer of new. (The video drummer looks like the live drummer. Are they the same person, in a technological synchronization?) The crowd is caught up in the moment. Ecstatic responses break out. Music bridges the Olympics past and present. Olympic rings of fire electrify the stadium's pool of water. Opposites come together in a new, artistic unity.

Music's Power to Unite

Celebrating the opening of the 1998 Nagano Olympic games, Beethoven's "Ode to Joy" finale from his 9th Symphony was simultaneously performed via satellite hookups from five continents. Choruses literally sang together from China, Japan, Berlin, Cape Town, New York, and Sydney (*Shinano Mainichi Shimbun* newspaper, 1998).

Beethoven's Symphony No. 9, composed in deaf solitude, united former enemies to celebrate one of the most pivotal events of 20th-century history. The Berlin Wall came down. On Christmas Day 1989, Leonard Bernstein conducted Beethoven's Symphony No. 9 in Berlin's historic Schauspielhäus (Beethoven, composer, and Bernstein, conductor, 1990). For this celebration, the well-known "Ode to Joy" was changed to "Ode to Freedom." The German word *freude,* meaning "joy," was sung as *freiheit,* meaning "freedom." Musicians were selected from both the East and West sides of the Berlin Wall. Furthermore, orchestral players and singers represented both sides of the World War II combatants, and the conductor was of Jewish heritage. These symbolic unions of former foes artistically endeavored through music to promote understanding between peoples. The finale chorus of singers included a children's choir from East Germany, who at their young ages had never experienced life beyond the Wall. Having watched a video recording, the sights and sounds create a collective life spirit that transcended years of separation, and even the music itself.

Music's Power to Empower and Transform

Music can empower us at life's most challenging moments. It can voice one's darkest struggles. Music can transform one's core spirit (Hesser, 2001). Oppression can become vision. Despair can become determination. Many African-American spirituals were sung as signals for the Underground Railroad: "Steal Away," "Follow the Northern Star," "Swing Low, Sweet Chariot," and "Keep Your Lamps Trimmed and Burning."

Children imprisoned by the Nazis in the ghetto of Terezin, Czechoslovakia wrote poetry, created drawings, and music. "If in barbed wire things can bloom, why couldn't I? I will not die, I will not die." Fifty years later, their poetry and artwork were set to music by Charles Davidson in the concert and VCR titled *The Journey of the Butterfly*, performed in 1991 by the American Boys Choir at the fiftieth commemoration of the ghetto's establishment. A few children who survived told their story in film (Frye, Davidson, Litton, & Children of the Terezin Jewish Ghetto, 1996).

Many readers remember the unifying, nonviolent powers stirred by singing throughout the Civil Rights Movement. "We Shall Overcome." "Oh Freedom." "Keep Your Eyes On the Prize ... Hold On." "This May Be the Last Time." "I'm On My Way to Freedom Land" (*Sing for Freedom*, 1992; Horner & Sweet Honey in the Rock, 2000). Energies were focused and freed. Closed ears and eyes were summoned to new truths. These songs had passed from generation to generation. They sang out personal stories and community histories of tragedy and triumph. They rang out "it's time" to change.

Our Western music history books neglect our rich African-American genres and legacies all too often (Reagon, 1992). Perhaps these songs confront a collective national conscience at places only the brave dare explore. (Paradoxically, Francis Scott Key's national anthem, written in our 1814 slavery era, ends with "o'er the land of the free, and the home of the brave.") Bernice Johnson Reagon, scholar, singer, social activist, and founder of the internationally acclaimed Sweet Honey In The Rock vocal group, sings on: "We who believe in freedom cannot rest until it comes" (Reagon, 1993).

Music's Power to Comfort

What would a community memorial service be without music, especially when the loss is tragic and unbearable? Reflect on TV reports of funerals, candlelight vigils, and community services for those who were tragically affected by the Oklahoma City bombings, the Columbine shootings, 9/11, war, and tragedies within your own community. What distinctive themes of loss and grief emerge (Lattanzi-Licht & Doka, 2003)? When communities gather to mourn, music can engage everyone in shared moments of thought, emotion, and meaning. Individuals can join together in humming or singing together. A new memory is created that can comfort in more private moments ahead. What music moments do you recall? My local newspaper reports:

> Singing hymns in English and in Dinka, accompanied by African drums and a pipe organ, hundreds of people gathered in Louisville last night to mourn a Sudanese refugee whose American dream ended with his murder on Friday. More than 300 people crowded into the Highland Baptist Church for the funeral of James Kuch Mangui, praising him as a free-spirited yet ambitious man who had worked hard to learn job skills and make his way in this country.... Mangui's ordeal began in 1986 at age 7, when he was separated from his family during Sudan's civil war. He fled the country on foot with other boys and lived 13 years in refugee camps in Ethiopia and Kenya before coming to Louisville with about 125 other Sudanese men in 2001. (Smith, *The Courier Journal,* September 1, 2004 p. B1)

Hear the power of the Western and Dinka music, African drums and pipe organ. Hear the "com-" (coming together) "-unity" (one-ness) in using music to coexpress diverse cultures. I know this church, and many of the people there. Vibrations of the music moved the core essence of each person present.

One person's voice can comfort the masses. On September 6, 1997, Elton John wrapped a nation (and more) in a musical blanket when he sang "Goodbye, England's Rose" at Princess Diana's funeral. Internationally, individuals instantly recognized his melody. They hummed, followed, and easily joined in their minds and hearts to Elton's already familiar popular song, "Candle in the Wind." He gave ready, sensitive expression to their voices, joining together nationalities, races, religions, and generations in an outpouring of sorrow.

Some tragedies curtail our standard rituals for mourning, both privately and as community. Multiple natural disasters prevented normal rituals to mourn: the December 2004 Asian Tsunami; the 2005 Hurricanes Katrina, Rita, and Wilma; the October 2005 Afghanistan and Pakistan earthquakes, and ongoing disasters. Priorities focus on finding survivors. There is no time to mourn. There is no time for reflection or support. No time for Taps to mark an ending and move us into quiet rest.

Perhaps these crises evoke a deeper "music." Not soothing sounds of song, but rather cries of sirens, anguish, and fear. Can we hear that music? Are its sounds too threatening? Can we find ways to join the refrain?

Music's Power to Transcend Tragedy

In 1968, a simple folk song written by Richard Holler and recorded by Dion DiMucci rapidly peaked as Billboard's number 4. The song? "Abraham, Martin, and John" simply and poignantly reflected a nation's grief just after the assassinations of John F. Kennedy, Martin Luther King, Jr., and Robert Kennedy (Holler, 1968). It voiced personal and community despair, with an enduring hope for a better future, and a vision that transcends even death.

The ballad begins with a historical soulfulness and simplicity. Like our earlier descriptions of searching for the loss, the singer asks, "Have you seen my friend?" A close, personal warmth moves back and forth between the listener and the song's bigger-than-life personas. Embedded in the decade of the Civil Rights Movement, echoes ring of Abraham Lincoln's 1860s battles for human rights: "Oh freedom, oh freedom, oh freedom over me! And before I'll be a slave, I'll be buried in my grave, and go home to my Lord, and be free!" Reverberations resound of Martin's 1960s nonviolent protests: "Deep in my heart, I do believe, we shall overcome some day."

This song's simple lyrics stir collective experiences and personal memories. For old-enough readers, where were you when JFK was shot? What TV images instantly come to your mind? What did you feel? Fear?

Back to "Abraham, Martin, and John" (and Bobby). As their names unfold, we focus not on their tragic deaths, but on their heroic lives. Themes and paradoxes interweave in the lives of these four men and their impact on this nation's history. Civil War and Civil Rights. Power by politics and power by religion. Yankee bred and Southern bred. Rich in money through breeding and rich in soul through bleeding. Unity and purpose.

Shot-down, yet still raised up. Despair in my larger world and closer in my intimate, personal world. No sense. A sense that whatever this chaos is, we're in it together. A hope and promise of a reunion with those we've loved and lost, with those who have suffered before us and whose beliefs tenaciously live on through us.

This song's power multiplied as other singers expressed it in their own voices and personal styles. "Abraham, Martin, and John" was rerecorded by Marvin Gaye, Ray Charles (Charles, 2002), Harry Belafonte, Smokey Robinson, Andy Williams, Kenny Rogers, Mahalia Jackson, Moms Mabley, Miguel Rios, Cliff Richard, Eartha Kitt and the 100 Voice Gospel Choir, Ray Conniff, Frankie and the Fashions, and Bob Dylan. Even now, most baby boomers hearing the song go right back in time to their personal memories of these national events, and the meanings they took from them. For readers, where does this song take you? To your past? Your present? Anywhere in your future?

☐ Global Expressions

For any examples I have given from Western music, countless more exist for all other civilizations, cultures, religions, generations, and genres. Our exciting age of technology and artistry can unite us through increased awareness and understanding of each others' music. We can experience first-hand both the uniqueness and universality of our musical expressions.

Multiple resources reflect both our cultural individualities and kindred ties. The 2002 IMAX production of *Pulse: A Stomp Odyssey* masterfully weaves these together, from street performers in New York City, to taiko drummers in Japan, gumboot dancers in South Africa, tabla players in India, bell ringers in England, and many more (*Pulse: A Stomp Odyssey*, 2002). Numerous world music compilations can take you around the world in 80 minutes or less, like international lullabies (Mendelssohn, collector & editor, n.d.) and funeral commemorations (Charno, 1998).

Sensitively hearing another's music can foster societal understanding and change (Small, 1996). Even without recordings, compare in your mind Tibetan Buddhist chants, Gregorian Roman Catholic chants, Jewish chants, Muslim Qawaali, and Appalachian lined out hymns (Titon, Cornett, & Wallhausser, 1997). Similarities sound aloud.

The following examples were noted within a contained space of time (see teaching guide 6.7). Hear the intertwined elements of personal and community expressions, in these global examples, only within a few weeks of each other.

August 15, 2005 — An Assassination and Funeral

Sri Lanka's Foreign Minister, Lakshman Kadirgamar, was assassinated on August 12, 2005. He was a humanitarian, with concerns for children of war, world wide. He had proposed "Vesak Day" to the United Nations as a day of international celebration. His state funeral, today, reflected his strong interests in world religions and efforts for peace. It began with a military band and the service included Hindu, Buddhist, and Christian elements of mourning, reflecting his efforts for world peace. His body was cremated, in accordance with his Buddhist heritage (details gleaned from various TV and Internet news reports).

September 2, 2005 — New Orleans

NBC and MSNBC televised an initial relief concert for victims of Hurricane Katrina. Native New Orleans musicians sang and played their music: Harry Connick, Jr., Aaron Neville, Wynton Marsalis, Faith Hill, and Tim McGraw. Faith Hill, raised in Mississippi, sang of personal tragedies, of holding on and finding faith, in her well-known song, "There Will Come a Day" (Luther, Mayo, & Lindsey, 1999). Its words struck new meaning (Associated Press, September, 2005). Little did we know, Hurricanes Rita, Wilma, and other natural disasters were still ahead (Associated Press, September 5, 2005).

October 8, 2005 and Days Following — Devastating Earthquakes

Over 50,000 are killed in Afghanistan and Pakistan earthquakes. No time exists for funerals. No songs except for cries of desperation and grief.

October 19, 2005 — Café du Monde, New Orleans

Café du Monde in the French Quarter reopens after the floods. This 143-year-old landmark represents history and survival. The feast fills one's senses with longed-for smells and tastes of beignets, chicory coffee, and sounds of Dixieland jazz. The jazz trio played "When the Saints Go Marching In" and "Down by the Riverside" (Reuters, 2005).

November 2, 2005 — Rosa Parks's Funeral

Four thousand gathered in Detroit, Michigan, to mark Rosa Parks's death and celebrate her life. Brenda Jackson sang a "soaring rendition of The Lord's Prayer." Aretha Franklin sang about one world being a better place because of Rosa Parks. The gathered community stood, held hands, and sang "We Shall Overcome" (CNN.com, 2005).

November 15, 2005 — Earthquake Relief Concert

An estimated 1,400 people gathered in Amsterdam to raise money for relief efforts. Death tolls from Afghanistan and Pakistan's earthquakes now stand at over 70,000 persons. Over 3.3 million were left homeless. Leaders of the concert put forth: "We're here to discover what's common between us — from Palestine to Israel to Morocco to Ethiopia to Sudan to Syria…. There are no borders here tonight. We must be united, people to people." The project was a multiethnic fusion of Israeli, Ethiopian, Sudanese, Hebrew, Aramaic, Amharit, French, and other international music (Shuster, 2005).

November 17, 2005 — Debut of *All the Saints*

Truly composing life out of loss, a commissioned work was debuted, *All the Saints*. It was composed by the Grammy-nominated and Billboard award-winning jazz trumpeter, Irvin Mayfield. Its form includes a Jazz Funeral, Memorial, and Processional, and is premiered by the New Orleans Jazz Orchestra (NOJO), at the city's Christ Church Cathedral on November 17, 2005. Its date coincides with the church's bicentennial of its first services in 1805. Christ Church was the first non-Roman Catholic congregation in the 1803 Louisiana Purchase. This musical premiere marks a reunion for NOJO musicians since their evacuations. This is the city's first major cultural event since the hurricanes.

> Mayfield notes that the historic music will be a blues piece that will include Negro spirituals, chain gang chants, call-and-response, and field hollers rolled into a big jazz funeral event. Acknowledging his use of blues in this jazz piece, he reminds everyone that blues is to jazz as blood is to the body.
>
> "Jazz comes from the blues, and the blues comes from slaves taking European Christian hymns and making it their own," Mayfield said.

"The healing comes from dealing with the pain. Through the blues, you take the pain and suffering and turn it on its head, look at it, celebrate its passing through as a part of life, and move on. That's what jazz teaches. That's the blues that you can find in jazz." (NOJO, 2005, Retrieved on November 19, 2005 from http://www.thenojo.com/saints.html)

☐ Ode to Expressions of the Soul

From Ricky's personal "I want you to love yourself no matter what" to Tom's "No one else on earth," and from the Civil Rights collective "We shall overcome," to Mayfield's *All the Saints,* music can express the soul. Music can open closed off emotions, empower the powerless, transcend tragedy, comfort, and unite us in purpose. Music can strike hope in the ashen soul.

May we all find ways to love ourselves and others, no matter what.
May we express ourselves in ways that overcome division and hatred.
May our lives create *freude* (joy) and *freiheit* (freedom).
Amen
Peace
Shalom
Solh
Shanti
Peoning Hwa
Vrede
Wolakota
Hoa Binh,
Spokoj
Paix
Let It Be[2]

FIGURE 6.1

The Final Cadence

I realize the people I love most will all be gathered at my memorial service, but I won't be there. I'll never see most of them again.

**Judy, a hospice patient, as she chose music
for her memorial service.**

☐ Music of the Soul at Life's End
☐ Final Cadence Endings
☐ More Final Cadences
☐ Music with the Dying
☐ CORE Principles: Care, Ownership, Respect, Empowerment
☐ Physical, Psychosocial, and Spiritual Care
☐ The Music Therapist with the Patient and Family
☐ Final Moments

Thus, spoke Judy. Even as her hospice chaplain, I felt stunned. She courageously voiced finalities of her own endings, with sadness and sacred awareness. As we began to play her glorious choice of "Autumn" from Haydn's "Seasons," I gently invited Judy to close her eyes and picture those same loved ones in the room with us. I offered to take her words of awareness to her loved ones at her memorial service, when they would be gathered, grieving her death.

About a month later at Judy's memorial service, I invited Judy's family and friends to bring Judy's music full circle. I told them of her words and how their love for her brought supportive presence in her last days. As we experienced her music together, we both grieved her absence and celebrated the gifts of life Judy had given each of us. Thus, the already triumphant music that sings, "Raise your glasses to toast the harvest"[1] (Judy's description), transformed itself into transcendent soul-connecting moments, earlier with Judy in her small room, and later with her loved ones at her memorial service. Her absence was real. Her essence was present.

☐ Music of the Soul at Life's End

What setting might you want when you are dying? Chaos and crisis? Calm and companionship? Solitude? What sounds, music or otherwise, might you want? Not want? Whom might you want with you, knowing your nuances, sensitively hearing your heartbeats and breaths, and giving witness to this final moment, your final release?

Music at life's end is found in virtually all civilizations, cultures, and religions (Charner, 1998; Irish & Lundquist, 2003). Common universal themes for music through the dying and at the commemoration include singing, playing instruments, praying, telling life stories, providing comfort, sending the person's spirit from this world into its next passage, and bringing community together in expressions of remembrance and grief. Styles and uses of music are congruent with the person's cultural and religious heritage, and contemporary context. So, back to you: What music would you want for your funeral? Why? (See teaching guide 7.1.) No doubt, your choices reflect something about who you are. Your ability to consider these questions says something about how you approach (or avoid) death. How we live and move into our current endings likely foreshadows how we will deal with our own dying, our own final cadence endings ahead.

☐ Final Cadence Endings

Continuing this book's many musical metaphors, let us explore the cadence. A cadence is a melodic or harmonic configuration that creates a sense of repose or resolution. Cadences mark the end of a phrase, a section, or a complete composition. The strength or finality of a cadence varies considerably, however. Musically, different cadences mark different kinds of endings: a bridge to a new section, a modulation to a new key, a deceptive cadence, a final ending cadence.

Back to basic music theory. A half cadence (ending on the V chord) brings a recognizable pause, but the listener knows "we're not done." A plagal cadence is the familiar IV-I "Amen" in church music. It offers an affirmation of "Yes. So be it." The full-fledged V7-I is called an authentic cadence. It can clearly communicate, "The End." A less known cadence, but especially appropriate to our metaphors, is the deceptive cadence. At the moment the cadence should end on the tonic (I or i), it lands on a different chord (usually the vi) with, "Surprise! You're not through yet."

Metaphors for Living

What great terminology. Surely, you have experienced your own deceptive cadence. You were engrossed in some type of saga that you expected to end, to be over, as soon as (fill in your own blank) happened. You wanted a clear-cut, authentic ending. Shock. In the flash of a moment, something happened and your almost-finished tale had a suddenly deceptive ending. The trauma and drama continued (see training guide 7.2).

Often, we do not explore our feelings of loss when something in life does not finish out the way we had hoped. Instead, we might fight the surprise ending or ignore it. We might become distrustful and disengaged from any future "cadences" that could go bad (or different from what we want). How might we understand and enter these cadence endings with more insight and understanding? Read on for a few metaphors and practical interventions.

Metaphors for Dying

The final coda (ending section) of the Western classical sonata and symphony forms an amazing parallel to a typical dying process (excluding some type of trauma, emergency, or surgery). It often flows something like this:

> The *coda* starts (the finale to the recapitulation, where main themes are recapped in the home key) → *accelerando* (speeding up) → *ritardando* (slowing down) → *fermata* on the final chord (hold, with an awareness that this is the end) → release at the *fine* (prounced fee'nay, and meaning the finish, completion).

Musically, audience members may wander off in their minds during the development section. The coda calls them back by signaling "we're at the end." Likewise, the terminally ill person's distanced relatives and close friends often join together, suddenly aware that an end is coming. An accelerando sets in, as decisions and difficult passages speed up and one's sense of remaining time shortens. In life, this is rarely a time for new thematic material. Rather, decisions and experiences should affirm the person's own style and being, as much as is possible. Often, the person's body slows down and moves into a fermata-like dying phase that clearly alerts, "the time has arrived." Family and friends gather to keep vigil, "holding" the person in a whole-note kind of care ("whole" care for physical, emotional, and spiritual care), and aware that "this is it." Movement into death emerges at one's personal *fine* release. "It is finished."

☐ More Final Cadences

Moving vans are loaded, and you walk through your empty apartment or house and close the door for the last time. You complete the last question on your last exam for a hard-earned degree. You sign and date your divorce papers. You watch a favorite building being torn down. You hug long-time colleagues at your own office farewell party. You take your pet to the vet and stay with her as she's put to sleep. As described before, you keep vigil with your loved one through his last days, hours, and breaths.

When such endings come, it does not matter if music is involved or not. What does matter is the "music" of the moment: being present, being aware. The important music here is not literal music, it is the life music of the person. The life themes, rhythms, and harmonies of the moment. One's being and essence. Personal and community expressions.

Spontaneous Music

Through the days of endings, literal music may gently emerge in one's mind, stirring emotion, memory, and meaning. Often, the music springs up in those grounding, routine moments, such as driving the car or taking a shower. A melody may pop in your head and you find yourself humming it, or you keep playing a particular CD again and again. Listen to yourself. Hear. Learn. It may be the song you gently sing to assure your loved one (and yourself) as you watch her breathing in and out, in and out, in and out … out … out.

Music and Media for Meaning

You can find and give meaning to the cadence you are experiencing through sight and sound. Simply telling one's story within a supportive community can be life affirming and life healing (Harvey, 1996; Harvey, Carlson, Huff, & Green, 2001). As life composer and conductor, you might make a video of photos paired with the just-right music and show it at a celebratory life transition like a graduation party or a wedding rehearsal dinner. You might have the just-right musician give a tribute at a move or retirement party. You can rewrite words to a familiar song and have everyone join in singing. Standard computer programs for business presentations provide easy, visual formats for pairing texts with photos. Today's laptop computers and home theater systems provide multiple modes for sharing such music and meanings (adhere to copyright laws). Perhaps most importantly, the active "doing" or putting together of the media presentation creates powerful ways to "be" in one's experiences, and to explore one's meanings (Rigazio-Digilio, 2001).

In today's geographically separated society, you may want to create a personalized website (Golden, 1999). Assure approvals from those involved. In light of today's web security measures, be careful with using maiden names, addresses, phone numbers, or other features that post more information than is needed. Or, make the website secure or password protected, and e-mail a link to family and friends you want to include. Add a guestbook for people to add in their remembrances and thoughts. My sisters and I did this for my parents' 50th wedding anniversary, because many of their family and friends through the years were scattered throughout the nation. The celebration and reconnections with important family and friends lasted for months, and were shared by all who visited the site.

Such music and media presentations can be played at a visitation-wake, or at other gatherings of family and friends. This might be a tribute created earlier, or one created with full awareness of a loved one's terminal illness. Creating the tribute can bring different generations together in interactive, meaning-making ways. For example, the older generations' life stories and photos can be gathered. Younger, technologically literate family members can create CDs, DVDs, or other modes of expression for the family. Photos of younger children within the family can be age-appropriate, meaningful ways to include the youngest members, who can feel included in the family relationships when seeing themselves in the photos. Meanings are gathered and explored by all generations. Grief and gratitude are paired in oscillation. Meanings are interpreted through the selections and sequencing of photos and music. The loss is not cut off. Rather, new stories and meanings add to the family's heritage (Attig, 1996; Harvey et al., 2001; Nadeau, 1998, 2001). Your "creation" can be revisited again and again in years ahead, with ever new meanings in new contexts.

Taking Judy's musical experience one step further, in the acclaimed *Tuesdays with Morrie* (Albom, 1997), family and friends affectionately gathered for a memorial service with Morrie while he was alive and alert, so he could experience their love and gratitude up close and personal. There was humor and laughter, memories and gratitude. Morrie and his gathered family and friends voiced many of those most important things to say: Thank you, I love you (Byock, 1997, 2004). In more private moments, further cadence completion can occur with, "Forgive me," and "I forgive you." As emphasized throughout this book, such uses of music or ritual can open a door for emotional connection and remembrances. Such music must be congruent with the person's interests, desires, and timetables. They should never be pushed or manipulated. This is not a time for venting or vengeance. It is a time for soul-searching and support.

Cadence Closure and Completion

We hear and speak about needing closure when loss occurs. We need to close a door. To let go. To not be stuck in the past. True. So true. And there is a time for closure, and a time for completion.

I understand grief's ultimate gifts to include closure, goodbyes, letting go, *and* integrations of the loss back into oneself in new and different ways. Parkes describes this as "reorganization" (1987, p. 27) or "gaining a new identity" (Parkes, 2001, pp. 89–106). Worden defines the final task of mourning to be that of "emotionally relocating the deceased and moving on with life" (2002, pp. 35–37). Neimeyer and other constructivist bereavement researchers explore it more fully as "meaning reconstruction," or constructing new meanings and sense of self out of the loss (Neimeyer, 2001).

The saying that time heals all wounds is an overused cliché. It doesn't. Some people choose to hold onto wounds, rather than risk moving on. Some losses continue to have lessons to teach, and the person moving on still has more to work out and learn from the loss. Sometimes, time itself is not enough to heal life's huge sorrows, regrets, limitations, tragedies, or inner brokenness. Can completeness be found in our incompleteness? Can wholeness or wellness fill our holes? At times, yes. There is a time. Not always. Not in all ways.

Cadenceless Endings

Some endings strike prematurely, before a life cadence moves us to an expected place of closure: an accident, an injury, a sudden death, a natural disaster, violence, suicide. Don McLean's "Bye, bye Miss American Pie" song of 1971 captures that abrupt halt. He sings of the plane crash deaths of Buddy Holly, Ritchie Valens, and J. P. Richardson ("The Big Bopper") in February 1959. He describes their deaths as being a day when music itself died. For us, whether through literal music or "life music," life as we know it stops. Dies. Life can never again be the same.

With a cadenceless ending, we cannot move through natural rhythms and harmonies of the loss. Still, we search for some ending to make sense of it all, to somehow finish it out. Often, we struggle with the "what if's" and "if only's" and desperately search to integrate meaning from them into who I am now and what I choose to do with my life ahead. Out of his horrific Auschwitz concentration camp internment, Viktor Frankl wrote: "Everything can be taken from a man but … the last of the human freedoms — to choose one's attitude in any given set of circumstances, to choose one's way" (Frankl, 1963, p. 104).

Music (literal music) can provide a unique language for expressing our paradoxes and soul struggles (see teaching guide 7.3). Music can stir pain and comfort, both at the same time (Berger, 1993). Music can help us enter into the dark places within, or with another, whether nice cadence-like endings are found or not. Sometimes, music can help us simply get through. A father whose son had unexpectedly died found focus and meaning in his grief through compiling music for and publishing three CDs titled *Before Their Time* (1999, 2002, 2004). These are unique compilations of songs, styles, and stories from many who experienced loss before there was time to prepare and let go. A theme resounds: sometimes, music can help us simply get through.

☐ Music with the Dying

With one who is dying (we are all dying and living, living and dying) — quality of life is a key concern. Research shows music therapy to improve quality of life for terminally ill patients, especially as music therapy is experienced in cumulative sessions (Hilliard, 2002). With the terminally ill, two often used scales for care are the Missoula Quality of Life Scale (Byock, 1998) and the Palliative Performance Scale (Kuebler, Davis, & Moore, 2005, pp. 456–457). Elements on these tools reflect several of the music of the soul themes we have explored: life review, life meaning, pain (physical, emotional, or spiritual), levels of doing activity and being engaged with life, and supportive relationships. With someone who is dying (and living) with a terminal illness, music can be used skillfully to relax or stimulate. Music can empower the dying person to voice emotion, to remember and reflect on life's meanings, to nurture connection with another, to venture into soul work, to heal grief, to pray, to be.

Hear again. Music can empower the dying person. Not, music should be imposed upon the dying person. Not, the dying person should be manipulated through music. In reality, music can be imposed and the music can manipulate another. But, music should not be used in this way. Rather, when all else is being stripped from the person, music can sensitively connect with one's life spirit. It can sustain the soul and affirm one's core essence. It can restore an internal locus of peace in the midst of chaos.

Caution: Stop

A key concern of this music therapist is that music should never be imposed upon another, especially the dying. For example, in long-term care, how often are radios mindlessly tuned to sounds of no relevance to the resident? Music therapists are clinically trained to discern the person's responses. Clinical practice pairs with research (Wheeler, 2005) to increase evidence-based practice techniques and skills (Aldridge, 1999). Especially when someone is in the later phases of dying, the patient's comfort must be in the forefront of care, with focused attention given to purpose, choice, and use of music. Too often, well-meaning clinicians, musicians, and other persons impose their musical, emotional, and spiritual assumptions onto others, especially when they do not adequately know the person.

Because music can go to such soul-depth places, extreme caution must be observed. Intensely painful emotions can be stirred in an instant. Anyone using music with someone dying — music therapists included — must be held to the highest levels of accountability against causing unwanted intrusions or imposed experiences. The actively dying patient is least able to say "stop." We musicians can too often assume our gifts are always good and wanted by others. Think again. Remember the diversity throughout this book of personal responses, life stories, and meanings. Hear that,Hear the person. Honor the soul.

Parkes and Markus identify fear and grief as two common emotions that arise in adult, dying patients (1998, p. 99). My relationships with the dying affirm that. I voice strong cautions about using music with the dying, because — as demonstrated throughout this book — music can evoke such powerful emotions, images, and meanings. A previously ordinary song experienced in a new context confronts the life-threatening illness and what it holds for the person. Again, the person's response is uniquely individual, and must be approached and responded to with sensitive care. Parkes and Markus identify common causes of fear in persons with a life-threatening illness:

Fear of separation from loved people/homes/jobs

Fear of becoming a burden to others

Fear of losing control

Fear for dependents

Fear of worsening symptoms

Fear of being unable to complete life tasks/responsibilities

Fear of dying

Fear of being dead

Fear of the fears of others (reflected fear) (1998, p. 99).

Similarly, Parkes and Markus name frequent "losses of patients with life threatening illness":

Loss of security

Loss of physical functions

Loss of body image

Loss of power/strength

Loss of independence

Loss of self esteem

Loss of the respect of others

Loss of future (1998, p. 102).

There is a time for music, and there is a time to not have music. One must be able to discern these different times. The objective is in-the-moment care of the person, not the musician's agenda for entertainment, performance, or an inflated sense of music's help. The music may be a catalyst for sustaining, confronting, healing, reconciling, guiding, or informing with sensitive care. The music may be a catalyst for being in and moving through the moment at hand. However, whose timetable is it, anyway — that of the person or the musician? Whose life and death is it, anyway? Whose present, past, and future is it? Effectively using music's power requires discerning when it is not helpful, and may be harmful (see teaching guide 7.4).

Caution: Go

During the Middle Ages, the original hospices were resting places for weary travelers. The term *hospice* is derived from the Latin term *hospitium*, and means "hospitality" and "host." The contemporary terms *hostels* and *hotels* are related. A hospice was a place along the journey to tend the dying. One's use of music with the terminally ill person and family is similar. The musician is not soloist, performer, or entertainer, but rather an accompanist with a person who is at a new phase of life pilgrimage. Any use of music is based on the patient's needs and desires, not on the merits of the music or musician. Furthermore, the skillfully trained music therapist serves as an ensemble player with the interdisciplinary care team.

Using music with a patient needs to be proportional and appropriate with who the person has been, and his current condition. Consider a few variables. Is the person alert and reflective? Lost in dementia, depressed, angry, afraid, or anxious? Is he or she accepting and ready for death? Is the person verbally unresponsive? Does he or she demonstrate nuanced responses of awareness? The hospice music therapist discerns these factors and initiates clinical care through music. The hospice music therapist hears and transcribes the person's life story into musical expression, through selections and reflections with the patient and/or family. She understands the importance of giving the conductor's baton for life music to the patient.

If you provide music to a terminally ill person, whatever your role or relationship, check your ego at the door. Enter with your best knowledge, understanding, and wisdom about music, living, dying, and the pulsing moments in between. Be open to surprise, learning, and soul transformation, for when we are fully present with the dying, one cannot *not* be stretched and changed (Hartley, 2001).

"The cancer has overcome my body, but I will overcome the cancer — even if that means death." That was the proclamation of Chris, a fiery African-American woman whose body no longer responded as she wanted. We had just experienced our own sort of communion, me with my keyboard near Chris, in her bed. She was in pain that day. So instead of our normal music and dialogue, we moved into our "direct" mode of music for pain (see chapter 2). I had just played about 20 minutes of Chris's soul music: from Edward McDowell's "To a Wild Rose" (Chris was no greenhouse rose), to Louis Armstrong's "What a Wonderful World," to Dorsey's "Precious Lord," to "Deep River," and improvisations on "We Shall Overcome." Chris was dying in the house where she had been raised, and in the bedroom where she had been born. In her invalid condition, she found validity. In her dependency, she found strength; in her chaos, she found peace. Chris's words ring in my ears. "The cancer has overcome my body, but I will overcome the cancer — even if that means death."

☐ CORE Principles: Care, Ownership, Respect, Empowerment

Synthesized from hospice patients and families I have been privileged to know, I offer a few core principles for serving the dying and soon-to-be bereaved. Whether one is relating in a professional role or a personal relationship, I find the following core principles central to one's decision making when giving care to one who is dying.

Care

Care for the person from a soul connection of common humanity. Care for yourself through whatever emotions and thoughts are stirred in the encounter. Care enough to hear another's interwoven life story themes, to adjust your rhythms to another's, and to be a calm, nonanxious presence in the life dissonances that cannot be fixed or easily resolved. Care through stretching beyond your comfort zone to understand another's style or expression that goes against your grain. Search for soul connection. Risk care, but know that without the following three principles, one's care can be less for the person, and more about one's own unresolved ego and self-care needs.

Ownership

Own your own experiences and responses, and give ownership to the other person of their experiences and responses. Do not assume to know how another person feels or thinks. Do not assume to know what she or he should do. Grant ownership of different life experiences, expressions, and styles. Another's responses do not have to match your expectations. Care enough to learn more of the other's context. When the person moves into a less responsive state of consciousness, continue to give ownership of one's body, emotions, thoughts, and prayers, to the person. Talk to the person when bathing or changing. Acknowledge the life spirit that is still breathing in the room.

When assisting a family with decisions, what documents had the person prepared, communicating his or her desires for this time of living and dying? (For downloadable Advance Directives for all 50 United States, visit http://www.caringinfo.org.) When needed, follow the next-in-line protocols for owning decisions: the spouse, an adult child, a health surrogate, or a durable power of attorney. Be sensitive to significant others who may not be legally recognized, but are significantly connected to the person, such as gay/lesbian partners, never-married partners, stepchildren, stepsiblings, stepparents. Again, what wishes has the person left in writing?

Support, educate, and encourage ownership of decisions and care giving. Offer choices, and inform the person(s) of likely outcomes. Ask questions. What do they already know? Want to know? Need to know? Who needs to know what and be involved in making decisions? Be sensitive to others' cultural decision-making norms that differ from your own. Be the professional, friend, or family member, but do not assume the role of guru with absolute answers. Remember, a cadence can go in many different directions. After the death, all persons involved will be left to live with the outcomes of their decisions. Facilitate their down-the-road bereavement process by honoring their ownership. Do not further complicate their later grief by taking over their processes now.

Respect

Respect the physical, emotional, mental, and spiritual rights of the other person, especially at a time when so many freedoms are being threatened or lost. "Sympathy" can come from a dangerous disrespect, as in putting oneself in an over-under, pitying role. "Empathy" combines care, owner-ship of the person's experience, and a respect for the person's rights. It can provide a foundation for exploring disagreements. It can transcend conflicted beliefs and actions.

"Respect" does not presume to know and feel the same emotion as another (which can lead to countertransference). It does accurately describe what the other person is experiencing, feeling, thinking, and coping with, and expresses compassionate human respect for the other.

Empowerment

Empower others. Whose death is it, anyway? As a hospice chaplain, I would often affirm, "If it's time for you to hold on, then hold on. If it's time for you to let go, then let go. This is your time. You will know what to do, and when, and how. For this moment, I send to you whatever you need: hope, peace, faith, strength, rest, holding on or letting go." Some death and dying literature gives techniques for urging the dying to move on toward the light, to just let go, and admonishes family members that they must give their loved one permission to die. While some family members may be ready for this, others are not, and should not be forced or coerced into doing something they will later question and regret. Care enough to acknowledge the other person's ownership of his or her experience. Are you asking or telling? Who does most of the talking in your time together? Give suggestions with a sense of choice. Respect another's time-table. Empower others to live their own lives, die their own deaths, or travel their own paths of care giving and mourning.

☐ Physical, Psychosocial, and Spiritual Care

As you read the above principles, did you question, "But these don't have anything to do with music?" Read again. These principles are core for the hospice physician, nurse, social worker, chaplain, nursing assistant, volunteer, child–adolescent therapist, and music therapist. They are core for the family member, friend, minister, or patient advocate. Providing music but overstepping or ignoring any of these can be harmful. Not harmonious. Not helpful.

The music therapist knows music's powers to connect with the dying person and family through timely selections and uses of music. The music therapist knows the nuances of relating, responding, and guiding.

Let's connect the music therapist within a dynamic paradigm of end-of-life care. Charles Corr identified the following "Four Primary Areas of Task Work in Coping with Dying":

- To satisfy bodily needs and minimize physical distress, in ways that are consistent with other values.
- To maximize *psychological* security, autonomy, and richness in living.
- To sustain and enhance those *interpersonal attachments* significant to the person concerned and to address the *social implications* of dying.
- To identify, develop, or reaffirm sources of *spiritual* energy and in so doing foster *hope*. (1991, p. 85)

These correspond to the standard hospice interdisciplinary team members for each patient and family. Central to all is the patient's unique self and needs.

The Hospice Interdisciplinary Team

The physician, nurse, and nursing assistant skillfully tend physical pain and symptom management, education, and support. The team's social worker utilizes resource awareness to maximize security, autonomy, and richness in living. Both the social worker and chaplain provide skilled counseling, support, and explore interpersonal relationship needs. The chaplain enters the person's spiritual struggles, fears, and hopes. Down the road, the bereavement counselor supports and guides those grieving the death. Collectively, the interdisciplinary team joins together to support the patient's and family's physical, psychosocial, and spiritual needs.

For example, the chaplain understands how a particular disease (i.e., ALS, AIDS, Alzheimer's) may uniquely affect one's spiritual journey. The nurse understands that one's faith background may affect decisions regarding total parenteral nutrition (tube feedings; TPN), or the use of pain medications. Does the person want to be more alert with a higher pain threshold? More sedated? Does the person believe that greater suffering before death may lead to a higher place in an afterlife? When Advance Directives have not been completed, one family member may want to continue every medical procedure available, no matter the potential suffering, "Anything to keep her alive." Another equal family member wants to allow a natural death to follow its course. How are these conflicts navigated? All hospice interdisciplinary team members understand the importance of educating and supporting caregivers through the dying, death, and initial bereavement process. Each team member brings to the table his or her own trained perspective and disciplined skills. Members work in ensemble with each other. (Am I hearing metaphors of a string quartet, or jazz group?)

☐ The Music Therapist with the Patient and Family

Dying, death, and grief are family affairs (Nadeau, 1998, 2001). A hospice music therapist brings unique tools to the bedside of the dying person: not pills, oxygen tanks, medicine patches, or pumps. The music therapist brings the person's and family's life stories together through song, expression, and meaning. Exploring life stories with each other is crucial to dealing with sorrow (Harvey, 1996, 2000; Harvey et al., 2001).

As a hospice interdisciplinary team member, the credentialed music therapist (Starr, 1999) brings evidence-based research and extensive clinical training to relax the body (Nicholson, 2001), stimulate dialogue and reflection, enter life review, help the dying person and their family and friends express their emotions and prayers, relate, and deeply "be" through music (Aldridge, 1999; Rykov & Salmon, 1998). Musical techniques with a more alert patient may involve singing, listening, playing an instrument, improvisation, lyric analysis, song analysis, composition, rewriting a text, or guided imagery. Often, the whole hospice team uses tools such as the Palliative Performance Scale (Kuebler et al., 2005, pp. 456–457) to help define levels of functionality and prognosis.

Music with a less responsive patient may foster a deep sense of presence; may engage gentle interactions with sensitivity to nuances of breathing, pain, and restlessness (Krout, 2003); and may provide a safe, contained space for meaningful, memorable moments for the family with the loved one. Music can provide a safe, contained space to transform experiences of suffering into those of meaning (Salmon, 2001). Musical interventions may be with the patient, the family, both (Hilliard, 2001), and may be at memorial services and bereavement care. Music can be a powerful tool to join generations, especially with creative and meaningful uses to include children and adolescents; especially if the dying person is the child or teen (Daveson & Dennelly, 2000).

Such music is not just playing music for an audience. It offers music with purpose and meaning. Music may stir humor, grief, thankfulness, fear, assurance, hope. The music therapist must be comfortable and skilled in traveling these diverse, oft-times painful, challenging paths.

Reread Corr's four primary areas of task work in coping with dying (listed earlier) in light of this book's chapters thus far: "Music of the Soul," "Rhythms of Body and Soul," "Themes and Counterthemes of Life Stories," "Harmonies and Dissonances of Healing," "Styles of Doing and Being," "Expressions of Self and Community," and the present chapter, "The Final Cadence." How might these translate to the dying patient and family? How might these provide guidance for the music therapist's own sense of artistry?

The following "Music Care for You" teaching sheet was designed for and used with hospice patients and families. It focuses on the patient's and caregivers' needs. It does not begin with certain CDs or music to use. It begins with the patient's own music of the soul. The left column, "I want to …," identifies a need, starting with physical needs. "I want" categories move into emotional and psychological needs, and then further into spiritual needs. (This progression reflects both Corr's tasks and Maslow's hierarchy of needs.) The right column, "I want to..." provides simple interventions for the identified needs. The paired statements "I want" and "I can" sets the stage for care, ownership, respect, and empowerment through music interventions (see teaching guide 7.5).

TABLE 7.1 Music Care For You

I want to ...	I can ...
Distract attention away from my pain	Play (radio, recording, instrument), sing or hum any piece of music I enjoy Ask someone to sing or play music for me that I enjoy, live or recorded
Relax better; sleep more deeply	Listen to a slow, soft piece of music, in a style I enjoy; lower distracting lights and noise levels Feel and listen to the rhythms of my breathing and pulse Breathe in and out with a piece of music's slower tempo Make a habit of playing the same piece of music when I take my pain medicine and begin to move into sleep (the same sound will begin to signal my brain that it's time to rest)
Find music to use	Ask a music therapist to help Ask a family member or friend to do an Internet search to find the recording, score, lyrics, or download (honor copyright laws)
Release pent-up feelings	Play a piece of music that expresses whatever I am feeling (sad, mad, glad, afraid) Find someone to experience the music with me, and to talk about what I am feeling (a family member, friend, or hospice team member)
Energize my body, emotions, or spirit	Play, sing, hum, or reflect on a piece of music that is faster, brighter, has a great beat for me Dance in whatever ways I can, like moving my arms, hands, fingers, legs, feet, toes, or head; "hand dance" with my loved one
Recall special people, events, or places	Recall, hum, sing, or listen to favorite music from years past; if my memory's weak, ask a family member or friend to select the music Enjoy the music, let the memories flow Let the feelings flow, whatever they may be Turn off the music if I feel too overwhelmed with memories and feelings; tell someone Have someone make a CD or cassette tape for me, combining many of my favorites
Explore meanings of my life's many paths	Combine my memory music with journaling, drawing, talking with my family or friends, exploring themes in greater depth with my hospice social worker or chaplain

(Continued)

TABLE 7.1 Music Care For You (*Continued*)

Experience spiritual nurture; pray	Play, sing, listen to music that validates my tears and fears, that voices my faith and beliefs Play, sing, listen to, reflect on music that I'm especially drawn to, or keeps popping into my head Let the music's sounds and words bathe my soul with sustaining comfort, peace, and hope
Reconnect with my faith community	Recall favorite music from my religious experiences Ask a leader or member from my faith community to lend me a hymnal, prayer book, or other item of meaning from my faith community (particularly from years past); reflect and talk with a trusted person about my faith journey through my past, present and future
Meditate on living and dying	Reflect on the rhythms, melodies, and harmonies of my life — my life's stages, themes, and relationships; create anew as I choose
Choose music for my funeral or memorial service	Talk with my family members, minister, or hospice chaplain If comfortable, experience the music with my family now in the present instead of just deciding it for later

The music therapist can go through this with the patient or caregiver, sensitively selecting and guiding appropriate interventions, rather than going through every category. Of note, the last intervention of choosing music for one's funeral may be too confrontational. Address this with care and sensitive timing. Simply say, "Some of these may not feel right for you right now, you can skip over them." Music may be provided in the moment, or suggested for later use. The patient's "doing" levels may be quite alert and interactive, or may require more "being."

Providing Music, as a Family Member, Friend, or Acquaintance

This tool can be used by others, when cautions listed earlier are observed. Again, do not misrepresent yourself as a music therapist, or as doing music therapy. Those skill sets are much more complex, and require board certification training (see http://www.cbmt.org). For example, a family member or friend will tend the person's physical care, but that does not make him or her a "nurse," or that the caregiver is doing "nursing" in a formal sense.

Still, like the family member who tends to physical needs, you can provide care, presence, support, and meaningful connection through music. You, the exhausted or emotionally stretched loved one, can create meaningful uses of music for your own self-care (see teaching guide 7.5).

☐ Final Moments

Presence. Breathing. A long pause. Is this it? Breathing again. Watching. Holding on. Letting go. Remembering. Preparing. When will the moment come? Will I be here? Can I be here or will I go crazy? What is that change? Is she in pain? What do I do? I experience calm and chaos, together at the same time. Where does he go when he goes? How will I live without her? Where is God? Is there God? Oh, God.

At this life ending, the best music of the soul is not literal music. It is the interwoven life themes, rhythms, harmonies, and dissonances, the doing and being, and the expressions of care gathered in a once only time and space. This music of the soul creates artistry by both digging deeply into one's human core and sending the life spirit soaring into death's release. This music of the soul can feel numb, cut off, simply moving through motions, or can feel extremely alive and aware. It is intensely personal and profound.

For those final moments when literal music is present, the experience can be extremely rich. Music may be sung or played just hours or minutes before death. It might synchronize with the actual moment of death. Most likely, it won't. Such timing should not manipulated, or expected to be some kind of a dramatic, cinematic moment. When it does occur, simply receive it as a gift. This vigil time can be filled with nuances of meaning and final gifts to and from the dying person (Callanan, 1997). I remember:

> ... a young African-American man letting go and moving into death as his sister sang to him a cappella, "I Believe I Can Fly."
> ... a patient I had known especially well, humming the alto part to "Blest Be the Tie," as I played her favorite hymns on my keyboard at her bedside. She had sung in her church choir for years. Now, she had not spoken in days. She died that night.
> ... walking into an inpatient room about three minutes after death occurred, with the most peaceful feeling and symphonic music playing nearby. The patient's wife described it: "It was as though the music orchestrated his dying." She described his increased breathing, a climax in the music and his responses, his release, and now the calm. His now still body and face portrayed a deep peace. Because we had CD/cassette players in each inpatient room, the patient's wife had taken his favorite classical music tapes. Months later, she donated many of his tapes to our library.
> ... Joan, with ALS (remember "My Fair Lady" earlier), immobile and actively dying, with a tear running down her cheek, and breathing out a loud, long sigh just as her pastor, family, and I ended singing and

playing her favorite hymn to her, "When We All Get to Heaven." Joan's daughter exclaimed, "Mom hears. She knows." At her funeral, the organist played this for the recessional of Joan's casket and family.

... Ida Mae moving her mouth and making sounds to sing with her husband, sister, and me, as we sang her lifelong theme song to her, "With a Made Up Mind." She had been in a coma for three days. She died three days later. At the funeral home, her husband thanked me profusely with, "I had one more moment with her."

... a 10-year-old girl requesting a nature relaxation CD at our inpatient unit to play for her mom to "help her." Suddenly within the next 15 minutes, her mom died. (No one expected death to arrive so soon.) We gave the daughter the CD to keep, to allay future guilt that she had somehow caused the death, and to assure her that indeed, she had helped her mom know that she (the daughter) loved her and was right there with her.

... on a Christmas day, a music volunteer (who was a medical student) singing "Silent Night" with the family to the patient (the patient was a pastor). In his coma, he took huge breaths right at the end of each phrase. "It was as though he was singing right with us." Our volunteer wrote a medical school paper on her cumulative experiences, identifying medical aspects of her supervised, volunteer experiences, and the patients' responses to music she had observed.

... personally delivering homemade cassette tapes to a teenage granddaughter and grandson, at their grandmother's casket, about an hour before her funeral. She had given me clear instructions to hand deliver these after she had died, and before she was buried. Weeks before, I had helped her tape about 20 minutes of her talking and singing her favorite songs (a cappella) to her grandchildren. Months before, she had also crocheted an afghan for each grandchild, for the great-grandchildren she would not know, but wanted to bless. We stood at the casket with arms around each other, with gratitude and loss.

... playing portions of Brahms *German Requiem* with a woman who was actively dying, who previously had kept hearing its music "stay in my mind," and "it won't leave me alone." As a first-generation American preschooler, she had been left to live with her non-English-speaking grandparents for several years in Germany. Weeks earlier, we had explored the requiem's text and meanings for her. Now, the music simply played, in German, "Wie Lieblich Sind Deine Wohnungen" ("How Lovely Is Thy Dwelling Place") .

... an elderly piano teacher in her final hours. Her daughter and son-in-law (both professional musicians) and her two adult grandsons lovingly surrounded her with her favorite music: hymns, live guitar (by a grandson), choral recordings, and classical piano music. They described her taking her last breath right at the end of Beethoven's "Moonlight Sonata." (How many times had she taught that piece to her piano students?)

Rahul, a 3-year old child who was actively dying, asked his mom and dad to sing to him, "Always There" from *The Land Before Time V,* his favorite VCR tape (Grosvenor, Tavera, & Brourman, & McBroom, 1997). He died within a few hours, on Christmas morning. Wisdom and love flowed to and from this child and his parents in his request and their singing. His father and mother — the right persons — were "always there."

There's more. Rahul's physician parents were from India and Spain. They wanted his funeral to reflect their rich interfaith and Rahul's beautiful spirit. Rahul's name meant "sun." Ironically, in approximately 350 A.D. Pope Julius I selected December 25th as the date for Christmas because of its pre-Christian meaning of the solstice, or "Day of the Sun." On this Christmas Day of Rahul's death and a few days later at his funeral, Rahul's loving grandparents and extended family were spread throughout our world, sharing the same daily sun, gratitude for Rahul's life, and soul-wrenching grief for his death. Like the rising of the sun and its setting of the day, even when we cannot know where the sun has gone, nor see nor feel it, for the sun has a way of being "always there."

At Rahul's funeral we played "Always There," along with "De Colores" (meaning the colors, in Spanish, another favorite song). We reproduced and gave to each person a copy of Rahul's colorful marker-drawing of the baby and parent dinosaurs in "Always There" in "The Great Green Valley."

A week before finishing this manuscript, Rahul's mom and I had an unexpected, chance encounter. It had been five years since Rahul's death. Our eyes and hearts were full. She shared a photo of their now 3-year-old daughter, whose favorite song is "De Colores." Now and forevermore a sense, a presence of Rahul is "always there."

As music therapist, I do not always have to be there, doing the music. Many times, the professional not being there at the moment can be better, in that the musical interaction is between the family and the loved one. Like the hospice nurse or other team members, the music therapist's role is to facilitate best care for the patient and family. For readers, what are your stories? Experiences? Hopes?

Final Meanings

Is this book for the living or the dying? Both. In experiencing dying, we can learn to live. In truly living, we can be more ready to die, without regret or fear.

When death arrives, one's true music of the soul has already been composed: those life-story themes, rhythms of movement, and sense of bringing harm or harmony to life's dissonances. Through bereavement's absence, that essence of soul is what others remember. It can be heard and played anew in a loved one's ongoing choices about living.

A Music Moment: Sounds of a Pope and Another Man of Soul

As I write this paragraph, a global vigil is being held for Pope John Paul II. Remembrances, reflections, meanings, and suppositions for ahead fill the airwaves. Newscasters have expected a ready death since the "grave" report of his condition. How long might this waiting last? Whatever one's religious or political choice, these present phenomena of music, prayers, life stories, and communal care bring new understandings of this man's formative years and his influences in this world. We learn early themes of Holocaust horrors and personal loss, and counterthemes of initiating reconciliation with Jewish and Muslim communities. Even on newscasters' reports, sounds of Catholic choirs, chimes, and pipe organs provide an audio backdrop, echoing sounds of communities and individuals gathered at St. Peter's Square and throughout the world.

This past year, another man of soul died, Ray Charles. He who was blind brought light into the dark of oh so many lives. Musically, Ray Charles mastered rock and roll, country, gospel, rhythm and blues, and jazz. His ultimate impact was not created through a recording studio's soundboard mixer, but rather through his soul's sounding board, as he continually played out his life's struggles, authenticity, and belief in the human spirit. Listen to his music. Hear.

How Do I End?

The stories could spin on. The guidelines could continue. Still, it is time to create a recapitulation summary and to move toward a coda's *fine*-finish for this book. (Does not death often arrive before all words are voiced? Before all tasks are done?)

What soul music will you imprint in the hearts and minds of your loved ones? What life themes and counterthemes, rhythms and harmonies of movement, styles and expressions of doing and being with others will you instill? We are creating them here. May we more fully hear. You are deciding now, you are living your music of the soul now. Do you care to make any changes? Dare to join your Creator in composing your life, dare to pick up your baton for what you can conduct, and to put it down for what you cannot.

I hope you dance, play, and sing.

"And when from death I'm free, I'll sing on, I'll sing on."

Southern Harmony folk hymn, "What Wondrous Love Is This"

Requested by my mother for her funeral.

8

Composing Life Out of Loss

My grief is beyond healing,
My heart is sick within me ...
Is there no balm in Gilead?

Jeremiah 8:18

Music gives peace to the restless and comforts the sorrowful.
They who no longer know where to turn find new ways,
and those who have despaired gain new confidence and love.

Pablo Casals, cellist

My life flows on in endless song, above earth's lamentation,
I hear the near though far-off hymn that hails a new creation.
Through all the tumult and the strife, I hear the music ringing,
It sounds an echo in my soul; How can I keep from singing?

Quaker hymn, Robert Lowry

☐ Redefining Self by "Relating" with the Loss
☐ Music Interventions at Different Seasons of the Soul
☐ Music's Keys to Our "Secret Gardens"
☐ Life's Endings and Beginnings — Life's Mourning and Morning
☐ Music of Morning
☐ Music of the Soul for Composing Life Out of Loss

Is your grief decomposing you, or are you composing life anew? Is there some interplay between the two? Music of the soul stirs grief and sorrow, memories and meanings, comfort and care, life and hope. It helps us re-member dis-membered life themes and counterthemes. It reels and rolls us through rhythms of chaos and grief. Music of the soul can help us be *in*, rather than bypass grief.

Thus far, we have explored these dynamics in grief–loss theories, music metaphors, historical examples, music therapy research and practice, case studies, tools, and reflective questions for readers. This final chapter compiles these grief concepts and musical metaphors into an overall metaphor of composing life out of loss. "Composing life" empowers one to explore what the loss means and then to choose and create one's life ahead.

Composing life out of loss references the phoenix archetype that created fire and life out of ash. It was mythologized in the Greek god, Orpheus, whose singing could tame fierce beasts, move trees, and bring life to stones. It is found in the Latino archetype, La Lobda, an old wild woman who collected bones in the desert taken for dead. She sang over them, asking: "What has happened to my soul voice? What are the buried bones of my life? … How do I make life come alive again? Where has La Loba gone to?… The old woman sings over the bones, and as she sings, the bones flesh out" (Estés, 1995, p. 33). Composing life out of loss is about transformation.

Composing life out of loss provides a contemporary phrase for our turn of the 21st-century humanities and liberal arts trained minds. It shifts yesterday's mythical legends into today's practical applications. When facing loss, the phrase *composing life* engenders empowerment, creativity, and hope. It honors the individuality of one's personal process, style, and "composition." It is not limited to a specific form or structure. Similar to musicians' language, it can shift concepts of grief "work" into grief "prac-tice" and "play."

Composing life out of loss gathers our previous music metaphors (see teaching guide 8.1). Composing music is not an absolute, linear progression of sequential steps. It may start with a melody, or a rhythm, or a lyric, or an emotion to express. It plays with going this way or that, rearranging something from here to there, and expressing oneself with personal style and expression. When composing music, one can get stuck. One can hear or visualize something in one's imagination, yet struggle with "how do I find it?" One interweaves these processes in highly individual ways. The composition reflects the composer, at a unique time in his lifespan and personal development.

Thus it is with composing or re-creating life. Bits and pieces. A driving emotion or dissonance that demands attention. A memory that keeps replaying itself. An unresolved conflict that keeps exploring different underlying harmonies and resolutions. A surprise twist or turn. A cadence ending that requires a pause before moving on.

With a finished music composition, the musician can come back and play the finished product again and again, each time with fresher understanding than before. Thus it is with composing life out of loss. As we move into new life experiences, we revisit our previous losses, "playing" them again and again to sharpen our skills and artistry for living in ever new changes and challenges. We talk of our loss history. What of our "beginnings" history? (See teaching guide 8.2.) Endings and beginnings. Loss's griefs and life's gifts. One's personal mournings and mornings.

☐ Redefining Self by "Relating" with the Loss

I have loved, I have lost. Who am I, now? Who am I in relationship with others?

My spouse dies and I am labeled a widow or widower, but I don't know how to be or do that. If I am a child and my parents die, I am named an orphan. Even if I am an adult and my parents die, and I feel lost in the world, can I still call myself an orphan? Or, if my child dies, who am I, what name can I give myself? Does death kill my self-identity as a mother or father (Miller & Ober, 2002)? Do I suddenly cut off my constant thoughts and concerns about my child? If others casually ask, "How many children do you have?" how would I answer, within myself and to others? Would I stop being a parent? Or, could I both grieve deeply and redefine what it means to proudly be my child's parent?

We easily toss around the word *loss*. I lost my dad. Within myself, do I cease being a daughter or son? Or, without the physical presence of my dad, can I reclaim my role as "daughter" or "son" in a new way? Certainly, I can reflect on my relationship with my dad and more fully understand how I relate with my spouse, my children, or other men. In doing so, I can choose those related aspects within myself more consciously. I can reclaim or rewrite those themes and rhythms between my dad and me in my relationships today. When I miss my dad, I can imagine what he might say to me now. I can imagine what I would voice to him now. How might those conversations affect me now? My doing and being? How might it affect my being in and moving through grief?

Many religions and bereavement rituals foster this ongoing conversation to or "with" the loss (Goss & Klass, 2005). Since the 1950s, many clinical therapists have incorporated this into the gestalt technique long known as the "empty chair" (*Encarta*, 2005). Apart from religions and clinical therapies, this conversation with the deceased person is found in various pieces of music. For example, several real-life stories behind these songs have already been described:

- "When I Lost You," by Irving Berlin after his wife, Dorothy, died
- "Tears in Heaven," by Eric Clapton after his son, Conor, died
- "Goodbye, England's Rose," by Elton John, to Princess Diana
- "Ask Heaven," by Heavy D after his brothers were killed
- "Wish U Were Here," by Jamie Foxx to his grandmother, who had raised him and died just before the overwhelming, international acclaim for his portrayal of Ray Charles in the 2004 movie, *Ray*

Our movie industry has popularized this dialogue in familiar songs, such as these:

- "Papa, Can You Hear Me?" from *Yentl*, recorded by Barbra Streisand
- "You'll Never Walk Alone," from *Carousel*, by Rodgers and Hammerstein
- "Wind Beneath My Wings," from *Beaches*, recorded by Bette Midler
- "You'll Be In My Heart," from *Tarzan*, recorded by Phil Collins
- "My Heart Will Go On," from *Titanic*, recorded by Celine Dion
- "For Always," from *Artificial Intelligence: AI*, recorded by Josh Grobian

Other genres conducive to talking to the lost love include tragic opera, the blues, jazz, and country music. Additional examples include Billy Holiday's "Gloomy Sunday," Nina Simone's "I Get Along Without You / Except When" and *Rent*'s "Without You." (See teaching guide 8.3.)

An excellent example of a two-way dialogue and its healing effects is an obscure song, "How Could I Know" from the musical of *The Secret Garden* (Simon, Schulman, Norman, & Landesman, 1991). Archibald (the uncle) has been emotionally paralyzed by his wife's death during childbirth, some 10 years earlier. He frantically tries to escape emotions and shut out any remembrances of her, to no avail. While opening up this "dialogue" to his wife, she "appears" to him and expresses her pain in having left him, and in having caused him such grief and loss. She asks him to find a new way to love her, and to care for the child of their love. Their duet leads the uncle into an affirmation of moving on into life with their son; healed, reconciled, and sustained by new meanings of their love for each other.

Let us move deeper into redefining oneself. An athlete suffers a career-changing injury and faces his most strenuous physical, mental, and emotional challenges ever. Does he stop being an athlete, or can he reclaim and redefine his athletic identity in a new way, strengthening him to get through?

In the Preface, I described injuries to my classical pianist hands and arms. Every part of my being grieved. Would moving on mean no longer being a musician? Those years ago, I believed, "Yes, my core musician self can companion and teach me about loss and healing. I'm willing to enter my darkness of the soul, my practice rooms of grief. It's OK to get stuck, like when learning that new piece of music." That's where I asked, "what can I do, where are my limits, and what artistry can I create?" (Attig, 2001; Berger, 1993; Stroebe & Schut, 2001).

In loss and grief, I can relearn and redefine who I am. Please note, I used the word *can*, not *will*. This process includes choice. I *can* relearn my world (Attig, 1996, 2001). Parkes describes this process as "reorganizing" oneself (1987). Worden describes the tasks "to adjust to an environment in which the deceased is missing," and "to emotionally relocate the deceased and move on with life" (2002). Robert Neimeyer describes ongoing interactions that engage and facilitate persons to reconstruct meanings in their lives after loss (2001).

☐ Music Interventions at Different Seasons of the Soul

Throughout this book we have examined multiple ways that music can help us be in and move through our seasons of grief. Music provides an easily accessible, inexpensive, powerful mode to access and engage one's evolving, reconstructions of meaning. While definitive, linear trajectories of grief cannot be applied to all persons in all losses and mourning, some patterns can be gleaned by revisiting this author's seasons of the soul (chapter 2).

Through an autumn or initial season of change, one's present experience is shifting to the past. Changes are coming that cannot be stopped. Present experiences are shifting to past memories. Music can provide moments of accepting the reality of the loss (Worden, 2002). Whatever its lyrics or melodies, its mere presence usually confronts a truth that the loss has indeed occurred. For musicians, funeral officiants, therapists, or other professionals, any such confrontational experiences of music must be accompanied by personal, relational sustaining and support. One's purpose is not to deny the loss, but to allow the reality to be real, within a container of social, emotional, and spiritual support. If the music confronts without appropriate validation and support, the person may react with a defensive cut-off. This reaction is not limited to music at a funeral. For example, if someone is going through a divorce and hears a love song from earlier years, the truth can hit hard: my relationship is ending.

Time moves us on into a barren season of winter. The cold is colder. The nights are longer and darker. Music can be a catalyst that, like fire, warms or burns. Music can evoke deep emotions with no notice. Physiologically, fight or flight responses can kick in. Panic can suddenly hijack whatever else is happening. The person can feel especially vulnerable and powerless. To empower instead of be overpowered, intentionally set aside a time to hear the music associated with the loss. Offer a similar container or safe, trusting experience for another. One's doing (experiencing) music and one's being (presence) with another can powerfully validate another's mourning. One may need silence. Whether sound or silence or some combination of the two, give another your attention. Hear. Empower. Affirm. Learn.

Winter into spring provides a time to clear out a space and prepare oneself for growth. This is a time for both chaos and creativity (Bridges, 2001, 2003). Music experiences give us time, space, and tools to explore what a loss and its new challenges mean to us, now. It intersects with our everyday world, simply in the CDs we buy and the songs we sing in the car or shower. Try my friend's question, "What music are you listening to these days?" What music are you drawn to and why? Intentionally listen to the music that attracts your attention. Tune into what your subconscious is saying.

Music can provide non-threatening ways for us to interact with our community while redefining, "Who am I now?" Ask yourself, "What do I do that's creative?" Risk something new. Attend musical events with a conscious awareness of the absence of your loss and the presence of your larger world. Be in the presence of expressive musical sounds, with a privacy of not having to disclose anything about yourself. Join a music group that fits your music interests and skills. Try something you have wanted, but were prohibited from doing or inhibited about before the loss occurred. Compose yourself. Create variations or whole new movements out of your life themes, rhythms, harmonies, and styles for doing life and being in your world.

Spring into summer announces a season for new life and ongoing growth. Within this, Memorial Day anniversaries of the loss and firework celebrations present important times to remember the loss in one's new context. Many effects and meanings from losses cannot be known until years later. A transplanted professional has been promoted and is moving again. While packing, she comes across a box of treasured LPs and cassettes from her teen and college years. While playing a few and boxing them yet again (how many moves have they survived?), she tunes in to her early dreams and passions. These decades later, she counts the costs. She has been more successful than she could have dreamed, yet at huge sacrifices that she could not have known then. She experiences a bittersweet peace with her past paths and a wise hope for her future.

The cycles continue into more autumn seasons and cycles of life. While a father sings to his infant son during a late-night crying, he suddenly connects with the divorce he experienced as a young child. He realizes he's singing "Danny Boy," what his dad used to sing to him. As he rocks and sings his son to sleep, he reflects on his rocky relationship with his wife and the challenges they face. They argue all the time, bitterly and divisively. This is not new. While singing to his son, he deeply feels pains his parents must have struggled with at that time in their marriage. Emotions roll through his body, with grace for his parents, and for himself those years ago as their young child. He cradles his son into the crib, and slips back into bed with his wife. Profound awareness and understandings of their choices ahead settle within. Changes have to happen if their marriage is to last. He reclaims his commitments to his wife and son, knowing that unsettled paths lie ahead for all. "Tis I'll be here in sunshine or in shadow, oh Danny boy, oh Danny boy, I love you so."

One's music can teach "there is a time" for countless moments of memories, mourning, meanings, and moving on.

☐ Music's Keys to Our "Secret Gardens"

No one's terrain of loss and grief is exactly like anyone else's. Each person's responses are personal, with fences and defenses to protect oneself; with gates and private entries into one's feelings and thoughts; and with soils and seeds to nurture one's growth. Each has our own stuff that has been decomposing. Again, like Mary's robin in *The Secret Garden* (Burnett, 1911/1998), music can call us into garden places of the soul's soil, compost and all. Here are a few "keys" I hope this book passes on to you:

- Music can evoke moments of memories, emotions, and/or meanings from the past.
- Music can create new moments of emotions and meanings for the present and future.

- Emotions stirred by music can be especially intense. One's timetables and internal defenses must be honored.
- The music, most often, needs to reflect a musical language and style of the person (i.e., classical, popular, gospel, et al.).
- Music should be used within the context of one's role and relationship with the other person.
- Music experiences should not be imposed onto another.
- Music can help unlock one's expressions and creativity. Again, another's inner timetables must be honored.
- Music can teach or instill new understandings, through lyrics or other elements that stir "aha" moments of insight within the person.
- Music moments can occur without formal instruments, music scores, or recordings. Such moments may occur in one's imagination or dialogue. "If there is a time, place, or person you would like to revisit, what music would take you there?" "What about that time connects for you with this loss, now?"
- One's presence matters. If you are providing music for another, you must ask: am I egocentric or emotionally centered? Is this about me or them? Does my attitude convey judgment or affirmation and exploration? Does my presence convey distraction or engaged participation?

Literal music provides tools for expression and exploration. One's best music can be one's life and living. While Nat King Cole's musical genius is certain to have been lauded in his eulogy, consider this statement at his funeral, in February 1965: "Sometimes death is not as tragic as not knowing how to live. This man knew how to live and how to make others glad they were living" (quoted in Benoit, 2003, p. 415). In the midst of loss, how might we learn to live?

☐ Life's Endings and Beginnings: Life's Mourning and Morning

Which comes first, beginnings or endings? Endings or beginnings? Let's explore.

Endings

A job, an illness, a relationship, a house and city, a dream, a belief that no longer works, a child growing up and moving out, a parent growing old and moving in, a death: Some endings are chosen, others are not. Some seem natural and expected, others challenge the depths of one's core self and dare to reshape one's daily doing and being.

Beginnings

Return to the earlier paragraph and reread the endings as beginnings.

Every ending signals a beginning, and each beginning marks an ending (Bridges, 2001, 2003). Rather than being two separate entities, life's endings and beginnings are inextricably intertwined. How I deal with one affects how I encounter the other. Similarly, let's explore two seemingly contradictory words: *mourning* and *morning*.

The words *mourning* and *morning* have the same Latin root, *mer*, which has meanings of "to die" and "to flicker." It refers to "dim lights of illumination," "darkness," "twilight," and "morning." The word *morning* means the entire period from midnight to noon — from darkest night through dawn and into the fullness of day. The word *mourning*'s extended root, *smer*, means "to remember," and is directly related to the Germanic, Old Norse Mimir who was a "giant who guards the well of wisdom" (*Webster's Third International Dictionary*, 1976).

These paradoxes of "mourning" and "morning" illuminate the grief process (Berger, 1993). Mourning ("smer"), is filled with remembering and can become a well of wisdom. Morning, the new day, is an ageless emblem of healed grief: "Weeping may remain for a night, but rejoicing comes in the morning" (Psalm 30: 5, NIV). A Native American morning blessing begins, "To be a human being is an honor, and we offer thanksgiving for all the gifts of life" (Swamp & Printup, 1995). Miles Davis, legendary jazz trumpeter who had battled a heroin addiction, affirmed: "My future starts when I wake up every morning.… Every day I find something creative to do with my life" (Davis, quoted in The Quotations Page, 2005).

How do we get from grief to gratitude? How might we move from darkness to light?

Being In and Moving Through Mourning

Being in, being with, being. Moving, not rushing, not going under, around, or over grief, but moving through grief. Most moving through grief does not plunge ahead and leave the loss behind. Rather, most moving through grief means journeying back and forth between the familiar past, the unknown future, and the displaced, disrupted present.

Most moving through grief means being with the changes. Life themes and counterthemes abound.

Moving may be at largo tempos (very slow) — simply breathing, in and out, in and out, in and out and in again. "Moving" can mean finding one's equilibrium to sit or stand or move again, in a different way from before. You find a balance, but in everyday encounters you get knocked back down, sometimes even harsher than before.

Moving through loss and grief can feel stuck. Paralyzed. You can neither go back, nor step ahead. Trying to survive trauma to one's whole being, the self moves into its own intensive care mode. Still, infinitesimal vibrations in the brain fire off neurons of activity. Unseen heart valves pulse life through the body, whispering, "hold on — breathe — live."

Moving may mean the intermezzo[i] pause and shift between a final cadence and a new movement. At a symphony concert, the silence and waiting between two musical movements is a crucial transition. Revisiting our sonata and symphony forms, the musician marks an ending, letting the reverberations of the music be heard and felt. The conductor brings the baton down; the pianist removes her hands from the keyboard. Everyone shifts and adjusts, before preparing for the next movement's beginning. Time-out, before time in.

Moving may mean being thrust back into doing everyday tasks and routines before you are ready physically, emotionally, mentally, and spiritually. The rest of your world acknowledged your loss and moved on. Perhaps, you courageously forged ahead and you have been doing well, but suddenly the pains crash in. One step forward, three steps back, another off to the side somewhere. And you are still moving. Life's dance has changed and you are forever changed and changing. You knew the dance steps with your partner, or whomever, whatever is lost. You now adapt and learn new skills and moves. You find your current rhythms of body and soul. You embrace those recurring life themes and counterthemes that make you who you are, and rearrange them into the now and new.

Moving through grief does not mean reaching a whole new destination without memories or meanings from the loss. Rather, it means composing and playing life anew with a broader understanding of oneself. It means moving through life with more flexible rhythms, and with greater adaptability to life's changing tempos and meters. Moving through grief means stretching one's vocabulary of life's dissonances, and finding a beauty, or at least a peace, in endings that are not totally resolved. It means living more authentically out of one's own "styles" and expressions.

Moving through grief means becoming. Be coming. Being. Coming. Being with oneself or another in the depths of loss and grief. Coming through the emotions and thoughts and questions with meanings for living life now. Creating, composing, playing, singing, and dancing life anew. The heartbeat pulses on.

An Audio Diary: The Kitchen Table Guitar

Jerry's teenage daughter was killed in a car crash just one week after his wife died from cancer. Terry was their only child. Jerry was devastated beyond description, and considered joining them himself. He told our hospice bereavement counselor he often sat at his kitchen table through the night with his cigarettes, his Pepsi, his gun, and his guitar. Standard suicide risk assessments and interventions were done, especially regarding his gun. I was called in as music therapist because of his guitar.

Though Jerry's wife had tried every available cancer treatment, he had prepared, as much he could, for her death. His daughter's sudden death broke life into a million pieces.

Jerry welcomed my visits, but he did not want to play his guitar. He had played in a country music band for years, but could not play or sing at all right now without breaking down. Still, his guitar brought him comfort. This guitar had been his companion since he was a teen. We talked. No music. Not yet.

Jerry had never written music, but he could not even listen to his music from before: "It just hurts too much." Little by little, Jerry picked up his guitar and created his own lyrics.

- "Does God Cry Tears?"
- "Are You There?"
- "Where Are You?"
- "Can You Hear Me?"

In a poignant song titled "Cardboard Box," Jerry described going through his daughter's room and finding keepsakes to save in a box. He gathered her little girl princess tiara, a 13th birthday photo with her mom, the ribbon from her brand new puppy's neck. Terry was 4 when they got the dog. She and the dog had grown up together. The dog had been killed by a truck just two years earlier. "It hit me: this cardboard box. It was like I was putting her body in that coffin in the ground all over again."

Jerry's music was private to him. He was open to telling me about his music and recalling his lyrics, but hesitant to play it for me live. That was fine. We continued to talk at his kitchen table, meeting every few weeks over the next year. He began to keep a list of the titles on a couple of pieces of notebook paper. His list became a safe entry for me into his anger, sadness, and fear. He began to keep a cassette recorder at the table, and recorded his songs as he created them. He affectionately called these tapes his "audio diary." He began to play tapes for me, and we would talk about his songs and stories behind them. I followed his stream of conscious creativity versus putting out predictable patterns of how he "should" and could mourn. Jerry was on his path.

During my visits, Jerry's guitar sat silently nearby, and that continued to be fine. This was about his timetable and comfort level. He was working out his grief in solitude with his guitar and in supportive trust with a few persons. Our bereavement counselor continued regular visits, for grief education and support. My music therapy role was not to teach him how to compose or help him arrange music, or to help him get it published. My role was to bear witness to his grief through his music: to sustain, confront, heal, reconcile, guide, and inform Jerry, the person, as fit each moment. My role with music was to preserve and encourage his strengths, not take over any of his musical processes with my own compositional knowledge or skills. Jerry had tools for healing within himself (see teaching guide 8.4). More songs unfolded:

- "My Empty Kitchen's Filled with Pain"
- "A Walk Back Down Our Road"
- "Remember When"
- "If We Could Go Back."

Jerry's audio diary voiced sorrow, questions, and fear. Survival and bits of humor began to surface:

- "God's Gotta Alot'a Talkin' Ahead"
- "Our '65 Chevy at the Levee"
- "Count Me Down But Don't Count Me Out."

Occasionally, Jerry began to sing his songs from years earlier. Still, holidays and anniversaries were terrible. Every few weeks seemed to be another anniversary, focused more on this time last year than this time in the present. At Christmas he bought a small tree from the drugstore. He ceremoniously placed Terry's princess tiara on top, as his star. This time last year he was preparing for his wife's death, but not for his daughter's, too. He wrote a spin-off from a traditional song, "I'll Be Home for Christmas, but Baby, Where Am I Without You?"

Jerry's former band buddies came over, unannounced, on the one-year anniversary of Terry's death. No music. "It was kind of awkward, and a lot of talk about nothing. Nobody mentioned Terry's name, but they were here. And we all knew why."

More songs emerged. Within a year, Jerry had written over three hundred songs, from scratch, as they say. Or, from pickin' and scratchin' as

Jerry would say: "pickin' up the pieces from the day and scratchin' out some way to get through the night."

Back and Forth

Back to our rhythms of body and soul, our themes and counterthemes of life stories, the harmonies and dissonances of healing. Loss can throw one into utter chaos. One's inner sense of flow, connection, and direction can feel more like an atonal cluster than a grounded tonal structure. Life's "music" suddenly transposes us into a foreign key we've never played. Or, the "score" I have followed is damaged beyond belief.

On we go into the loss. This isn't happening! This is. I can't go on. I can't go back. I can't go. I can't stay like this. Where's home? I can't find it. All has changed. Oh, God! Where is God? Is there God? We look for familiar ways to comfort ourselves, yet the loss itself took away that partner, best friend, belief, or ways of doing and being in one's everyday world that brought identity, security, and meaning.

Back to ancient wisdom: there is a time to despair. "For everything there is a season, and a time for every matter under heaven; a time to be born, and a time to die, a time to laugh and a time to weep." There is a time to hope.

Forward into contemporary theories and therapies: we can learn grief's patterns, personalized factors, and sensitive interventions that help us be in life's loss. In time, through time, and when "it's time" — we can move through life's losses into healing.

Back and forth, back and forth, can we feel it less as a yo-yo's yanking around, and more as a normal, calming rocking chair kind of rhythm? Back and forth. Back and forth.

I hear gentle movements back and forth between mourning and morning in Billy Joel's "Lullaby" (Goodnight, My Angel) to his young daughter, as divorce was moving into their lives. I hear and see them in Garth Brooks's "The Dance" video (Arato, Miller, & Ball, M., 1991). Through sound and sight, poignant familiar images pair with lyrics that lift up the joys of risking love over fearing loss. The endings of Dr. Martin Luther King, John F. Kennedy, the Space Shuttle Challenger crew, and others teach us not to fear death, but to love life.

Stroebe and Schut describe a dual process for coping with bereavement through our experiences of everyday life. Their research demonstrates that healing loss occurs best with oscillations back and forth between loss-oriented grief work and restoration-oriented tending to life's changes (2001; see teaching guide 8.5). Back and forth.

I experience that rocking back and forth when I rehear, sing, or play music that was meaningful to me at an earlier time, especially if the music is directly connected to my loss. (Do you remember Amy's "I'm So Glad You Were Born"?) I experience the music with fresh (perhaps raw) emotions and meanings in this new present. I may feel sad and glad, afraid and hopeful, all at the same time, with gentle oscillations back and forth between them all. Today's contexts bring new expressions, new understandings, and create new memories for moving into the future. Back and forth. Back and forth. Back deeper and forward further. How high can I swing?

☐ Music of Morning

Sing a song full of the faith that the dark past has taught us
Sing a song full of the hope that the present has brought us
Facing the rising sun of the new day begun
Let us march on til victory is won. (Johnson & Johnson, 1900/2002)

This turn-of-the-century song signaled a new day. "Lift Every Voice and Sing" was written in 1900 by brothers James Weldon Johnson and J. Rosamond Johnson for a celebration of the anniversary of Abraham Lincoln's birthday, and was first performed by children in Jacksonville, Florida. In the 1920s it was pasted into hymnals throughout the nation. It was known through that period of American history as the "Negro National Anthem."

On August 28, 1963, at the Lincoln Memorial, Dr. Martin Luther King's "I Have A Dream" speech was prefaced by music: "We Shall Overcome," "Oh Freedom," "I Been Buked and I Been Scorned," "How I Got Over," "He's Got the Whole World In His Hand." Singers leading the crowd stretched out across the Washington Mall included Mahalia Jackson, Marion Anderson, The Freedom Singers, Joan Baez, Bob Dylan, and Peter, Paul and Mary (Music of the Civil Rights Movement, 2005). Over 250,000 people demonstrated a peaceful protest by lifting every voice and singing. Echoes were heard round the world. Another new day had begun.

What other music signals beginnings? (See teaching guide 8.6.) Here are but a few, from different styles and contexts:

- "Happy Birthday to You"
- "Auld Lang Syne"
- "Reveille"

- The children's song, "Are You Sleeping, Brother John?"
- J. S. Bach's "Sleepers Wake," Chorale
- African-American spiritual, "In that Great Getting' Up Morning"
- Edvard Grieg's "Morning," from *Peer Gynt Suite*
- Sergei Rachmaninof's *Spring Cantata*
- Igor Stravinsky's *Le Sacre du printemps (Rite of Spring)*
- Benjamin Britten's *Spring Symphony*
- Aaron Copeland's *Appalachian Spring*
- Cat Steven's "Morning Has Broken"
- Louis Armstrong's "What A Wonderful World"
- Godspell's "Day by Day"
- *Les Misérables'* "One Day More"
- Smashing Pumpkins' "Today"
- Billy Joel's "River of Dreams"
- Gloria Estafan's "Reach"
- Tracy Chapman's "New Beginning"
- Des'Ree's "You Gotta Be"
- Mary Chapin Carpenter's "Grow Old Along With Me"
- Eminem's "Lose Yourself"
- Bruce Springsteen's refrain to "My City of Ruins"
- India Arie's "Ready for Love"
- Celine Dion's *Miracle* CD and DVD, celebrating birth
- Loreena McKennitt's *To Drive the Cold Winter Away*
- Michael Stillwater and Gary Malkin's *Graceful Passages*
- Faith Hill's "There Will Come A Day"
- Neil Diamond's "What's It Gonna Be" and "Create Me"
- *Seasons* music by Antonio Vivaldi, Joseph Haydn, The Byrds ("Turn, Turn, Turn"), various Windham Hill artists, and "Seasons of Love" from the musical *Rent*.

As I write, the sky outside my window is shifting from night to morning. It is a spring morning. A symphony of bird songs calls me away from my thoughts. My own new day. Today. This day. Never before. Never again. Here's to today.

Life Out of Loss

Orpheus sang and brought life to stones. La Lobda sang over bones and new flesh appeared. The African-American spiritual, "Dry Bones," joyfully sings of Ezekial's vision in the desert, connecting dry bone to bone for new life. Clinically, Parkes compares healing bones to healing grief: "broken bones may end up stronger than unbroken ones, so the experience of grieving can strengthen and bring maturity to those who have previously been protected from misfortune" (2001, p. 6).

Similar to the musical activity within those myths, a growing body of research and clinical literature validates music's tools to facilitate some type of good, i.e., comfort, healing, and fostering quality of life in the midst of loss (Aldridge, 1999; Berger, 1993; Bertman, 1999; Bonny, 2002; Bright, 2002, 1986; Hilliard, 2001; Lipe, 2001; Loewy & Hara, 2002; Marshman, 2003; Rykov & Salmon, 1998; Salmon, 2001; Smeijsters & Hurk, 1998; Starr, 1999; Wheeler, 2005).

These music therapy interventions do not represent sterile, laboratory research, but rather re-searching out what occurs in those interactive, person-to-person life-giving experiences. Of note, the National Academy of Recording Arts and Sciences (the Grammy's home base) underwrote support for the American Music Therapy Association to provide music therapy services to children, adults, caregivers, and families affected by the losses of September 11, 2001. Over 7,000 music therapy interventions were provided by 33 professional music therapists in the New York City metropolitan area. Additionally, a nine-week music therapy-based program, "Caring for the Caregiver," was created for relief workers, police officers, medical professionals, social workers, psychologists, and survivors. Sessions included music-facilitated experiences paired with trauma and grief training. Through music these traumatized caregivers explored personal and professional coping with anger, depression, stress, grief, and other effects of trauma (Loewy & Hara, 2002). These interventions were built on past research, and were recorded for ongoing learning (Lowey & Hara, 2002). They provide a wealth of new insight and information for future "singing over the bones."

Focused more directly on grief and loss (without music), researchers Frantz, Farrell, and Trolley have identified five major ways that good can come out of loss:

Many bereaved persons report they "learned to appreciate the value of life more than they ever did before."
Many describe having become stronger because of surviving death's pains and "stepping forward to handle things that previously were done by the deceased person." Many describe themselves as being "more independent, mature, self-reliant, and self-confident now and often express surprise at their newfound and unexpected strength."
Many "found themselves much closer to their loved ones and family than before the death."
A small but noticeable minority exists for "whom the death had left significantly worse off than before."
Ninety-six percent of the bereaved persons "said that they had done things to help themselves that worked and made at least some positive

difference in coping with their loss." Two general types of efforts emerged: "On the one hand, they faced their grief, felt it, expressed it, cried about it, and strove to keep their loved one's memory alive; On the other hand, they avoided it, throwing themselves into work, school, child care, travel, exercise." Additionally, the "ones who best cope with death may be those who both embrace and avoid grief, at times feeling the pain and at other times finding ways not to" (Frantz, Farrell, & Trolley, 2001, pp. 204–5).

Mourning and morning, endings and beginnings. Morning and mourning, beginnings and endings. I hear a rhythmic pulse, a search for resolutions. I hear dissonances and blue notes and modulations toward a new home key. Variations and developments on lifelong themes. Personal style and essence coming through. Expressions from self and with others. We commonly call persons going through grief, "mourners." I wonder, might we also think of them, and ourselves, as "morners"?

Recapitulation and Moving Toward the Coda

This book's composition is moving toward a final cadence. Let us recap its core themes for using music to compose life out of loss by reviewing this author's summary chart. Again, the following chart can be read both horizontally and vertically. Now, some seven chapters and numerous musical examples since it was first presented, how have its patterns played out in your "music of the soul" reflections and experiences? How might you use them to compose your future, both personally and professionally? What portions stand out as something you want to explore further? Write them down. Use the teaching guides at the end of the book to further your "composition" (see teaching guide 8.7). Whatever your styles are of doing life, adapt these principles to your life losses and your life music. Sing it. Play it. Dance it. Live it.

Being a Musician of the Soul

We have explored extensively one's "music of the soul." I offer to you the concept of being a musician of the soul, not through a magical, fantasy-powered whim, but rather through a grounded, relational presence. The musician of the soul sensitively hears the person's whole self — life themes, disrupted rhythms, dissonances, styles of coping, and expressions from community that do or don't jive. The musician of the soul offers music to sustain and confront, to heal and reconcile, to guide and inform. The

TABLE 8.1 Music of the Soul: Composing Life Out of Loss

Seasons of the Soul (Berger, 1993) Processes of Grief (Parkes,1987/2001) Tasks of Mourning (Worden,1991/2002)	Music for being in and moving through grief's seasons of the soul	Care of the soul An active presence
Fall Rich colors emerge as the potential loss is signaled. The loss begins. Change is here, and cannot be stopped. Individual timetables of letting go. Visible reminders are strewn around. Times for harvest & thanks. Birds fly south. Winter sets in.	**Process:** shock, numbness, denial **Task:** to accept the reality of the loss	**Music for Memories/ Memorializing** At initial loss (i.e., funeral or other ritual), meaningful musical expressions; reality oriented; comfort, hope, strength; affirmation both of faith and that a significant loss has occurred; favorites appropriate when designated as such, not for mere sentimentality; musical styles need to reflect the person.	Primarily **SUSTAINING** the shock and **CONFRONTING** the loss
Winter Cold, dark, empty. The nights are longer and days are shorter. Venturing out can be dangerous, unlike before. Hibernation. Need for hearth-heart places of trust and emotional safety. "How long, oh how long?"	**Process:** longing, yearning, pining, searching for the loss **Task:** to work through the pains of the loss	**Music for Mourning** Memories frequently emerge at sensory, physiological, emotional levels. Invite the person's favorite music & associated memories. Provide a container for intense pain and catharsis. Empowerment, safety, security, and trust are crucial. Respect the person's timetable.	Primarily **GUIDING** to validate and express inner pains Initial **HEALING** (cleansing and bandage of the emotional wounds)

(Continued)

TABLE 8.1 Music of the Soul: Composing Life Out of Loss (Continued)

Winter into spring	Process:	Music for Meanings	Primarily GUIDING & INFORMING
Daily process. Clearing away the dead. Tilling the frozen soil of the soul. Planting with a sense of risk, trust, and nurture. Surprise storms. Gentle growth. New birth.	disorganization and despair **Task:** to adjust to an environment in which the loss is missing	More of the same; move toward re-collecting memories and discovering their interwoven meanings. Introduce more music which is new to the person. "Reframe" or reinterpret the past. Meanings guide toward re-formation of self.	More **CONFRONTING** than before
Spring into summer	**Process:**	**Music for Remembering & Moving into Life**	**HEALING & RECONCILING** of the former
Fruition of new life. New growth is rooted and sturdy. A time for vacations from the work of mourning; new memory making.	reorganization **Task**: to emotionally relocate the loss & move on with life	Music at memorials marking losses, or celebrations marking beginnings. Affirm having come through, and what has been learned. Use same music from an earlier catharsis. Use new music that expresses life "now" and ahead.	**GUIDING & INFORMING** toward the new

Meaning reconstruction (Neimeyer, 2001): Ongoing exploration of meanings for the present and future

CORE Principles through all Seasons of the Soul: Care, Ownership, Respect, Empowerment (Berger, 1999)

HEALing Techniques through all Seasons of the Soul: Hear, Explore, Affirm, Learn (Berger, 1999)

Sources: Berger, J. S. (1993). *Music as a catalyst for pastoral care within the remembering tasks of grief.* Ann Arbor, Michigan: ProQuest/University Microfilms, Inc., [Pub. #9406295]. Berger, J. S. (1999). *Life music: Rhythms of loss and hope* [VHS]. Cleveland, OH: American Orff-Schulwerk Association. Neimeyer, R. A. (Ed.). (2001). *Meaning reconstruction & the experience of loss.* Washington, DC: American Psychological Association. Parkes, C. M. (1987/2001). *Bereavement: Studies of grief in adult life* (2nd and 3rd American ed. Madison, CT: International Universities Press. Worden, J. W. (1991/2002). *Grief counseling and grief therapy* (2nd and 3rd ed.). New York: Springer.

shared moment of a song's text or meaning can give a simple "yes," "uh-hmm," an "I understand," and "I'll walk or stand or sit or simply be with you in your grief."

A musician of the soul empathically hears one's deep vibrations within, however delicate or volcanic they may be. She can provide presence in aching stillness. He can create a safe hearth-heart place for warmth through winter's mourning. She can hear the call of hope and signal life anew. He can create a safe, nurturing space to transform grief's despair into a phoenix song that dares to rise up and out from fiery ash. A musician of the soul can provide this care, but does not impose it on another. She knows that her own style is not for everyone.

The musician of the soul feels the rhythmic dance between life's endings and beginnings in one's bones, even when the body is weary and the spirit is broken. A musician of the soul understands silence. A musician of the soul listens not to discriminate between "good" or "bad" music, but to discern life stories and understand one's styles for being and doing life.

A musician of the soul does not per-form life for others' applause. Rather, she creatively forms and trans-forms life's endings into beginnings. He does not conduct others' life music for power and prestige. Rather, he serves as a conductor for sparking life energy and group synergy. Meaningless despair can move into meaningful action. Musicians of the soul choose not to overpower another through musical stimulus, but to empower. They choose to give sensitive care. Courageous care. Artistic care. Soul care. Whole care.

☐ Music of the Soul for Composing Life Out of Loss

Hear the word *compose* without its musical context, as in *compose yourself.* It usually means to calm and ground oneself; to gather oneself together. Think of this "compose yourself" not as a Queen Victoria's 19th-century dark-clad, stoic "compose oneself," but rather as a 21st-century, creative, globally connected, "compose yourself" in this day and time, whoever you are, and wherever you are in your life composition. You are the instrument, your being and doing is the music. I invite you to join me in composing and playing your next movement.

A rhythm rocks back and forth. Life and loss, loss and life. Dare to risk. Learn to lose. Learn to live again. Move with soulful rhythm. A theme recurs. Music of the soul is about better knowing, understanding, and being with each other through life's ongoing themes and variations. It is about literal uses of music, and about the metaphoric music of how we live. A countertheme cautions. With our individual musical gifts and relational roles come responsibilities to choose and use our music wisely. This means not assuming, imposing, or manipulating another through music. It means being aware of one's talents, skills, and limits.

A harmony resolves and a dissonance moves us on. A jazz blue note captures that just-right-in-the-crack sound or life-experience you did not expect. A style captures that essence of who you are, who you've been, and perhaps new shifts in your process. An expression voices who and what matters to you and what you mean to others.

A cadence brings the coda into a *fine* ending. My best cadence is to spark your creativity.

There is a time — here is the time — for my finale.

Pick up your composer's pen
Open your instrument case
Put on your dancing shoes
Hear the harmonies in your head
Feel the rhythms in your bones
Sing the song in your soul

There is a time — here is the time — for your music.

Through the Ages: A Timeline of Western Grief Music

9000 BCE, China. Date attributed to the oldest playable flute, made from the hollow bone of a red crane bird, with holes carved out for fingering. Six flutes and 30 more fragments were recovered from the Jiahu Neolithic archaeological site. Though this is not considered "western," this Jiahu site reveals that these persons had established village life, with parts of the settlement being used for different community functions. Additionally, this musical craftsmanship notes a sophistication and importance of the arts in everyday life.

4500 BCE, Babylon. Oldest known bell found near Babylon.

3100 BCE and following, the Egyptian "Dynastic" or "Pharaonic" period. Hieroglyphics and other artwork document the use of music for the temple, entertainment, the battlefield, and for the tomb. They indicate singing, playing flutes, rattles, drums, harps, flutes, reed instruments, hand clapping, and a variety of percussion instruments. Music was an integral part of religious worship.

1500 BCE, Northeast Ireland. Bronze horns have been found in various sites, with designs and tuning being indicative of their geographical locations.

800–146 BCE, Greek musical culture. There was extensive use of music, singing, instruments, vocal modes, including Pythagorus' beliefs about music's powers. Specific to mourning and grief was the elegy, a poem or musical work lamenting the loss of someone. Later vocal examples were composed by Josquin, Beethoven, Schumann, and Mahler; instrumental examples by Fauré, Dussek, Liszt, and Stravinsky. An "Elegy for Martin

Luther King, Jr.," was written by David Ward-Steinman and performed at a community commemoration just days after King's death, April 1968.

800–146 BCE, Greek origin, *epicedium* or *threnody.* A funeral-like hymn or dirge. Later used in Blow's "The Queen's Epicedium," 1655 (death of Queen Mary II); Penderecki's "Threnody for the Victims of Hiroshima," 1960.

625 BCE–476 AD, Ancient Roman empire, classical examples, *Nenia* (Latin). A funeral dirge in honor of the dead, sung to the accompaniment of flutes, at first by the relatives, in later times by hired mourners. Additionally, funeral processions were elaborate, and led by musicians. Centuries later, Schiller's "Nänie" poem was set to music by Gotz (1874), Brahms (Opus 82, 1880–1881), and Orff (1956).

Biblical Hebrew music/Early Christian music. Descriptions of early Hebrew music reflect findings of similar geographical areas during those times; that is, instruments used for temple worship, celebration, and mourning. Early Christian music began with Jewish chants, and gradually incorporated Greek and Roman musical and cultural influences.

Through the centuries, numerous folk examples, *lament.* It was generally a broad term for a song or instrumental piece of mournful character, including all other forms in this list. More specifically, domestic music of mourning — such as the Irish and Scottish Caoine, Coronach, and Ho-hoane (bagpipe forms)—, developed from lament melodies. Bagpipes continue to be a powerful instrument at funerals.

814 AD, *Planctus* (Latin), *planh* (Provencal). A medieval song of mourning, such as "Planctus Karoli," written shortly after Charlemagne's death (d. 814). Later medieval plancti were of the three Marys at Christ's tomb.

Dark and Middle Ages, Medieval religious rites, *Dirge* (Latin). A mournful song, hymn, or musical composition with a slow and repetitive quality, used to accompany or portray burial rites; for example, Antiphons in the Office of the Dead; Vaughn Williams's setting of Whitman's "Dirge for Two Veterans" in his "Dona Nobis Pacem" (1936).

1000 AD–Present, *requiem.* The term *requiem* means "rest eternal"; requiems began in earliest Catholic liturgies for the dead, in plainchant style. The requiem's performance styles and practices have developed with the times on into 20th-century atonality. Representative composers include Palestrina (1554), Schutz (1636), Mozart (1791), Berlioz (1837), Brahms (1868), Fauré (1887), Durufle (1947), Britten (War Requiem, 1962), Stravinsky (1966), and Rutter (1986).

1250 AD, *Dies Irae* **settings.** Meaning "Day of Wrath," and a standard component of the Latin Requiem Mass. Attributed to Thomas of Celano (d. c. 1250), with a distinct melodic pattern. Used as thematic material in various other orchestral or choral works, such as Berlioz's *Symphonie Fantastique* (1830), Liszt's *Symphonie zu Dante's divina Commedia* (1867), Rachmaninoff's "Rhapsody on a Theme by Paganini" (1936), and Penderecki's

Dies Irae (1967) which commemorates the Holocaust victims. Penderecki's *Dies Irae* was first performed at Cracow and Auschwitz, sites of Nazi concentration camps.

1377 *Deploration* (French). A musical setting of a poem that laments someone's death; for example, Deschamps's poem "Armes, Amours" on the death of Machaut (d. 1377), set by F. Andrieu.

1525 *Dump* (England). Lute, keyboard, and viol laments from the 16th- to early 17th- centuries; for example, "My Lady Carey's Dompe" (ca. 1525).

1608 *Lamento* (Italian). A song of great sadness in Baroque Italian operas and cantatas; for example, Monteverdi's "Lamento d'Arianna" in *L'Arianna*, 1608.

17th–18th Centuries, *Apotheose* (French). A work glorifying a deceased composer; for example, Couperin's "L'Apotheose de Corellie" (1724).

17th–18th Centuries, *Plainte* (French). Certain 17th- to 18th-century French works which use unusual techniques to portray sadness (e.g., downward glissando on the violin).

1600–Present, *Tragic Opera*. Opera's massive combination of vocalists, orchestra, elaborate sets and costumes, staging, and complex plots engage the audience into stories of dramatic proportions. Suicide after the loss of a love is a frequent plot in opera. Classic examples of tragic opera include Mozart's *Don Giovanni* (1787), Verdi's *La Traviata* (1853), and Wagner's *Tristan und Isolde* (1865) with its "Motif of Death."

17th–19th Centuries, *African and Caribbean funeral rites*. Typically, three days of dancing, singing, and playing instruments helped transition the spirit to its new world. American slavery brought increasingly rigid restrictions. The days were shifted to shorter periods of time, and then to night. Dancing and playing of instruments was banned, in some places, by law. The unaccompanied spiritual grew out of these.

17th–20th Centuries, *Tombeau* (French). Meaning tomb or tombstone, a miniature memorial piece; for example, Gaultier's "Tombeau de Mademoiselle Gaultier" for lute (1655); Ravel's "Le Tombeau de Couperin" for piano (1914–17).

18th–19th Centuries, *Spirituals*. African vocal music within a Eurocentric, American context: Songs by and for slaves, expressing grief, sorrow, faith, and hope. Enormous impact on American music. "Sometimes I Feel Like a Motherless Child," "Nobody Knows the Trouble I See," "In My Trials, Lord Walk With Me."

19th Century–Present, *Gospel Songs* (American). Protestant songs of faith. Developed from the sol-feg shaped note tradition, into revival songs, and blended with popular music styles into praise choruses. "It Is Well," by Horatio Spafford (1874), "Precious Lord, Take My Hand," Thomas Dorsey (1932), "Because He Lives," William Gaither (1971).

19th–20th centuries, *Blues* (African American). Vocal and instrumental music created out of the slave spirituals, less spirituality, more about the hardships of everyday life and love. Regional styles, such as New Orleans, Chicago, Country Blues. Artists include Charley Patterson, Blind Boy Fuller, Leadbelly, Mississippi John Hurt, Ma Rainey, Howlin' Wolf, Muddy Waters, T-Bone Walker, and B. B. King. Basis for many other jazz genres: boogie-woogie, jug band, rhythm and blues, rock, soul, hip-hop, and rap.

Renaissance–Present. Almost any other genre of Western music includes pieces written out of, or expressing some type of grief/loss. They may be instrumental or vocal, choral, or symphonic, folk or classical, rap or religious. Countless examples can be found in country ballads, soul, hymns, liturgical forms, gospel, folk music, top-40 music, music theater, cinematic music, patriotic, holiday music, and world music. Such examples may have been written, performed, or experienced within contexts of loss and grief. Examples are given throughout this book, particularly drawing from popular styles that likely will be easily recognized by and accessible to this book's readers.

APPENDIX

My Music Menu

Name _____ Date _____

How I enjoy music

☐ Home ☐ Community ☐ Radio ☐ Singing

☐ Car ☐ Faith Community ☐ CDs/Cassettes/LPs ☐ Playing _____

☐ With Friends ☐ Concerts ☐ MP3/IPod/Other ☐ Dancing

☐ Outdoors ☐ Recitals ☐ TV & Movies ☐ Writing My Own

All-time music favorites

_____
_____
_____
_____

Feel good/energizing music

_____
_____
_____
_____

"Crying" music

_____
_____
_____

Music of memories

_____
_____
_____

Music of comfort and hope

_____
_____
_____

If there is a time, place, or person you'd like to revisit, what music would "take" you there?

_____
_____
_____

If there is a time, place, or person you envision visiting in your future, what music would "take" you there?

_____
_____
_____

APPENDIX

C

Keyboard Quality of Life: "Highs" and "Lows"

Name _____ Date _____

Lows   Middles   Highs

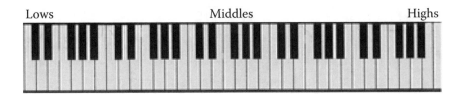

If possible, use a portable keyboard that the person can actually play. The real keyboard fosters visual, tactile, aural, and social stimulation.

Ask questions relevant to the person's context, using words *high* and *low* to focus on and measure a relevant quality of life issue: Pain? Mobility? Emotions? Activities? Relationships? Demonstrate as needed.

Have fun. Develop rapport, validation, and trust through your interactions. Engage the caregiver or others present. Focus on giving voice to the patient, as she or he is able.

Ask: If you want something to change, like a low emotion to move up, what key would you want it to get to? In our time together (or your time next week), what might help that happen?

Transfer the responses to a printed copy like this. Such record keeping can provide an informal "diary" of sorts for the person/caregiver, and a more formal record-keeping baseline and outcome measurements for the clinical professional.

Note: The range of keys on this display uses the same keys as on my portable keyboard. Adjust any paper copies to the range on the keyboard you use.

D

My Do-Be-Do-Be's

Today's Date _____

TABLE APPENDIX D.1 My DO-BE-DO-BE-DO-BE's		
My To DO List	**My To BE List**	**Today's top DO-BE-DO-BE's**
		1.
		2.
		3.

Directions (See chapter 5, "To Do or To Be: Is That the Question?")

Identify "To DO's" for your day in the left column.

Identify "To BE's" for your day in the middle column.

Play with possible combinations between the left and middle columns.

Prioritize your top three DO-BE's for the day and write them in the third column.

Then, DO the tasks while BE-ing the person you want to be.

Check In at the Day's End

How was your day?
Did you DO your main tasks? What's left?
Were you BE-ing who you wanted to be? What else crept in?
Did you find yourself choosing smaller "DO-BE's" through the day?
For tomorrow ... start envisioning (visioning within).

CORE Principles (Being) and HEALing Techniques (Doing)

☐ CORE Principles: Care, Ownership, Respect, Empowerment

Care

- Care for the person from a sense of common humanity.
- Exercise balanced initiative within your role and relationship with the person(s): as therapist, music therapist, hospice team member, colleague, music educator, performer, minister, family member, friend, volunteer, etc.
- Seek whole truths, not mere sentimentality. Use music to integrate heart and head and soul, not to manipulate emotions.
- Follow up the musical intervention or experience with continued care.

Ownership

- Know, tend, and learn from your own losses and beginnings.
- Get to know the person's history of loss and grief, and styles of coping.

- When engaged with another, let your own self-awareness and empathy for the other play in duet. When do you accompany? When do you take the lead? Find the relational beat. Tune in.
- Select music that is congruent with or complementary to the person's musical background.
- Use music to validate the person's current "season of the soul."

Respect

- Respect your self, even when your rhythms are out of sync and dissonances are unresolved.
- Respect another's unique self, welcoming and learning from another's styles of doing life.
- Respect another's musical tastes and uses of music, even when different from your own.
- Ask questions about others' life events, stories, and meanings related to the music. Learn more of the other's core self through their music.
- Respect another's timetables and defenses that are foreign to you.
- Respect that another's "there is a time" may have its own wisdom.

Empowerment

- Offer the person a choice to participate or not in the musical experience.
- Establish parameters for the person to leave or stop the music as needed, respecting pangs of flight or fight that can be stirred.
- Guide and inform persons to identify their own seasons, processes, and tasks.
- Ask questions. Take your leads from the person. Serve the person with a sustaining sense of discovery and guidance, versus an attempt to fix as an all-knowing superior.
- Empower persons to create their own musical rituals for their ongoing endings and beginnings.

☐ HEALing Techniques: Hear, Explore, Affirm, Learn

Hear

- Use background music to stimulate verbal interaction, when it is appropriate to the setting.
- Rehear a specific piece of music that evoked an earlier catharsis.
- Tune into emotions stirred within you during a musical experience.
- Hear deeper meanings. Reflect your thoughts back to affirm or revise your understandings.

Explore

- Provide an opportunity for the grieving person(s) to express feelings and thoughts through making music, listening, or dialoguing about a musical experience.
- Spark deeper levels of meanings by exploring one's associations to a particular piece of music.
- Use musical metaphors: rhythms, themes and counterthemes, harmonies and dissonance, musical styles, cadences, etc.
- Sort through your stored-away music scores and recordings. (Check out that piano bench or instrument case.) What persons, places, emotions, and meanings emerge? What music do you want to keep out for the present and near future?
- Pair music with photographs, VCR/DVD camcorder moments, personal artwork, or other visual images to gather one's life-stories and explore their meanings.
- Create a "musical scrapbook," or audio diary. Compile your significant life-story music into a CD, or video/DVD paired with photos. Tell the stories through the CD liner, photos, or captions. Sequence (organize) the materials in a format that supports the meanings you want to convey.
- Reframe an earlier memory by writing new words or creating musical variations to familiar music.

Affirm

- Educate others about grief by choosing a particular genre of music, and then selecting music that illustrates each season/process/task.
- Affirm another by selecting music that reflects the person's experience.
- Write and use a community litany that is appropriate to the group and setting (i.e., a faith community, a memorial service, a retirement party, a gathering for a celebration or blessing). Alternate a musical theme or stanzas with community readings or reminiscences. This can invite emotional, thoughtful, intimate, humorous, depth responses. It allows both personal and community expression. It creates a memory for everyone through changes ahead.

Learn

- Use musical experiences to get to know yourself, and others. What new knowledge, understanding, and wisdom emerge for you? For yourself with others?
- Know your grief–loss history, and expand your understanding through reputable resources.
- Know, nurture, and expand your own musical history, styles, skills, and uses of music in everyday life.
- Continually hear, compose, conduct, and dance to your own core, your essence, your music of the soul. This is your life. Who do you want to be and how do you want to live?

TEACHING GUIDES

Welcome to your practice room. Conservatory or university music students typically practice in small rooms, large enough to hold a piano and a music stand for a singer or instrumentalist. The musician learns the music here through rigorous practice before taking it to the recital or concert hall. Any of the following questions or exercises should be used with you, first, in developing your self-awareness and understanding, before ever using them with anyone else. These teaching exercises are intended by this author to be used appropriately within one's professional role (i.e., not assuming the role of a music therapist), and one's relationship with the person (family member, friend, colleague, client–patient, musical audience).

CORE Principles and **HEAL**ing Techniques apply to each exercise. Any use of music with someone dealing with loss must be grounded in:

- **Care** for the person
- **Ownership** of another's musical tastes, emotions, meanings
- **Respect** for another's worth, inner timetables
- **Empowerment** of another to be in and move through his or her loss.

Any musical experiences you might offer to another in the midst of loss should not be imposed, but rather focused on the following:

- **Hear** the person's experiences and meanings.

- **Explore** the person's experience with empathy. Grasp what the person's experience is like from his or her context, emotions, thoughts, culture and beliefs.
- **Affirm** and validate the person's experience. Check with the other to see if your understanding is accurate or not.
- **Learn,** continually, from your life's losses and healing, and from those of others.

You will enliven these teaching exercises by incorporating music that has meaning for you, or other group members. Look through your own recordings or musical scores. Memories and life stories abound. Additionally, you can easily find music resources on multiple Internet sites. For example:

- For music recordings, search http://www.amazon.com (or other clearing houses), using a title, performer, composer, song, or other key words.
- For downloadable sheet music, go to http://www.musicnotes.com. Often, you can order the music in a transposed key.
- For lyrics, go to http://www.google.com and search a key phrase.
- Many genre specific search engines exist. Mark any favorites for your ongoing use.

☐ Teaching Guides for Chapter 1. Music of the Soul: Creating Life Out of Loss

> **CORE** Principles
> Care - Ownership - Respect - Empowerment
> **HEAL**ing Techniques
> Hear - Explore - Affirm - Learn

1.1 Catalyst Question: Revisit Your Life

If there is a person, place, or time in your life you would like to revisit, what music would "take you there"?

The questions below move in a progressive flow. They can be used informally in a conversation, or more structured in a group exercise. The leader's voice and body language easily sets a tone for "where to go." Depending on the group, this can serve as a fun, getting-to-know-you, trust-building interaction. For groups that have already formed, this can quickly go to deeper, supportive reflection and expression about a loss. For both, partner group members for 1:1 sharing. Encourage members to sing or hum phrases together. Allow time for processing. Typically, stories unfold and roll. Bring everyone together in a large group and invite responses.

- Identify the person, place, or time.
- Identify the music that would "take you there."
- Sing, hum, or recall phrases of it, within yourself or with another. You don't need to have an actual musical score or recording. Simply recalling it in your imagination can "take you there."
- What memories are stirred? Emotions? Meanings?
- How does this music, and the person, place, or time you identified connect with you today, in this moment? (This question requires higher self-reflection skills.)

1.2 Time Line Your Losses

Create a time line of your loss/grief history. Draw a line across a piece of paper, with arrows at both ends. Write in the words below at each end: (1) Family Losses Before My Birth, and (2) Probable Losses Ahead.

Family Losses Before My Birth	Important Losses for Me A Death, Move, Job, Relationship, Health, Goal/Dream, etc.	Probable Losses Ahead

Next, think of this time line as your life, thus far. Identify significant losses and write them in. You may want to "measure" out periods of your life, such as decades, or childhood, teen, young adult, etc. Be sure to identify "Family Losses Before My Birth." For example: death at war, miscarriages/stillbirth/infant death, divorce, the Depression, bankruptcy, death of a parent or sibling, a trauma that affected the family system. This leads to understanding losses and ways of coping that shaped the person's experiences and coping of grief.

Depending on trust levels and maturity of the individual(s), look at "Probable Losses Ahead." These might include death of a parent, a child growing up and going to college, a chronic illness that likely will progress, or other aspects of aging or anticipated changes.

This does not have a right or wrong. If you use this with others, as a leader, quietly observe how different individuals organize their time line. Encourage the person(s) to refer to this through later exercises. This easily pairs with teaching guide 8.2, which time lines your beginnings (and healing), versus losses.

Music Note: For the musically adventurous and highly conceptual, make your single line into a five-lined staff. You may want to graph your life experiences, with "highs" and "lows." You are creating a metaphor "score." Avoid getting overly caught up in the music "score" being just right. Real life does not fit strict "measures." Keep your focus on understanding your losses.

1.3 Journal Your Journey

Approach this book as your journey of self-reflection and growth. A key phrase throughout is to "be in and move through grief." Let yourself be and do both.

Go through this book at your own pace. Keep a specialized journal nearby. Respond to numerous questions and exercises throughout the book. Date and list any music you find yourself experiencing (i.e., listening to, singing, playing or composing). Look for connections between the music and (a) your everyday world; (b) a specific loss you are grieving; or (c) your broader span of loss/grief history.

- Identify music moments that empower you to "be in" your loss more fully.
- Identify music moments that guide you to "move through" your loss.
- Over time, go back and reread your entries. What movement do you hear and feel in yourself?

Music Note: Beethoven carried sketchbooks of staff paper with him, wherever he went. He was able to capture those fleeting ideas, whenever they came, and to continually work them out. Here is your opportunity to do the same.

1.4 Group Meetings or Book Club

Move through this book with a group, such as a book club, one chapter at a time. If you are the group leader, first assess the needs and goals of your group's participants, and select or adapt these teaching guides accordingly. If you are a group of peers, then share leadership. Be sure to include some type of musical experience, as described within a chapter or these teaching guides.

Seek to get to know others more fully through their music. Listen to others' music choices with curiosity, but do not critique them. Affirm others' life experiences. Have someone keep a list of the various pieces of music identified in the group. Over time, go back and reflect on the list itself, and what it says about your group and your group process.

Music Note: What type of music group does your group resemble? For example: partners, as in a jazz improvisation group or a string quartet; a teacher and students, as in a school chorus or band; professionals who hone their skills and create artistry for others; or something else?

1.5 Create a Musical Scrapbook

Create a musical "scrapbook" that tells part of your life story. Draw from the time line you created in exercise 1.2. Numerous possibilities exist, depending on what you want to express and explore. Here are some guidelines.

- Identify the life-experience(s) you want to capture:
  - a significant loss from your past or present
  - developmental age spans (early childhood, school, teen, young adult, etc.);
  - a specific relationship, place, role, or other aspect important to you.
- Decide your format, based on your musical background and skills. For example, if you are a music listener try any of the following.
  - Compile your relevant LPs, cassettes, CDs, or other recordings in a box or other container. Attach Post-it notes or other labels to the recordings. Perhaps, share these with a friend or a younger family member.
  - Burn a CD with your favorites (honor copyright laws; do not sell or distribute illegally). Create a CD liner, and tell the stories behind your selections.
  - Do the same with a VCR tape or DVD, especially if you have recorded images that relate to your loss.
  - Be creative and intentional in what you select and how you organize your content. What do you want to express? Is it strictly for you, or to be shared with others (as in family and close friends)? What impact do you want it to have? What emotional pacing?
- If you are a musician, compile your musical scores related to the loss; or more simply, your favorite music through the years.
  - Write down thoughts, emotions, and memories about the music itself.
  - We musicians focus on learning to perform the music. Ask, "What qualities within you did it take to bring this music to life?": belief that you could; hearing the score in your head even though your fingers or voice had not figured out its patterns; practice, practice, practice; risk; ongoing listening to yourself; polish; playing it from "heart and soul."
  - What did you learn about yourself through this music: self-worth, shame, perseverance, artistry?
  - Which of those qualities can you draw from for coping with this loss?
  - What meaning(s) does this music hold for you today and ahead?

1.6 Make Music

- You are the musician. Whatever your musical ability, carve out moments or larger time frames in your day or week to sing, play, move or dance to, or compose your own music.
- Listen to, sing, play, or move to any music in this chapter. Tune into your responses and journal your reflections.
- Identify additional music related to any concepts in this introductory chapter. Listen to, sing, or play it. Tune into and journal your reflections.
- Create your own music: vocal, and/or instrumental. Write it down, whatever your music notation skills may be.
- Share your music and reflections with another.

☐ Teaching Guides for Chapter 2.
Rhythms of Body and Soul

CORE Principles
Care - Ownership - Respect - Empowerment
HEALing Techniques
Hear - Explore - Affirm - Learn

2.1 Catalyst Question: It's Time — It's Not Time

Related to your loss, where in your life are you saying "it's time" and where are you saying "it's NOT time?" Write it down. Reflect on your lists. Which individual items can you have an effect on? Which ones are not yours to control?

For the musically brave, tap a steady beat, using one hand as the drum and the other hand to tap it. You may want to beat a 2-pattern (**1**-2-**1**-2-**1**-2-**1**-2-) or a 3 pattern (**1**-2-3-**1**-2-3-**1**-2-3-**1**-2-3-). Above the steady beat, speak your words, in a rhythmic pattern that's comfortable for you, like:

It's **TIME**, to **GET** some **HELP.**
It's **TIME**, to **FEEL** my **GRIEF.**
It's **TIME** to **WRITE** my **THOUGHTS.**
It's **TIME** to **BE** there for my **KIDS.**

and

It's not **TIME,** to **CUT** it **OFF.**
It's not **TIME,** to **HEAR** cli-**CHES.**
It's not **TIME,** to **KNOW** how this **ENDS.**
It's not **TIME,** to **GIVE** up **HOPE.**

For contrast, you may want to switch hands at the "It's not time" portion. Be comfortable with leading this. The rhythmic exercise instills responses into memory banks, and creates interactive validation. Depending on your setting, voice these with another trusted person or people. If you lead this in a group setting, be sure to introduce this with a sample group experience. When using people's actual responses, first let them work out their words and patterns by themselves or with a partner. If you invite responses into the large group, engage volunteers. Do not put anyone on the spot. Respect privacy and timetables. If a loss affects the entire group (i.e., a serious illness of a group member or a community crisis), use this as a group exercise to define group members' responses to the loss, at that given time.

2.2 Calendar Composing

Be aware that grieving and mourning can zap enormous amounts of energy: physically, emotionally, mentally, and spiritually. Its tasks (like care giving or funeral arrangements) can also give you shots of adrenalin. Your everyday rhythms for functioning can get thrown way off balance. While you cannot totally control what will be required from you, what can you anticipate and prepare for? How can you ground and steady yourself when life seems to twist you around in tornadic whirlwinds? Try this.

Pull out your calendar and write in some musical symbols that correspond to energies needed of you to function in everyday life. You might focus on one day, or several weeks. If you see a *presto* moment (extremely fast) or a *szforzando* meeting (heavily accented), write it in. Score in some rests, or *ritardandos* (slow down) and *fermatas* (stretch the moment), and then protect them. This is your time. Own it. Claim it. Is not your loss teaching you how valuable time is? Do you have some type of *andante* (walking speed) or *adagio* spaces (even slower) in your day, week, or month? Where is an *allegro vivace* week (fast and full of life)? Can you create some *largo* breathing space (extremely slow) the next week? You are the composer. Give yourself good pacing. Know when you will need extra reserves of energy, and when you can rest and renew yourself.

Oscillate between expending and recovering your energies. This is a key to building one's capacity to "perform" in the midst of increasing stress (Loehr & Schwartz, 2003). Again, tap into your own, "this is the time" and "this is not the time." You are the composer. This is your life, your loss, your timetable, and your healing.

2.3 Match It and Move It

Most exercise videos use patterns of (a) a warm-up exercise; (b) moving into high-intensity movement; and (c) a final cool down. Both the physical movements and the background music match this pattern. Create your own musical backdrops for your common physical or emotional "movement." You might simply identify these pieces in your head, or to sequence them onto a CD, computer drive, or IPod. For example:

- What music energizes you? Gets you moving, exercising, or serves as a great background for chores or exercise? Use that Walkman or IPod. Crank up the speakers. Or, wherever you are, sing. Select music that nurtures your body and soul.
- What music can you readily recall (or sing, or pop in your player, or play on an instrument) to help steady and ground you when you feel scattered or "lost"? Identify it ahead of time. Create your own recreative rituals.
- What situation often triggers panic or another painful response in you? What music would you select to create your own "Match It and Move It" CD? Remember, the purpose is not to escalate the pain, but to provide a safe container to acknowledge and channel or shift it.

2.4 My 3 Ds of Music for Pain Management: Distract, Divert, Direct

Identify for what, when, and how you might use these basic "3Ds of Music with Pain Management." For example, are you or a loved one coping with a serious illness? Is the pain related to the disease's symptoms, or its treatments? That can affect your mental approach and pain threshold. If the pain signals symptoms of increased illness, you may feel increased loss: loss of control, loss of future, and fear. If the pain is caused from treatment side-effects, it may signal hope and healing. When, specifically, might music help: before treatments, during, or after? During sleepless nights? For an afternoon nap? Tune in to your body's rhythms. Adapt the 3 Ds to your needs.

Distract. Identify music that distracts you and brings pleasure to you. It brings humor or comfort to you in this specific situation. Keep your music close by. Let someone else know where it can be found for you, as needed.

Divert. Identify music that diverts your attention from physical pain. It calls forth your emotional, mental, or spiritual strengths; helps you enter those places of pain within yourself. When you release tears and fears, your body can relax. When you explore emotions, thoughts, and beliefs of what the pain or loss means to you, you can find purpose and hope in the midst of suffering (Frankl, 1963).

Direct. Identify music that directs your whole being toward deep relaxation. Experiment with different CDs or IPod downloads for deep relaxation. Find what suits you best: nature, new age, classical, et al.

Musically, it probably will be slow, soft, and smooth (legato). New age music tends to be more free-floating, with less defined rhythms or melodies. For some, this creates openness; for others, it feels too loose. Classical music tends to have more predictable rhythms and harmonies. For some, this feels more secure; for others, too stuffy. Some music has guided imagery, with spoken suggestions. Some simply has acoustic, electronic sounds sequenced to affect your brain waves. Find what works for you.

Create a ritual of using this music at specific times: an afternoon nap, going to sleep at night, with earphones in the waiting room before or during a treatment, or when coping with painful side-effects. Note your pain levels before and after the intervention.

2.5 Seasons of the Soul

Identify a loss through which you have already come. Relate the "Seasons of the Soul" to your grief process. What metaphors connect with and describe your experience? What other grief/loss language from the chart helps you understand your grief experience (i.e., Parkes's processes of grief, Worden's tasks of mourning, and Neimeyer's reconstructing meaning)?

Identify a current loss you are experiencing. Identify any "Seasons of the Soul" you have experienced and any ways you have used music thus far. (Remember, this chart is not a rigid timetable, but more like the changing weather throughout any day, within a broad season.) What needs, interventions, or creativity stir within in you? What music might help you be in and move through your current loss and grief? Journal and dialogue your thoughts with others.

2.6 "There Is a Time" for Opposites Paired Together

Take the final reading in chapter 2, and create your own "there is a time" lines. Simply, find two opposites that pair together, within the experience you are describing: a death, an illness, a move, a retirement, a divorce. Also, the "time" may be a celebration: a birth, marriage, remarriage, a blessing ceremony, a move, a graduation, or any type of a "coming through" commemoration. Find phrases that describe unique qualities of your experience.

If this is for a public service, include as many different persons and experiences as you can. You may want to turn this into a litany or responsive reading, where all persons read the bold text, and selected individuals read the line(s) relevant to their roles. Keep it focused on the experience and the persons for which it is intended.

- Reflect within yourself on the experience of writing your "there is a time." Did it move you to better, steadier, sturdier "rhythms" within yourself? Do you feel more chaotic about life's many options, or calmer and more open, more in sync with your life?

2.7 Make Music

You are the musician. Whatever your musical ability, carve out moments or larger time frames in your day or week to sing, play, move or dance to, or compose your own music.

- Listen to, sing, play, or move to any music in this chapter. Tune into your responses and journal your reflections.
- Identify additional music related to any concepts in this chapter, "Rhythms of Body and Soul." Listen to, sing, or play it. Tune into and journal your reflections.
- Create your own music: vocal or instrumental. Write it down, whatever your music notation skills may be.
- Share your music and reflections with another.

☐ Teaching Guides for Chapter 3. Themes and Counterthemes of Life Stories

> **CORE** Principles
> Care - Ownership - Respect - Empowerment
> **HEAL**ing Techniques
> Hear - Explore - Affirm - Learn

3.1 Finish That Phrase

Play with "Finish That Phrase," as described in the first paragraphs of chapter 3. Take it to a level of interaction, trust, and openness that is congruent with your context, role, and relationship with the person. The purpose of this exercise is to experiment with using music as a springboard for deeper reflection within oneself, and richer dialogue with others. Do not assume another's meanings. Let the other person finish the phrase. Validate and affirm the other's thoughts and emotions even if they do not concur with your own. Hear another's musical themes and life stories, especially when they counter your own.

3.2 Gonna' Take a Sentimental Journey

This easily creates an informal, low-threat "Getting to Know You" exercise. Write each title on a small piece of paper. Fold the papers, and put them in a bowl. Have someone select a song title and lead everyone in singing whatever melody, phrase, or lyrics they can recall. Lead a fast-paced recall of memories, people, places that are brought to mind.

- "Take Me Out to the Ballgame"
- "I'll Be Seeing You"
- "I Love Lucy"
- "Rock Around the Clock"
- "Danny Boy"
- "Gilligan's Isle"
- "Let It Be"
- "I Will Survive"
- "New York, New York"

- "Sesame Street"
- "Taps."

Keep it moving. As a leader, use your own energy and expression to set the tone and respond to the levels of openness group members express. Adapt this to your group's size and length of time, for example, (a) select titles more familiar to your group; (b) create 1:1 partnering for more depth recall and reflections, letting them choose which pieces stirs the most within; (c) gather CD examples or MP3 downloads to enliven the musical experience. For live music, http://www.musicnotes.com provides downloadable sheet music.

3.3 Catalyst Question: Today's Music

What music are you listening to these days? Ask yourself, an individual, or a group. Within a group, start with 1:1 partners and then invite responses with larger group sharing. Take it beyond the actual music, to everyday real life. What draws you to the music? How does it to connect to your mourning and healing? What speaks to you: a key quality about the music, its lyrics, something about the performer or the music's context, or specific musical moment?

3.4 My Music Menu

Use appendix B, "My Music Menu," with yourself and others. Adapt how you use it, according your context and purpose. For example, you might have the actual sheet, or you might simply ask the questions. In a group context, you might have people partner and go through it together, or you might put out questions for group responses. To enliven the experience, invite people to sing a phrase and have others join in. Pace it according to the energy you want the group to have. Use this as tool to get to know the group, to let group members get to know you, and to set the tone for future exercises that require one's own recall and reflections.

3.5 Themes and Counterthemes

Find a recording of Beethoven's 5th Symphony, first movement. It should be available at any music store that sells classical recordings. Use this exercise with yourself, before venturing into it with any kind of group.

For yourself, as you listen to the recording, simply raise your right hand anytime you hear the main theme ("da-da-da-dum"), and then raise your left hand when you hear its lyrical countertheme. The first theme will recur with humorous repetitions.

For a group, assign one-half of the group the first theme, and the other the second theme. Similarly, have them raise a hand when they hear their theme. Splitting this into two groups creates a more visual contrast, and cuts down on visual "mirroring" confusion, as in using one's right or left hand. (This makes for a great, pick-up-the-energy exercise.) Use enough of the music to get into the flow, and for members to experience the contrasts between theme and countertheme. Upon stopping the music, ask for descriptions of the two themes. Ask what the music would be like with just one of the two themes. Does the play between the two themes bring life to the music?

Next, for yourself or the group, apply the theme and countertheme concepts to one's life. Affirm that this exercise is based on trust, confidentiality, and support for each other. Invite people to go into this as they feel ready.

Identify a core theme and countertheme that recurs in your life (refer to this portion of chapter 3). If this is a loss–grief context, focus this toward a theme and countertheme that emerges when you experience loss and grief. For example:

- desperate loneliness or peaceful solitude
- being rigid or being flexible
- feeling controlled by the loss or open to it
- owning what I can change or accepting what I cannot (AA/Serenity prayer)
- uncontrollable floods of emotions or emotional flow
- feeling angry at _____ or feeling relieved that _____
- being absorbed in my own world or being open to another's experience of the loss
- fear or faith
- holding or letting go
- risk or security
- name your own.

As befits the context, your role and relationship with the individual or group, facilitate dialogue about those patterns in one's life. Move toward accepting these parts of oneself. Affirm one's choice toward "developing" (another metaphor from our sonata and symphony forms), exploring, and reworking these parts of oneself.

Leading this exercise requires *guiding* and *informing*. The person will *confront* one's own patterns, and should experience *sustaining* support from the leader and group. It can lay the groundwork for future *healing* and *reconciling*. These qualities are explained further in chapter 5, "Styles of Doing and Being."

3.6 Five R's for Relating with Memories through Music

Role-play this process. Have one person be the person with dementia and another person be the musician, who either sings or has an instrument that is simple-sounding and nonintrusive (guitar, Q-chord, choir chime et al.). Interaction is as important as the actual music.

The person role-playing the person with dementia needs to identify with the group common characteristics of the disease, and to decide what level of disease progression the role-play will include: early, intermediate, or advanced. As a group, set the stage for this person's age, cultural context, and faith system, and the person's use of music earlier in life. For example, this person sang in a community choir, played piano, went to classical concerts; he or she was a kindergarten teacher, a jazz enthusiast, and so on.

The person using music describes to observers the following:

- One's role and relationship with the person (i.e., caregiver, family member, friend, music volunteer, professional music therapist)
- What she or he knows about this person's life story and current condition
- What she or he knows about this person's musical preferences and previous musical activities
- How one hopes to relate with the person through music.

Depending on the training level and purposes of the group you may want to send the "musician" out of the room while the initial descriptions of the patient are decided.

Let the role-play begin. Note the progression (or not) of this author's "5 R's for Relating with Memories."

- **Respond:** the person responds (or not) to the musician's greeting, presence, or musical sound. Note nonverbal communication, like body language, a startling or gentle entry into another's world. The person responds (or not) through eye contact, nodding or tapping to a rhythm or another physical, observable response.
- **Recognize:** The person noticeably recognizes you, or the music. A sense of familiarity is observed.

- **Recall:** The person is able to recall a phrase or melody, by singing a text or humming a melody (experiment with music that connects with the person's life-history).
- **Reflect:** The person is able to reflect at some level on the music or the memories it stirs. The musician asks questions that springboard from the music. Choose open (narrative) or closed (short answer) questions, depending on the person's ability to communicate. Make this successful for the patient. Do not push it to a level where the person feels increased frustration and anxiety. If grief emerges, be present. Know your abilities and limits.
- **Revision:** The person is able to voice some type of hope for the future. This is not a time to stir someone's existential fears and then leave the person in a more frightened darkness. This is a time for connection, security, and assurance that she or he is known, safe, and valued.

After the role play, process it. Learn from it. Identify cautions. More specific cautions are identified and discussed in chapter 7, "The Final Cadence," at "Caution: Stop." Balance your expectations with the stage of dementia; a simple "respond" may be a huge gift.

3.7 Make Music

You are the musician. Whatever your musical ability, carve out moments or larger time frames in your day or week to sing, play, move or dance to, or compose your own music.

- Listen to, sing, play, or move to any music in this chapter, "Themes and Counterthemes of Life Stories." Tune into your responses and journal your reflections.
- Identify additional music related to any concepts in this chapter. Listen to, sing, or play it. Tune into and journal your reflections.
- Create your own music: vocal or instrumental. Write it down, whatever your music notation skills may be.
- Share your music and reflections with another person.

☐ Teaching Guides for Chapter 4. Harmonies and Dissonances of Healing

> **CORE** Principles
> Care - Ownership - Respect - Empowerment
> **HEAL**ing Techniques
> Hear - Explore - Affirm - Learn

4.1 C-major Chord

Play a C-major chord (C-E-G) on your piano, electric keyboard, guitar, or other instrument. As you continue to repeat the chord, sing with it the nursery song: "Are you sleeping, Are you sleeping / Brother John, Brother John / Morning bells are ringing, Morning bells ringing / Ding dong ding, Ding dong ding." Experiment with other well-known songs. Doubtless, you will find few other songs that work well with only one chord. (For the adventurous, try "Row, Row, Row Your Boat" and "The Farmer in the Dell." Note that these songs with only one chord are for toddlers and preschoolers.)

On the piano or other keyboard add to your C-major chord (C-E-G) a B flat and hold it. Play it several times. (If you are playing guitar, this is a C7 chord.) What does your ear tell you to do? Resolve it. Shift this chord to C-F-A, otherwise known as F major. Hear its resolution. Try again. Take the C7 chord (C-E-G plus B flat) and resolve it to F minor, C-F and A flat. How does that sound similar or different from the C7 to F major resolution? Try one more. Start with the same C7 chord, and resolve it to C-E-A (A minor). This resolution is a deceptive cadence (it does not sound complete), and will be discussed further in chapter 7, "The Final Cadence."

Journal your thoughts and discuss the following metaphors. Interface these metaphors with your personal, life experiences.

- Life would be boring if it were all a C-major chord.
- Dissonance is not necessarily bad. It can stimulate movement.
- Resolving dissonance usually has numerous options, choices, and outcomes.

Pull out your list of personal harmonies and dissonances in teaching guide 4.1. This is not a time to completely figure out or resolve those personal dissonances. This is a time to identify them, accept them with a fresh perspective, and open yourself to your choices ahead. What new insights do you experience for yourself?

4.2 Catalyst Question: Harmonies and Dissonances in My Life

Today, what in your life feels "in harmony," and what feels "dissonant"? Apply this question specifically to a loss, a relationship, or an aspect of your life like your family, job, career, finances, or life goals. Do you hear those dissonances in your life as being bad? Can you hear your dissonances as something calling for movement and motion? Where will you take it? (For musical illustration, see the previous exercise.)

4.3 Finding Home — Finding Healing

Identify as many songs as you can that describe "home." Here are a few:

- "Home, Home On the Range" (Folk Song)
- "My Old Kentucky Home" (Stephen Foster)
- "Going Home" (Folk/Spiritual; Dvorak's *New World Symphony*)
- "... and grace will lead me home." (from "Amazing Grace")
- "Baby, Won't You Please Come Home" (Sam Cooke)
- "Can't Find My Way Home" (Joe Cocker)
- "Sweet Home Alabama" (Lynard Skynard)
- "Take Me Home, Country Roads" (John Denver)
- "Homeless" (Paul Simon)
- "Bring Him Home" (sung by the character Jean Valjean in *Les Misérables*)
- "I'll Cover You" (sung by the characters Angel and Tom Collins in *Rent*)
- "Nobody's Home" (Avril Lavigne)
- "Sing Me Home" (Tim McGraw)

Note how each song reflects something about the singers and their sense of home, at least what we know of them through their public personas or stage characters (as in the examples from Broadway). Note the variety of moods: some reminisce, others move toward the future, each exudes personality, emotion, and meaning.

Journal or discuss with others how your sense of "home" is being challenged and changed by your loss. What is similar from before? What is different? What new sense of "home" are you seeking? This is not about wishful thinking, but rather a deep, passionate hope that is rooted in reality and open to transformation. For those who understand music theory, what modulations and transpositions will you need to go through to reach that new home?

Like the music listed above, what piece of music describes that newer sense of home that you seek? It does not have to use the word *home*. It might be instrumental. It might be something you create. Mainly, it envisions and articulates what your own healing might be. Any healthcare professional knows about setting goals and objectives. This does much the same, but in creative, musical, soulful language versus a clinical, objective, documentation style language.

Get your music and keep it nearby. Play it. Sing it. Explore what it means to you, and how you might rearrange your aspects of your life to create that new home. Revisit it through the remainder of this book, and again after you have finished reading this book's last page.

4.4 Revolutionary Dissonances in My Life

Refer to chapter 4's section on "Beethoven and the Beatles," and the revolutionary changes they made to music by adding elements considered to be dissonant (at that time). Similarly, what dissonant experiences in your life revolutionized you? Your family system? Your workplace? Your community? For example, after fully experiencing a major "dissonance," you can no longer hear or see life in an innocent, overly simplistic "harmonic" framework. Perhaps you experienced a trauma, the death of a child, the long illness of a parent that involved great suffering, a betrayal, a job loss, a divorce, a broken relationship with a close friend or relative. Whatever and however painful it was, you challenged and revolutionized who you are and how you do life.

Today, you embrace those bitter experiences as significant turning points that shaped much of who you are now. You are wiser. Your values and belief system have shifted. Even if your life suddenly, magically became as it was before the loss, this new you would cope differently from the way you coped before. Journal and discuss what you learned from your loss, and any transformations you have experienced.

4.5 Being with Your Chaos Clusters

Recall a time when your pain was greeted with clichés. Someone told you what you should do to fix it, or turned your story into their own once-upon-a-time saga. They grabbed your "music" and drowned it out with their own. (Or, have you done this to others?) Here is your chance to hear and "be with" your chaos for as long or short a time as you want, without someone else taking it away from you.

At a piano, hold down the right pedal and then create a crashing sound by letting your whole hand slam down on a cluster of random notes. Listen to its sounds. Unlike the quick chord resolutions in guide 4.1, these dissonances are beyond repair. (Note: Such atonal clusters are common to formal 20th-century composition techniques, though they may be more foreign to the untrained ear.) Simply hear the sounds without resolving, stopping, or judging them. Play clusters again, somewhere else, randomly crashing as life sometimes hits us. Relate these sounds to clusters from your loss, or other clusters in your life that feel like this. Name them, play them again. Say what you need and what you do not need. Guard yourself against emotional fight or flight responses. Be with the sounds. Take them in. Let them be.

In your own past, how did you feel someone was fully present to you and with you in your chaos and pain? The other person resonated with you. She was somewhat like the sturdy soundboard of a grand piano, or the safe encasing of a cello or guitar. He gently let his heart and mind resonate with yours, without judgment, nor control. Ultimately, which mode was more helpful to you in your healing, the person who took it from you to fix it or the one who was present to you?

Today, what chaos clusters in your life are seeking your attention? Your full presence to yourself is your best present to yourself. Today, what chaos clusters in someone close to you might you need to hear? How might you be present?

4.6 It Is Well

Identify a significant loss from your past, one that felt as though it would never heal. What "is well," now. "Well" does not mean that it never again hurts. "Well" does mean that overall, you experience a healing, a strength and peace that calls you to give yourself to life and living.

Identify a significant loss you are coping with today, now. What sorrows are rolling like a storm at sea? What, for you, in the midst of the storm, is "well"? Remember, being "well" does not necessarily mean being happy or celebratory. Being well means experiencing more of a sense of whole-ness in the midst of loss. It might be comfort and assurance in the midst of horrendous pain. It might be a sense of presence in the midst of absence.

Wellness and healing do not mean a return to life as it was before. They do not dismiss turmoil or trouble. It means accepting life's harsh realities, and finding a place within to breathe, to hope, to believe, and to live.

Do you know a piece of music that voices that for you? Find it. Play it. Sing it. Compose it. Journal about and experience your music with a trusted person or group.

4.7 Make Music

You are the musician. Whatever your musical ability, carve out moments or larger time frames in your day or week to sing, play, move or dance to, or compose your own music.

- Listen to, sing, play, or move to any music in this chapter, "Harmonies and Dissonances of Healing." Tune into your responses and journal your reflections.
- Identify additional music related to any concepts in this chapter. Listen to, sing, or play it. Tune into and journal your reflections.
- Create your own music: vocal or instrumental. Write it down, whatever your music notation skills may be.
- Share your music and reflections with another.

☐ Teaching Guides for Chapter 5. Styles of Doing and Being

> **CORE** Principles
> Care - Ownership - Respect - Empowerment
> **HEAL**ing Techniques
> Hear - Explore - Affirm - Learn

5.1 Catalyst Question: My Styles of Coping with Loss

What musical styles describe how you cope with your loss? For example: jazz improvisation, classical structure, gospel faith, grassroots folk, country ballads, R&B soul, explosive rap, a rock driving beat, dramatic opera, easy listening, new age flow, rhythmic reggae, or something else? Perhaps, even silence. Note: the adjectives are this author's adjectives to illustrate the concept of style. Change them to whatever fits you, best. Journal or discuss with others the following.

- How are those styles of music similar to how you cope with your loss?
- Do they work well for you?
- Do your styles of coping with loss work for or against you in your relationships with others?
- Are they creating wellness for you as you move through your loss?
- Would other styles stretch you and add to your coping strengths and skills?

If you answered "yes" to the last question, find some top-quality music in that style. You may want to find a rendition of one your favorite songs (search the Internet for options). If you have a friend or colleague who enjoys the style you are exploring, ask for recommendations. Listen. Hear. Take it in. You may want to move or dance. Journal and discuss these with others.

On another note, listening to any music you associate with your loss may be too painful right now. You may want to explore other styles of music that provide something completely different.

5.2 Claiming My Own Style

Before the group meeting, identify a variety of musicians with distinctive styles, who would be familiar to your group. For example: Aretha Franklin, Placido Domingo, Usher, Celine Dion, Louis Armstrong, Bob Dylan, Norah Jones, Stevie Wonder, Dolly Parton, Bobby McFerrin, the Vienna Boys Choir, Elton John, John Williams, Cher, George Winston, Eminem, or even ol' Kermit the Frog. Write their names on individual pieces of paper. Fold the papers and put them in a bowl.

In the group, discuss how our styles of dealing with loss are personal, unique, and rooted in our styles of doing life. Others may try to impose their styles on us. We may find we need to try something new. We might need to reconnect with our personal style that's been disrupted.

In the group, have the person (or group members) identify a personal, favorite song. Let everyone respond. Encourage them to sing the first few phrases. This can be a fun, community building exercise. Be sensitive to anyone who does not want to sing or feels put on the spot.

As a group, decide on one easy-to-sing song that is familiar to all. Discern appropriate levels of emotional vulnerability to the song itself. Pull out the bowl. Have individuals pick a paper, and then have the group play with singing the song in this new style. Again, be sensitive to vulnerabilities. Involve members with each other in fun, supportive interactions.

As you move through this exercise, create teachable moments. Primarily, even though the names on the slips of paper are professionals at their own styles, they cannot impose their style onto someone else. If you have not already read out all of the names in the bowl, do so now. Note that both applause and criticism could be put on any one singer.

Ask members to describe their own style. What is working for you? What is not?

Music artists, whatever their style, are subject to critical reviews.

Do you feel subjected to others' free criticisms of how you should or shouldn't cope with your loss? Good questions are, "Whose loss is it, anyway?" and "Ten years from now, who will still be affected by how I cope, now?" (The answer is likely to be yourself, your children, and possibly your spouse/partner.) Claim your rightful ownership of your loss, and your style of being and moving through this, and your choices.

Sing the opening phrase of the selected song again, with each person singing it his or her own way, and the group joining in together for one more round.

5.3 Learning from Others' Styles

Identify someone whose ways of coping with loss inspires you. Describe what you know about that person, his or her loss, and what you see that you value. Is this person still alive, and accessible for dialogue? If not, is there someone close to this person with whom you can talk? Perhaps this person is your own grandparent, parent, or some other close, personal relationship. If she or he has died, engage conversations with this person in your imagination (see chapter 8, pp. 143–145).

Ask questions. Listen and learn. What similarities do you hear with you and your loss? What differences? What do you want to take and try on for yourself, practicing and incorporating into your own everyday doing and being?

Doubtless, any successful musician has had teachers and mentors along the way. Still, a best teacher will call forth the talent, skills, and expression of the student. This is not a place for creating clones. This is time and place to find a new way of living.

5.4 My Do-Be List

Refer to chapter 5, p. 82–83, and appendix D, "My Do-Be-Do-Be List." Practice your Do-Be's in manageable, measurable time frames, like a day, or even a morning or afternoon. Once you feel more comfortable with them, apply them to larger time frames, like a week, month, several months, or even next year. This tool helps you define and create your own style. You are not being tossed around by life haphazardly. You are not rigidly controlling life. You are becoming more aware of your emotions, responses, and choices. You are composing better ways to do life's tasks and to be present to yourself and others. Do-be-do-be-do-be.

5.5 What Do You Do That's Creative?

Ask yourself, "What do I do that's creative?" It does not have to relate to music. You might find creativity when you cook, garden, or make improvements to your home. You might find creative energies when you problem solve, take photos and edit them (especially with digital technologies), paint, write, design a new room, or redesign an existing one. Perhaps you love to journal or draw. You read novels or poetry. Maybe you enjoy attending theater, art galleries, museums, or concerts. Maybe you re-create yourself through nature by walking, enjoying a sunrise or sunset, spending time at a lake or beach, hiking, or camping out for a few days.

Your creativity might be musical. You may sing, play an instrument, dance, or compose. Whatever it is you do, your creativity re-creates your core being. You feel enriched, restored, and refueled.

Too often, we think of grief and loss in pathological terms. Often, it is dark, painful, and challenging. Often, at the right season and time, it can be a catalyst for creativity and transformation. The doing of a task can be one's way of working out one's personal, profound aspects of the loss.

Again, "What do you do that's creative?" Identify what feels doable and re-creative for you at this time. This is your time to do and be your creative self in your own way.

5.6 Care of the Soul

Identify a personal encounter with someone who exhibited any of the following to you at some time during a significant loss:

- **Sustaining:** the person's presence with you comforted and strengthened you within. You felt supported.
- **Confronting:** the person stood with you in accepting a reality. This does not mean a forceful, "in your face," confronting. It means taking in and "getting" the truth.
- **Healing:** the person's interactions with you reworked or healed wounds within yourself.
- **Reconciling:** the person's interactions with you reworked or healed wounds between you and another person or people.
- **Guiding:** the person's presence and interaction with you evoked memories, emotions, and meanings from the past.
- **Informing:** the person's presence and interaction with you instilled a moment of insight, information; of new understanding or meaning for your present and future.

Identify a time when a piece of music has moved you to similar places within. If relevant, relate it to significant loss.

- **Sustaining:** the music both comforted and strengthened you.
- **Confronting:** the music confronted and evoked strong realities about the loss.
- **Healing:** the music brought insight or meaning that helped heal a wound within yourself.

- **Reconciling:** the music created a relational moment with you and someone else that held great meaning. It was "healing" between two or more persons.
- **Guiding:** the music evoked memories, emotions, meanings from the past.
- **Informing:** the music instilled an insight or new meaning for your present and future.

5.7 Make Music

You are the musician. Whatever your musical ability, carve out moments or larger time frames in your day or week to sing, play, move or dance to, or compose your own music.

- Listen to, sing, play, or move to any music in this chapter, "Styles of Doing and Being." Tune into your responses and journal your reflections.
- Identify additional music related to any concepts in this chapter. Listen to, sing, or play it. Tune into and journal your reflections.
- Create your own music: vocal or instrumental. Write it down, whatever your music notation skills may be.
- Share your music and reflections with another.

☐ Teaching Guides for Chapter 6. Expressions of Self and Community

---

CORE Principles
Care - Ownership - Respect - Empowerment
HEALing Techniques
Hear - Explore - Affirm - Learn

6.1 Highs and Lows

Refer to appendix C, "Keyboard Quality of Life: 'Highs' and 'Lows.'" Go through this worksheet on your own or with a group. It can provide a fast, easy check-in tool for you at a given time. You may want to make multiple copies and include them in your journal. They can be a great tool for tracking your patterns, shifts, and changes through your loss. In contrast to a standard graph chart, this allows both "highs" and "lows" to coexist with each other. The shifts, over time, do not have to always go higher to mark improvement.

This also works with a client or group. A portable, battery or electric keyboard provides a visual, aural, and tactile tool. Great questions can be, "in our time today, where would you like us to go (play it on the keyboard)" and "what do you think might get us there?" You are calling both expressions and expectations of the other, versus assuming or imposing your own.

6.2 Catalyst Question: One Song for Today

If you could hear, sing, or play on an instrument only *one* piece of music today, what would it be for today? Why?

If you could express yourself to only one person today, who would that be and what would you say?

Apply these same questions to your past six months, or another time frame relevant to your loss. Apply these same questions to your next six months, or another time frame relevant to your loss.

6.3 Music Symbols: Score Your Day

Write down musical symbols that describe your day, today. For example: *pp, ff, accelerando, ritardando, dolce, furioso, fermata, repeat*. Relate them to specific time frames and/or activities. Identify musical symbols that represent what you want for the remainder of your day, or for tomorrow. This is similar to chapter 2's teaching guide, "Calendar Composing." However, it expands self-awareness beyond rhythms and pacing to multiple nuances of expression.

6.4 Silence

What music can you *not* listen to right now, because it is too painful? What solace do you find in silence? This question requires a supportive relationship, trust, and sensitivity to the person's response. It requires appropriate timing, and should not be casually tossed out. Simply asking the question forces the person to "listen" to (in one's head) that which has been silenced.

With those cautions in mind, this question may be a catalyst for being in and moving further into one's grief. Again, it may be a closed door that cautions, "Don't go there, at least not now." It may provide an opportunity to invite, "If a time comes when you want to experience the music, I'm here." Use of this depends on one's role, relationship, and context with the person.

6.5 Choose Your Own Tools for Working with Children

Multiple exercises are given at chapter 6, "Tools for Professionals Who Work with Children." Select one or more tool and use it with yourself, first. Explore either a current loss, or one that you experienced as a child. Journal or discuss with another person your emotions and insights that stir.

6.6 Learning to Say Goodbye

Listen to a recording of "How Can I Help You Say Goodbye" (Taylor-Good & Collins, 1993). Similar to its three stanzas, write out messages you have learned about loss and grief, (1) as a child, (2) as a young adult, and (3) through a recent, current loss.

Reflect on how well those messages are or are not working for you in your current loss. For more depth examination on various survival messages, explore Paul Valent's tables in Charles Figley's *Compassion Fatigue* (Valent, 1995, p. 32).

To what modes of coping might you "say goodbye"? For example: "I have fully learned how to be independent, and now I'm ready to learn about depending on others." Another might be, "I learned to run from or cut off my emotions, and that protected me from some pretty overwhelming stuff. Now I am ready to say 'goodbye' to emotional cut offs that damage me. I want to say 'hello' to experiencing my emotions and thoughts about the loss."

6.7 Noteworthy News

Identify examples of music that appear in the news over a period of time. Make this a group project (preferably at the beginning of the group process). Tune into ways that different cultures use music to mark life's celebrations, sorrows, commemorations, and everyday living.

6.8 Make Music

You are the musician. Whatever your musical ability, carve out moments or larger time frames in your day or week to sing, play, move or dance to, or compose your own music.

- Listen to, sing, play, or move to any music in this chapter, "Expressions of Self and Community." Tune into your responses and journal your reflections.
- Identify additional music related to any concepts in this chapter. Listen to, sing, or play it. Tune into and journal your reflections.
- Create your own music: vocal or instrumental. Write it down, whatever your music notation skills may be.
- Share your music and reflections with another.

☐ Teaching Guides for Chapter 7. The Final Cadence

> **CORE** Principles
> Care - Ownership - Respect - Empowerment
> **HEAL**ing Techniques
> Hear - Explore - Affirm - Learn

7.1 Catalyst Question: What Music Do You Want For Your Funeral?

Imagine you are dying. (First, how do those words and thoughts affect you? What different ways might they affect someone else?) What kind of setting would you want, a hospital, home, a particular room, or other space?

What sounds and activity would you *not* want around you? What sounds and activity would you be likely want to have around you?

Who would you want with you? What parameters for visitors might you want, and who might be your best gatekeeper? Most likely, these reflect relationships and patterns for how you live your life, now.

Would you want music? If so, what music might you want? What music would you definitely not want?

What might you want to express to someone else through music? Might it be perhaps, a lullaby for your son or daughter, a love song for your spouse, a teen song for lifelong friend?

What music might you want at your wake/visitation, funeral, or memorial service? Why? Is there a particular musician you want involved? Especially if that is a family member or friend, talk with him or her now. Such an experience may feel too overwhelming, or might be a wonderful outlet for expression. How might you experience this music, now?

Dialogue your responses with other group members. Note similarities and unique differences. Debrief your vulnerabilities in doing this exercise. Discuss parameters for when you might ask these questions to someone, and when you would not. For what persons/roles/contexts might this catalyst question easily fit, and for what persons/roles/contexts would this probably intrude?

7.2 Deceptive Cadences

In music, a cadence is a series of harmonic progressions (chords) that signals an ending. The musician and listener are prepared. It marks "The End" like in a storybook. This exercise pairs with descriptions of deceptive cadences in chapter 7. It is also a continuation to teaching guide "4.1 C-major Chord." Using the same instrument as before, play the C-major chord (C-E-G), then play C7 (C-E-G-B flat), and then resolve it to A minor (C-E-A). For those with a basic music theory background, try the following.

- Accompany any basic song familiar to you and your group on piano, keyboard, guitar, Q-chord, or another instrument.
- When you get to the next to the last chord (usually a V7), switch the final resolution to the submediant (vi) chord. Here is your deceptive cadence. Hear its unsettling, unresolved ending.
- To simplify finding that "deceptive" chord, simply take the 6th scale degree of your key, and build a 1-3-5 chord from it. (It will usually be minor.)
- Another trick is to take the 5th of your tonic chord, and raise it a whole step. (You get the same notes, in an inverted position.) For example:
  - Change C-E-G (C major) to C-E-A (A minor, inverted)
  - Change F-A-C (F major) to F-A-D (D minor, inverted)
  - Change E flat-G-B flat (E flat major) to E flat-G-C (C minor, inverted)
  - Change G-B flat-D (G minor) to G-B flat-E (E diminished).

If you plan to use this in a group, practice it ahead of time. You want to create a surprise ending, that does not quite end. Use this as a springboard for dialogue, such as:

- Describe a deceptive cadence that happened to you. How did you feel? How did you switch gears?
- What difference did that deceptive cadence make in the big picture? It may have simply delayed the same outcome. It might have completely changed a direction.
- Do you consider that pivotal "chord" to have been negative or positive?
  - Name a forthcoming "cadence" in your life that could be hijacked by a "deceptive cadence." How might you cope?

7.3 Final Cadences versus Cadenceless Losses

Musically, any of the compositional elements described throughout this book can help create that rich ending. For example, that last phrase might repeat the melodic theme, or rhythm patterns are stretched out. It might have a creative harmony. It might be a poignant lyric that brings a surprise meaning. How might those musical endings relate to life?

- Identify a piece of music that you feel has a beautiful, complete ending.
- Reflect on musical elements that make that musical ending so rich. Is it the rhythm, melody, harmony, style, or lyrics, or is it an interplay of all of those elements?
- Identify a significant loss you have experienced that had a clearly defined cadence or ending. Use our music metaphors to describe your preparation for the loss, and what made it a "good ending," even though it was a significant loss.
- Identify another loss you have experienced that did not have that sense of "cadence" preparation and movement. This loss abruptly crashed your world with no chance to say goodbye. Or, this loss has been a no-end, ongoing saga, like a missing person who is never found, or a limited recovery after a physical trauma. What musical metaphors, thus far, describe this loss?
- Explore the differences between your two different cadence endings. What do you learn about preparing for the loss, when time was given to you to create that just right ending? What do you learn about coping with the loss when you could not have prepared? Might you create smaller cadence markers for yourself, now?
- What music, readings, or rituals would help you acknowledge and commemorate those losses (like at a funeral)? Whom else would you include?
- If this exercise is used in a group, include time for partnered or small group sharing. Listen. Learn.

7.4 Caution: Stop and CORE Principles

Journal or discuss the cautions listed described at chapter 7, "Caution: Stop." Identify for yourself a moment when music was extremely painful to you. Ample materials and questions earlier in this book can help you identify those.

Refer to chapter 7's section on "CORE Principles." An advanced learning technique is to identify contraindicators, or opposites. One might easily describe ways to provide care, ownership, respect, and empowerment, but one might not be able to discern boundaries for when one's actions or intents overstep.

Identify the opposite for any potential uses of music with another. Incorporate concepts throughout this book of hearing others' music, life stories, timetables, and meanings. Ask yourself:

- In my role as _____ , and my relationship with _____ , I might use music to _____ . I would not provide *care* if I _____ .
- In my role as _____ , and my relationship with _____ , I might use music to _____. I would not provide *ownership* if I _____ .
- In my role as _____ , and my relationship with _____ , I might use music to _____. I would not provide *respect* if I _____ .
- In my role as _____ , and my relationship with _____ , I might use music to _____. I would not provide *empowerment* if I _____ .

7.5 Music for You

Refer to chapter 7's chart titled, "Music Care For You." Examine the left column's progression from physical to mental, to emotional, to spiritual aspects. Note that while these are broken out for needs assessment and intervention, much overlap can occur.

Explore how any two of you might approach dying differently from one another, and how music might or might not be welcomed by you. What does that teach you about using music with the dying?

Examine which pieces of this might be more appropriate for professionals from different disciplines to use: the person who is dying, a family member, a caregiver, a nurse, a social worker, a chaplain/minister/rabbi, a nursing assistant, a therapist. Which pieces might be misused or imposed? How might you prevent this?

7.6 Make Music

You are the musician. Whatever your musical ability, carve out moments or larger time frames in your day or week to sing, play, move or dance to, or compose your own music.

- Listen to, sing, play, or move to any music in this chapter, "The Final Cadence." Tune into your responses and journal your reflections.
- Identify additional music related to any concepts in this chapter. Listen to, sing, or play it. Tune into and journal your reflections.
- Create your own music: vocal, and/or instrumental. Write it down, whatever your music notation skills may be.
- Share your music and reflections with another.

☐ Teaching Guides for Chapter 8. Composing Life Out of Loss

> **CORE** Principles
> Care - Ownership - Respect - Empowerment
> **HEAL**ing Techniques
> Hear - Explore - Affirm - Learn

8.1 Catalyst Question: Composing Life Out of Loss

Refer to chapter 8's descriptions of age-old archetypes for composing life out of loss: the phoenix rising out the ashes, Orpheus singing and bringing life to stones, and La Lobda singing over bones taken for dead. Create quiet, reflective time and space for yourself. Journal and/or dialogue: *What do I want to create out of this loss, in my life and my larger world?*

Listen. Hear.

- What rhythms are pulsing through me?
- What themes and counterthemes are playing around inside?
- What dissonances have the potential to get something unstuck and moving in a new direction?
- What do I want to uniquely, personally express?
- How do my styles of doing life and being me adjust to my loss?
- What cadences have occurred, and which ones do I need to create or complete?
- What "music" from before can I always carry within and arrange a new?

8.2 Time Line Your Beginnings

This exercise pairs with "1.2 Time Line Your Losses." Use the same methods as before. Now, create a time line of your significant beginnings. "Family Beginnings Before My Birth" might be: my parents left their hometown for military life; my mom went to college and became a professional; when my parents met my dad was widowed with two children and my mom was divorced with no children; my grandfather survived the Holocaust and started life all over.

Family Beginnings Before My Birth	Important Beginnings for Me A Death, Move, Job, Relationship, Health, Goal/Dream, etc.	Probable Beginnings Ahead

Identify important beginnings for you, and probable beginnings ahead. Compare this time line with your loss time line. What patterns do you see? For example, do you jump right into a new relationship or job to avoid confronting pain or conflict from a loss? Do you allow yourself transition time between the old and the new? Do you wallow on and on in the old before you ever risk anything new? What do you learn about yourself from both time lines?

Do you want to follow those same patterns, or to compose something new?

8.3 Redefining Self by "Relating" with the Loss

Refer to chapter 8's list of music that portrays a conversation from the singer to the deceased. Listen to any of the pieces of music, or another example. Simply, the song is being sung to the person (or thing) that has been lost. What lyrics connect for you? What emotions and thoughts are stirred? Pair your responses with various discussions throughout this book about the importance of continuing to explore what the loss means to you, instead of simply cutting it off and moving on. Do you experience any "aha" moments or insights regarding your grief journey?

You can be your own composer or lyricist: "If you could say something to someone or something you have lost, what would it be?" Let your imagination flow freely. Write your words. You may want to write in some expressive musical symbols, like *sfz* for a strong accent, or *dolce* for sweetly, or *pp* for softly.

What would you want to hear back? What would you likely hear back?

Write your dialogue. You may want to put it to music, in some type of vocal soliloquy or duet. You may prefer an instrumental piece that conveys for your messages. Creating literal music is a powerful mode for expressing your deeper self. It can be an intimate way to work through your questions, your inner dissonances and harmonies within. With or without a literal music setting, its transforming qualities for you are in voicing what matters to you.

8.4 Your Audio Diary

Like Jerry's audio diary, you too can create your own simplified version, in various ways. The main objective is to gather various moments, memories, and meanings of your grief journey, itself. Reflect on where you have been, where you are now, and what you want to move toward. This is especially beneficial if you are nearing an anniversary of the loss, or another significant life event that stirs emotions and memories of your loss (like a wedding, graduation, et al).

a. Collect various pieces of music that have been significant to you through this grief journey. For example, include:

- Music from before the loss but associated with the person or that part of your life
- Music associated with the loss itself (such as music from a funeral)
- Music from throughout your mourning, such as sorrow, gratitude, fear, or hope.

The music might be recordings you hear or scores you play. It might be music you have composed. Whatever it is, compile it through lists of titles, scores that you readily revisit, or through burning a personal CD or loading your IPod with your selections sequenced. (Adhere to copyright laws.) Add photos or videos and make a video or DVD. Personalize your creation. It is personal. It is your creation.

b. For variation, imagine that you are a country music writer. The lyrics and title say it all. Create a time line about your loss, similar to your time lines at teaching guides 1.2 and 8.2. Identify significant moments throughout your loss and healing. Give these moments titles, as if they were country music ballads. (Or, choose another style.) You are the storyteller. Here is your chance to infuse unabashed sorrow, sap, and humor. You do not have to actually write music, just the titles. Let your emotions and thoughts roll. Open yourself to free exploration.

c. Share your music with someone who understands you and your paths through grief, or someone who might understand you better through your music. In doing so, you are creating a ritual. You are validating where you have been and clearing a path for new growth ahead.

8.5 Back and Forth — Mourning and Morning

This exercise follows up teaching guide "2.6 There Is a Time." This is similar, though more focused on the back and forth motion between "mourning" and "morning." Draw a line down the center of a piece of paper. On the top left side write "Mourning" and on the right write "Morning." In the left column, brainstorm as many adjectives as you can for the "Mourning" part of your experience. Do the same in the right column for "Morning."

With a basic drum, beat an ongoing 3/4 pattern: **1** – 2 – 3 - | **1** – 2 – 3 - | **1** – 2 – 3 - | **1** – 2 – 3. If you are in a group, have others beat as well, using drums or simply clapping. Start on your right side. Alternate from right to left to right to left at each measure (**1** – 2 – 3 -); or you can lean back and forward and back forward. Simply, you are rocking back and forth.

When the beat and movement are steady, read your list together, alternating back and forth between a "mourning" and "morning" adjective. Say each new word or phrase on beat 1.

Note: the list of words probably will not pair together nicely and neatly as in "2.6 There Is a Time." However, that too is indicative of real life grief. We move in and out, back and forth, and all around. Use your energy, voice, and body language to set an inviting, creative tone, and to guide the group through the exercise. At its conclusion, reflect with the group on new insights they experienced through the exercise.

8.6 Identify Your Music of Morning/Beginning

Numerous pieces of music are listed that indicate some kind of morning, or beginning. What music does the same for you?

You might pull out a catalyst question from chapter 3: "What music are you listening to these days?" At a subconscious level, you may be drawn to music that calls you toward a deeper meaning or a direction to be heading toward. What, within yourself, is drawn to that same song, over and over again?

What music from earlier "seasons" in my loss might I pull out now, and hear in my newer context, today? Through what have I come? Where am I now, and where can I go? Where do I want to go? What do I need to get there?

8.7 Make Music

You are the musician. Whatever your musical ability, carve out moments or larger time frames in your day or week to sing, play, move or dance to, or compose your own music.

- Listen to, sing, play, or move to any music in this chapter, "Composing Life Out of Loss." Tune into your responses and journal your reflections.

- Identify additional music related to any concepts in this chapter. Listen to, sing, or play it. Tune into and journal your reflections.
- Create your own music: vocal or instrumental. Write it down, whatever your music notation skills may be.
- Share your music and reflections with another.

Notes

Chapter 1
1. A *fermata* is the musical term for holding a note or chord for longer than the notated beat(s).
2. Pronounced *fee-nay*. The Italian musical term for the finish, the end, the completion. Or, with a double meaning, the English term *fine*, meaning excellent; of quality or worth.

Chapter 2
1. Adapted from Ecclesiastes 3 by Joy Berger, Louisville, Kentucky, 1994 to present; personalized for hospice funerals and memorial services (see teaching guide 2.6, 2.7)

Chapter 3
1. The theme and variation is a common musical form, in which the main theme is varied in numerous ways, for example, melodically, rhythmically, harmonically, while maintaining its main characteristics. A well-known example is Pachelbel's "Canon in D Major."
2. Amyotrophic lateral sclerosis (ALS), often referred to as "Lou Gehrig's disease," is a progressive neurodegenerative disease that attacks nerve cells in the brain and the spinal cord. For more information, visit http://www.alsa.org.
3. A fugue is a contrapuntal composition in which a short melody (theme) is introduced and taken up by others. A second melody (countertheme) is usually introduced and the two interplay throughout the composition, in polyphonic texture, using techniques of imitation, inversion, and tonal changes.
4. "Sonata," from "sonare" meaning "to sound," is a classical music form for one or more solo instruments (i.e., piano, violin and piano, flute and piano), usually in several movements. The first movement is often referred to as "sonata form," with three main sections: Exposition, Development, and Recapitulation. This same form is often used for the first movement of the classical symphony.
5. "Symphony" meaning "sounding together." As a classical music form, a symphony is an orchestral work in multiple movements. The first movement is typically in the standard sonata form of Exposition, Development, and Recapitulation.

6. The Q-chord is a portable, battery operated instrument often used in music therapy. It can be compared to the autoharp, yet with a variety of sounds, rhythmic accompaniments, and cartridges with prerecorded songs. It has a small, easily responsive pad for strumming, and is conducive for stimulating interaction, especially with elderly adults and children.

Chapter 4

1. Serenity prayer, "God grant me the serenity to accept the things I cannot change, the courage to change those I can, and the wisdom to know the difference" (Reinhold Niebuhr).

Chapter 6

1. *ppp:* pianississimo, extremely soft; *pp:* pianissimo, very soft; *p:* piano, soft; *mp:* mezzo piano, moderately soft; *mf:* mezzo forte, moderately loud; *f:* forte, loud; *ff:* fortissimo, very loud; *fff:* fortississimo, extremely loud; *crescendo* < : increasing in volume; *diminuendo* > : decreasing in volume; *largo:* extremely slow; *adagio:* slow; *andante:* walking speed; *allegro:* fast, lively; *presto:* extremely fast; *accelerando:* speeding up; *ritardando:* slowing down; *legato:* smooth; *staccato:* short and sharp, not smooth; *dolce:* sweetly, soothing; *furioso:* with fury; *sfz:* a sudden attack or sharp accent; *soli:* by oneself, the soloist, solitude; *tutti:* together, in orchestration with others.
2. "Peace," in English, Hebrew, Farsi, Hindu, Korean, Afrikaans, Lakota, Vietnamese, Bosnian, French, Paul McCartney's lyrics for baby boomers, and music's fermata.

Chapter 7

1. Translation from CD liner notes: "Thus nature, ever kind, rewards the pains of virtuous toil." Oratorio for three solo voices, chorus and orchestra (Haydn & Gardiner, 1992).

Chapter 8

1. An intermezzo is a shorter piece played between two larger works. It usually functions as a reflective pause.

Books and Articles

Aasgarrd, T. (1999). Music therapy as milieu in the hospice and paediatric oncology ward. In D. Aldridge (Ed.), *Music therapy in palliative care: New voices* (pp. 29–42). Philadelphia: Jessica Kingsley.

Albom, M. (1997). *Tuesdays with Morrie: An old man, a young man, and life's greatest lesson.* New York: Broadway.

Aldridge, D. (Ed.). (1999). *Music therapy in palliative care: New voices.* Philadelphia: Jessica Kingsley.

Aldridge, D. (Ed.). (2000). *Music therapy in dementia care.* Philadelphia: Jessica Kingsley.

Altilio, T. (2002). Helping children, helping ourselves: An overview of children's literature. In J. V. Loewy & A. F. Hara (Eds.). (2002). *Caring for the caregiver: The use of music and music therapy in grief and trauma* (pp. 138–147). Silver Spring, MD: American Music Therapy Association.

Amir, Dorit. (2004). Giving trauma a voice: The role of improvisational music therapy in exposing, dealing with and healing a traumatic experience of sexual abuse. *Music Therapy Perspectives, 22*(2), 96–103.

Angelou, Maya. (1997). *Gather together in my name.* New York: Bantam. (Original work published 1974)

Ashida, S. (1999). The effect of reminiscence music therapy sessions on changes in depressive symptoms in elderly persons with dementia. *Journal of Music Therapy, 37*(3), 170–182.

Associated Press. (2005, September 5). Stars offer heartfelt performances in benefit: Aaron Neville, Harry Connick, Faith Hill sing to help raise fund for victims. Retrieved December 26, 2005 from http://www.msnbc.msn.com/id/9146525/

Attig, T. (1996). *How we grieve: Relearning the world.* New York: Oxford University Press.

Attig, T. (2001). Relearning the world: Making and finding meanings. In R. A. Neimeyer (Ed.), *Meaning reconstruction and the experience of loss* (pp. 33–53). Washington, D.C.: American Psychological Association.

Benoit, T. (2003). *Where are they buried? How did they die?* New York: Black Dog & Leventhal.

Berger, J. S. (1993). Music as a catalyst for pastoral care within the remembering tasks of grief. Ann Arbor, Michigan: ProQuest / University Microfilms (Publication No. 9406295)

227

Berger, J. S. (2003). Music for your practice. *Home Healthcare Nurse, 21*(1), 25–30.

Bertman, S. (Ed.). (1999). *Grief and the healing arts: Creativity as therapy.* Amityville, NY: Baywood.

Bonny, H. (2001). Music and spirituality. *Music Therapy Perspectives 19*(1), 59–62.

Bonny, H., & Savary, L. M. (1973). *Music and your mind: Listening with a new consciousness.* New York: Harper & Row.

Bonny, H., & Summer, L. (Eds.). (2002). *Music consciousness: The evolution of guided imagery and music.* Gilsum, NH: Pathway Book Service.

Bowlby, J. (1980). *Attachment and loss: Vol. 3. Loss: Sadness and depression.* New York: Basic Books.

Bridges, W. (2001). *The way of transition: Embracing life's most difficult moments.* New York: Perseus.

Bridges, W. (2003). *Transitions: Making sense of life's changes.* New York: Perseus. (Original work published 1980)

Bright, R. (1986). *A handbook for those who care.* St. Louis, MO: MMB Music.

Bright, R. (2002). *Supportive eclectic music therapy for grief and loss: A practical handbook for professionals.* St. Louis, MO: MMB Music.

Brookes, D. (2002). A history of music therapy journal articles published in the English language. *Journal of Music Therapy, 40*(2), 151–168.

Brotons, M., & Koger, S. M. (1999). The impact of music therapy on language functioning in dementia. *Journal of Music Therapy, 37*(3), 183–195.

Burnett, F. H. (1998). *The secret garden.* New York: HarperCollins. (Original work published 1911)

Burns, D. S. (2000). The effect of the Bonny method of guided imagery and music on the mood and life quality of cancer patients. *Journal of Music Therapy, 38*(1), 51–65.

Burns, J. L., Labbé, E., Arke, B., Capeless, K., Cooksey, B., Steadman, A., & Gonzaels, C. (2001). The effects of different types of music on perceived and physiological measures of stress. *Journal of Music Therapy, 39*(2), 101–116.

Byock, I. (1997). *Dying well: Peace and possibilities at the end of life.* New York: Riverhead.

Byock, I. (1998). Measuring quality of life for patients with terminal illness: The Missoula-VITAS quality of life index (MVQOLI), *Palliative Medicine, 12,* 231–244.

Byock, I. (2004). *The four things that matter most: A book about living.* New York: Free Press.

Calhoun, L. G., & Tedeschi, R. G. (2001). Posttraumatic growth: The positive lessons of loss. In R. A. Neimeyer (Ed.), *Meaning reconstruction and the experience of loss* (pp. 157–172). Washington, D.C.: American Psychological Association.

Callanan, M., & Kelley, P. (1997) *Final gifts: Understanding the special awareness, needs, and communications of the dying.* New York: Bantam Books. (Original work published 1992)

Charno, J. (Ex. Producer). (1998). *Dancing with the dead: The music of global death rites* [CD & book]. Roslyn, NY: Ellipsis Arts.

Chase, K. M. (2003). Multicultural music therapy: A review of literature. *Music Therapy Perspectives, 21*(2), 84–88.

CNN.com. (2005). Rosa Parks' funeral, Pakistan quake toll, Nov. 3, 2005. In *CNN.com. Education with Student News.* Retrieved December 18, 2005, from http://www.cnn.com/2005/EDUCATION/11/02/transcript.thu/index.html#first

Corr, C. A. (1991). A task-based approach to coping with dying. *Omega — Journal of Death and Dying, 24*(2), 81–94.

Corr, C. A. (Ed.). (2004). Death related literature for children [Special issue]. *Omega, Journal of Death and Dying, 48*(4).

Crofton, I., & Fraser, D. (1985). *A dictionary of music quotations.* New York: Schirmer Books.

Daveson, B. A., & Kennelly, J. (2000). Music therapy in palliative care for hospitalized children and adolescents. *Journal of Palliative Care, 16*(1), 35–38.

Davis, C. G. (2001). The tormented and the transformed: Understanding responses to loss and trauma. In R. A. Neimeyer (Ed.), *Meaning reconstruction and the experience of loss* (pp. 137–155). Washington, D.C.: American Psychological Association.

Davis, C. G., & Lehman, D. R. (1995). Counterfactual thinking and coping with traumatic life events. In N. J. Roese & J. M. Olson (Eds.), *What might have been: The social psychology of counterfactual thinking* (pp. 353–374). Mahwah, NJ: Erlbaum.

Davis, C. G., Lehman, D. R., Wortman, C. B., Silver, R. C., & Thompson, S. C. (1995). The undoing of traumatic life events. *Personality and Social Psychology Bulletin, 21,* 109–124.

Davis, M. Retrieved December 18, 2005, from http://www.quotationspage.com/quotes/ Miles_Davis.

Diallo, Y. (1989). *The healing drum: African wisdom teachings.* Rochester, VT: Destiny Books.

Doka, K. J. (Ed.). (1995). *Children mourning, mourning children.* Washington, D.C.: Hospice Foundation of America.

Doka, K. J. (Ed.). (2002). *Disenfranchised grief: New directions, challenges, and strategies for practice.* Champaign, IL: Research Press.

Doka, K. J. (Ed.). (2003). *Living with grief: Children, adolescents, and loss.* Washington, D.C.: Hospice Foundation of America.

Dunn, B. (1999). Creativity and communication aspects of music therapy in a children's hospital. In D. Aldridge (Ed.), *Music therapy in palliative care: New voices* (pp. 59–67). Philadelphia: Jessica Kingsley.

Dyck, H. (n.d.). Consort Caritatas to raise funds for HIV/AIDS projects in Africa. In *Brahms requiem.* Retrieved December 18, 2005 from http://www.consort-caritatis.ca/brahms. htm

Einstein, A. (1941). *Greatness in music.* New York: Oxford University Press.

Einstein, A. (1969). *A short history of music.* (Rev. ed.). New York: Alfred A. Knopf. (Original work published 1917)

Encarta. (2005, December). Gestalt therapy. In *MSN Encarta — Psychotherapy.* Retrieved December 22, 2005, from http://encarta.msn.com/encyclopedia_761563630_4/Psychotherapy.html

Estés, C. P. (1995). *Women who run with the wolves: Myths and stories of the wild woman archetype.* New York: Ballantine.

Exley, H. (Ed.). (1992). *Music lovers quotations.* Watford, UK: Exley.

Figley, C. R. (Ed.). (1995). *Compassion fatigue: Coping with secondary traumatic stress disorders in those who treat the traumatized.* Levittown, PA: Brunner/Mazel.

Figley, C. R. (Ed.). (2002). *Treating compassion fatigue.* New York: Brunner-Routledge.

Frankl, V. E. (1963). *Man's search for meaning: An introduction to logotherapy* (I. Lasch, Trans.). New York: Washington Square Press. (Original work published 1946)

Frantz, T. T., Farrell, M. M., & Trolley, B. C. (2001). Positive outcomes of losing a loved one. In R. A. Neimeyer (Ed.), *Meaning reconstruction and the experience of loss* (pp. 191–209). Washington, D.C.: American Psychological Association.

Gaffney, D. (2002). Seasons of grief: Helping children grow through grief. In J. V. Loewy & A. F. Hara (Eds.), *Caring for the caregiver: The use of music and music therapy in grief and trauma* (pp. 54–62). Silver Spring, MD: The American Music Therapy Association.

Golden, T. (1999). Healing and the Internet. In S. L. Bertman (Ed.), *Grief and the healing arts: Creativity as therapy* (pp. 343–348). Amityville, NY: Baywood.

Goldman, A., Hain, R., & Liben, S. (Eds.). (2006). *Oxford textbook of pediatric palliative care.* Oxford: Oxford University Press.

Goldman, L. S., Myers, M., & Dickstein, L. J. (Eds.). (2002). *The handbook of physician health: The essential guide to understanding the health care needs of physicians.* Chicago: American Medical Association.

Goleman, D. (1995). *Emotional intelligence: Why it matters more than IQ.* New York: Bantam.

Goleman, D., McKee, A., & Boyatzis, R. E. (2002). *Primal leadership: Realizing the power of emotional intelligence.* Boston: Harvard Business School Press.

Goss, R. A., & Klass, D. (2005). *Dead but not lost: Grief narratives in religious traditions.* Walnut Creek, CA: AltaMira Press.

Greene, M. (1999). Michael Greene, President & CEO of NARAS — 1999 Grammy Awards. On *Quotes about music therapy*. Retrieved December 18, 2005 from http://www.music-therapy.org/quotes.html

Hagman, G. (2001). Beyond decathexis: Toward a new psychoanalytic understanding and treatment of mourning. In R. A. Neimeyer (Ed.), *Meaning reconstruction and the experience of loss* (pp. 13–31). Washington, D.C.: American Psychological Association.

Hall, M. P. (1982). *The therapeutic value of music including the philosophy of music.* Los Angeles: Philosophical Research Society.

Hartley, N. A. (2001). On a personal note: A music therapist's reflections on working with those who are living with a terminal illness. *Journal of Palliative Care, 17*(3), 135–141.

Harvey, J. H. (1996). *Embracing their memory: Loss and the social psychology of story-telling.* Needham Heights, MA: Allyn & Bacon.

Harvey, J. H. (2000). *Give sorrow words: Perspectives on loss and trauma.* Philadelphia: Brunner/Routledge.

Harvey, J. H., Carlson, H. R., Huff, T. M., & Green, M. A. (2001). Embracing their memory: The construction of accounts of loss and hope. In R. A. Neimeyer (Ed.), *Meaning reconstruction and the experience of loss* (pp. 231–243). Washington, D.C.: American Psychological Association.

Heitzman, J. C. (2005). Survival songs: How refugees and immigrant women experienced violence. Ann Arbor, Michigan: ProQuest Digital Dissertations. (Publication No. AAT 3172277)

Hesser, B. (2001). The transformative power of music in our lives: A personal perspective. *Music Therapy Perspectives, 19*(1), 53–58.

Hilliard, R. E. (2001). The use of music therapy in meeting the multidimensional needs of hospice patients and families. *Journal of Palliative Care, 17*(3), 161–166.

Hilliard, R. E. (2002). The effects of music therapy on the quality and length of life of people diagnosed with terminal cancer. *Journal of Music Therapy, 40*(2), 113–137.

Hiltner, S. (1958). *Preface to pastoral theology.* New York: Abingdon Press.

Hip Online. (2005). Biography Heavy D. *Hip online: artists: heavy d.* Retrieved December 18, 2005 from http://www.hiponline.com/artist/music/h/heavy_d/

Irish, D. P., & Lundquist, K. F. (2003). *Ethnic variations in dying, death and grief: Diversity in universality.* Philadelphia: Taylor & Francis.

Iwaki, T., Tanaka, H., & Hori, T. (2002). The effects of preferred familiar music on falling asleep. *Journal of Music Therapy, 40*(1), 15–26.

Jensen, K. L. (2000). The effects of selected classical music on self-disclosure. *Journal of Music Therapy, 38*(1), 2–27.

Juan, A. (2005, September 12). Requiem. *The New Yorker* [front cover].

Jung, C., & Adler, G. (1991). *The archetypes and the collective unconscious* (2nd ed., R. F. Hull, Trans.). New York: Routledge. (Original work published 1981)

Kane, L. (2005). *Lennon revealed.* Philadelphia: Running Press. (book and DVD)

Knights, W. E. J., & Rickard, N. S. (2000). Relaxing music prevents stress-induced increases in subjective anxiety, systolic blood pressure, and heart rate in healthy males and females. *Journal of Music Therapy, 38*(4), 254–272.

Koger, S., Chapin, K., & Brotons, M. (1998). Is music therapy an effective intervention for dementia? A meta-analytic review of literature. *Journal of Music Therapy, 36*(1), 2–15.

Krout, R. E. (2003). Music therapy with imminently dying hospice patients and their families: Facilitating release near the time of death. *American Journal of Hospice and Palliative Care, 20*(2), 129–134.

Kübler-Ross, E. (1969). *On death and dying.* New York: Macmillan.

Kuebler, K. K., Davis, M. P., & Moore, C. D. (2005). *Palliative practices: An interdisciplinary approach.* St. Louis, MO: Elsevier Mosby.

Lattanzi-Licht, M., & Doka, K. J. (Eds.). (2003). *Living with grief: Coping with public tragedy.* Washington, D.C.: The Hospice Foundation of America.

Lewis, C. R., Vedia, A. D., Reuer, B., Schwan, R., & Tourin, C. (2003). Integrating comple-mentary and alternative medicine (CAM) into standard hospice and palliative care. *American Journal of Hospice & Palliative Care, 20*(3), 221–228.

Lipe, A. W. (2001). Beyond therapy: Music, spirituality, and health in human experience: A review of literature. *Journal of Music Therapy, 39*(3), 209–240.

Loehr J., & Schwartz, T. (2003). *The power of full engagement: Managing energy, not time, is the key to high performance and personal renewal.* New York: Free Press.

Loewy, J. V., & Hara, A. F. (Eds.). (2002). *Caring for the caregiver: The use of music and music ther-apy in grief and trauma.* Silver Spring, MD: The American Music Therapy Association.

Magill, L. L. (1993). Music therapy in pain and symptom management. *Journal of Palliative Care, 9*(4), 42–48.

Marshman, A. T. (2003). The power of music: A Jungian aesthetic. *Music Therapy Perspec-tives, 21*(1), 21–26.

Mauk, L. (Ed.). (1995). *The essence of music — An ensemble of musical quotes.* Glendale Heights, IL: Great Quotations.

Metzger, L. K. (2004). Assessment of use of music by patients participating in cardiac reha-bilitation. *Journal of Music Therapy, 41*(1), 55–69.

Miller, S., & Ober, D. (2002). *Finding hope when a child dies: What other cultures can teach us.* New York: Fireside.

Minear, P. S. (1987). *Death set to music: Masterworks by Bach, Brahms, Penderecki, Bernstein.* Atlanta, GA: John Knox Press.

Moore, T. (1994). *Care of the soul: A guide for cultivating depth and sacredness in everyday life.* New York: Harper Perennial.

Morgenstern, S. (Ed.). (1959). *Composers on music: An anthology of composers' writings from Palestrina to Copeland.* New York: Pantheon. (Original work published 1956)

Nadeau, J. W. (1998). *Families making sense of death.* Thousand Oaks, CA: Sage.

Nadeau, J. W. (2001). Family construction of meaning. In R. A. Neimeyer (Ed.), *Meaning reconstruction and the experience of loss* (pp. 95–111). Washington, D.C.: American Psychological Association.

Neimeyer, R. A. (Ed.). (2001). *Meaning reconstruction and the experience of loss.* Washington, D.C.: American Psychological Association.

Nichols, T., & Wiseman, C (2004). *Live like you were dying.* [Book with CD]. Recorded by Tim McGraw. Nashville, TN: Rutledge Hill Press [Book] and Curb Records [CD single].

Nicholson, K. (2001). Weaving a circle: a relaxation program using imagery and music. *Journal of Palliative Care 17*(3), 173–176.

NOJO. (2005). TheNOJO.com —The official website of the New Orleans Jazz Orchestra. Retrieved November 19, 2005, from http://www.thenojo.com/saints.html

O'Callaghan, C. (1999). Recent findings about neural correlates of music pertinent to music therapy across the lifespan. *Music Therapy Perspectives 17*(1), 32–36.

Pacholski, R. A. (1986). Death themes in music: Resources and research opportunities for death educators. *Death Studies, 10*(3), 239–263.

Parkes, C. M. (1987). *Bereavement: Studies of grief in adult life* (2nd ed.). Madison, CT: International Universities Press. (Original work published 1972)

Parkes, C. M. (2001). *Bereavement: Studies of grief in adult life* (3rd ed.). Philadelphia: Taylor & Francis Inc. (Original work published 1972)

Parkes, C. M. (2002). Grief: Lessons from the past, vision for the future. *Death Studies, 26,* 367–385.

Parkes, C. M., & Markus, A. (Eds.). (1998). *Coping with loss: Helping patients and their families.* London: BMG.

Pearsall, P. (1998). *The heart's code: Tapping the wisdom and power of our heart energy.* New York: Broadway.

Randel, D. (Ed.). (1986). *The Harvard dictionary of music.* Cambridge, MA.: Belknap Press/ Harvard University Press.

Rando, T. (1993). *Treatment of complicated mourning.* Champaign, IL: Research Press.

Reagon, B. J. (Ed.). (1992). *We'll understand it better by and by: Pioneering African-American gospel composers.* Washington, D.C.: Smithsonian Institution Press.

Reagon, B. J. (1993). *We who believe in freedom will not rest — Sweet Honey In the Rock — Still on the journey.* New York: Anchor Books/ Doubleday. [Book & CD]

Reel Classics. (2005). The Pride of the Yankees. In *Reel Classics: The classic movie site.* Retrieved February 16, 2006, from http://www.reelclassics.com/Movies/Yankees/yankees.htm

Reuters. (2005, October 19). New Orleans Café du Monde and its beignets are back. On *Reuters AlertNet Foundation: Alerting humanitarians to emergencies.* Retrieved Oct. 22, 2005, from http://www.alertnet.org/thenews/newsdesk/N19543098.htm

Rigazio-Diglio, S. A. (2001). Videography: Re-storying the lives of clients facing terminal illness. In R. A. Neimeyer (Ed.), *Meaning reconstruction and the experience of loss* (pp. 331–343). Washington, D.C.: American Psychological Association.

Rorke, M. A. (2000). Music therapy in the age of enlightenment. *Journal of Music Therapy, 38*(1), 66–73.

Rowatt, G. W. (1989). *Pastoral care with adolescents in crisis.* Louisville, KY: Westminster/John Knox Press.

Rykov, M., & Salmon, D. (1998). Bibliography for music therapy in palliative care, 1963–1997. *The American Journal of Hospice & Palliative Care, 15*(3), 174–180.

Salmon, D. (2001). Music therapy as psychospiritual process in palliative care. *Journal of Palliative Care, 17*(3), 142–146.

Shinano Mainichi Shimbun Newspaper. (1998). Excitement arises among Olympic singers around the globe. On *Olympic Winter Games, NAGANO, February 6, 1998.* Retrieved December 18, 2005 from http://www.shinmai.co.jp/oly-eng/19980206/0005.htm

Shuster, Y. (2005, November 17). Fund-raising concert raises, draws thousands: Event held to raise money for Victims of Pakistan Quake. In Columbia Spectator — online edition. Retrieved November 19, 2005 from http://www.columbiaspectator.com/vnews/display.v/ART/2005/11/17/437c44e5d2c89

Small, C. (1996). *Music, society, education.* Middletown, CT: Wesleyan University Press. (Original work published 1977)

Smeijsters, H., & Hurk, J. van den. (1998). Music therapy helping to work through grief and finding a personal identity. *Journal of Music Therapy, 36*(3), 222–252.

Smith, P. (2004, September 1). Slain refugee's spirit and ambition recalled at service. *The Courier Journal,* p. B1.

Standley, J. M. (1991). *Music techniques in therapy, counseling and special education.* St. Louis, MO: MMB Music.

Starr, R. J. (1999). Music therapy in hospice care. *American Journal of Hospice and Palliative Care, 16*(6), 739–742.

Stokes, J. A. (2004). *Then, now and always — Supporting children as they journey through grief: A guide for practitioners.* Cheltenham, UK: Winston's Wish.

Stroebe, M. S., & Schut, H. (2001). Meaning making in the dual process model of coping with bereavement. In R. A. Neimeyer (Ed.), *Meaning reconstruction and the experience of loss* (pp. 55–73). Washington, D.C.: American Psychological Association.

Swamp, Chief Jake, & Printup, E. (Illust.). (1995). *Giving thanks: A Native American good morning message (A Rainbow reading book).* New York: Lee & Low Books.

Tagore, R. (1997). *Gitanjali: A collection of Indian poems by the Nobel Laureate* (p. 69). Mineola, NY: Dover Thrift Edition. (Original work published 1911)

Tedeschi, R. G., & Calhoun, L. G. (1995). *Trauma and transformation: Growing in the aftermath of suffering.* Thousand Oaks, CA: Sage.

Valent, P. (1995). Survival strategies: A framework for understanding secondary traumatic stress and coping in helpers. In C. R. Figley (Ed.), *Compassion fatigue: Coping with secondary traumatic stress disorders in those who treat the traumatized* (pp. 21–50). Levittown, PA: Brunner/Mazel.

Vink, A., & Enschede, H. (2000). The problem of agitation in elderly people and the potential benefit of music therapy. In Aldridge, D. (Ed.), *Music therapy in dementia care* (pp. 102–118). Philadelphia: Jessica Kingsley.

Waldon, E. G. (2000). The effects of group music therapy on mood states and cohesiveness in adult oncology patients. *Journal of Music Therapy, 38*(3), 212–238.

Walworth, D. D. (2002). The effect of preferred music genre selection versus preferred song selection on experimentally induced anxiety levels. *Journal of Music Therapy, 40*(1), 2–14.

Webster's third new international dictionary of the English language unabridged. (1976). Springfield, MA: G. & C. Merriam.

Wheeler, B. (Ed.). (2005). *Music therapy research* (2nd ed.). Gilsum, NH: Barcelona. (Original work published 1995)

Whipple, J., & Lindsey, R. S. (1999). Music for the soul: A music therapy program for battered women. *Music Therapy Perspectives, 17*(2), 61–68.

Worden, J. W. (1991). *Grief counseling and grief therapy: A handbook for the mental health practitioner* (2nd ed.). New York: Springer.

Worden, J. W. (1996). *Children and grief: When a parent dies.* New York: Guilford.

Worden, J. W. (2002). *Grief counseling and grief therapy: A handbook for the mental health practitioner* (3rd ed.). New York: Springer.

Scores, Recordings, and Videos

Afanasief, W., & Crokaert, L. (Lyrics), & Foster, D. (Music). (2002). Broken vow [Recorded by Josh Grobin]. On *Josh Groban in concert* [DVD]. United States: Reprise Records, Warner Music Group.

Anka, P. (1969). My way [Recorded by Frank Sinatra]. On *My way* [Album]. United States: Warner Brothers (CD release 1990).

Arato, T. (Words & music), Miller, J. S. (Director), & Ball, M. (Producer) (1991). The dance [Recorded by Garth Brooks]. On *Garth Brooks* [VHS]. Hollywood, CA: Liberty Records.

Armstrong, L. (2004). *Louis Armstrong* [CD]. St. Laurent, Canada: Madacy Entertainment Group. (Original recording, no date)

Bach, J. S. (Music) & Tureck, R. (1960). *An Introductions to the Performance of Bach.* London: Oxford University Press. (Original work 1725).

Bachelor, M. (Words) & Bliss, P. P. (Music). (1940). Go bury thy sorrow. In *The Broadman Hymnal.* Nashville, TN: The Broadman Press.

Barber, S. (Music) & Slatkin, L. (Conductor). (1989). *Music of Samuel Barber* [CD]. United States: Capitol Records.

Beethoven, L. V. (Music) & Bernstein, L. (Conductor). (1989). *Ode to freedom: Bernstein in Berlin, Beethoven Symphony No. 9 in D minor, Opus 125* [VHS & CD]. (1990) Hamburg, Germany: Deutsche Grammophon.

Before their TIME [CDs and liner notes]. (Vol. 1, 1999, Vol. 2, 2002, Vol. 3, 2004). Various artists. NH: Before Their Time.

Berger, J. S. (1999). *Life music: Rhythms of loss and hope* [VHS]. Cleveland, OH: American Orff-Schulwerk Association.

Berlin, I. (1912). When I lost you. New York: Waterson, Berlin & Snyder.

Berlin, I. (1984). Always. In *150 of the most beautiful songs ever* (3rd ed.). Milwaukee, WI: Hal Leonard. (Original song published 1925).

Bernstein, L. (Music), & Sondheim, S. (Lyrics). (1957). Somewhere. From *West side story.* United States: Amberson Holdings LLC and Stephen Sondheim.

Boubil, A., & Schonberg, C. M. (1989). *Les misérables: 1987 original Broadway cast* [CD]. United States: Decca U.S.

Brahms, J. (Music) & Mandyczewki, E. (Ed.). (1971). Intermezzo in A major, Op. 118, No.2. In *Johannes Brahms — Complete Shorter Works for Solo Piano* (pp. 143–146). New York: Dover Publications. (Original work 1893).

Charles, R., & Jones, Q. et al. (2002). *Ray Charles sings for America* [CD]. Los Angeles: Rhino Records.

Charno, J. (Ex. Producer). (1998). *Dancing with the dead: The music of global death rites* [CD & book]. Roslyn, NY: Ellipsis Arts.

Clapton, E. (1992). Tears in heaven. On *Unplugged* [CD]. United States: Warner Brothers.

Columbus, C. (Director) & Larson, J. (Music and Lyrics). (2005). *Rent* [DVD]. Culver City, CA: Sony Pictures.

Dorsey, T. (1981). Precious Lord, take my hand. In *Songs of Zion*, W. B. McClain (Ed.). Nashville, TN: Abingdon Press. (Original text written 1932)

Ephron, N. (Director). (1993). *Sleepless in Seattle* [VHS]. United States: Columbia/Tristar.

Floyd, P. (2000a). Wish you were here. On *Wish you were here* [Remastered CD]. United States: Capitol. (Original work recorded 1975)

Floyd, P. (2000b). Shine on you crazy diamond. On *Wish you were here* [Remastered CD]. United States: Capitol. (Original work recorded 1975)

Frye, R. E. (Director), Davidson, C. (Music), Litton, J. (Conductor), & Children of Terezin Jewish Ghetto (Words & Art, 1941–1945). (1996). *The journey of the butterfly* [VCR]. New York: Bolthead Communications Group, Ltd.

Grosvenor, C. (Director), Tavera M. (Music), & Brourman, M. & McBroom, A. (Song). (1997). Always there. On *The land before time — V — The mysterious island* [VCR/DVD]. United States: Universal Studios Home Video.

Haydn, J. (Composer) & Gardiner, J. E. (Conductor). (1992). So Lohnet die Natur den Fleiss, from "Der Herbst" (Autumn), from *Die Jahreszeiten (The seasons)* [CD]. Hamburg, Germany: Deutsche Grammophon.

Heavy, D. & The Boys. (1999). Ask heaven. On *Heavy* [CD]. United States: Universal.

Holler, D. (1968). Abraham, Martin and John [Recorded by Ray Charles]. On *Ray Charles sings for America* [CD]. Los Angeles: Rhino Records. (2002).

Horner, J. (Music) & Jennings, W. (Lyrics). (1997). My heart will go on. [Recorded by Celine Dion]. On *Titanic Music from the motion picture* [CD]. United State: Sony.

Horner, J., & Sweet Honey in The Rock. (2000). *Freedom song — Soundtrack.* United States: Sony. (Original TV video available on VHS)

Hurwitz, R., & Bither, D. (Executive Producers). (2005). *Our New Orleans 2005.* New York: Nonesuch Records.

Jernigan, D. (2000). I'm so glad you came. On *Worshiper's collection*, Vol. 4 [CD]. Nashville, TN: Here to Him Music. (Originally recorded on *No life is too small* [CD])

Joel, B. (2001). *Billy Joel — The essential video collection.* [VCR & DVD]. United States: Sony/Legacy.

Johnson, J. W. (Words) & Johnson, J. R. (Music). (1900). Lift every voice and sing [Recorded by The Boys Choir of Harlem]. On *The boys choir of Harlem sings hope and inspiration: We shall overcome* [CD]. (2002). United States: Tantivy Entertainment.

Judd, W. (1992). No one else on earth. On *Wynona* [CD]. Nashville, TN: Curb Records.

Larson, J. (Words & Music). (2005). *Rent* (2005 Movie Soundtrack) [CD]. United States: Warner Brothers, (Original, Broadway Cast, 1999)

Lennon, J., & McCartney, P. (1967). Strawberry fields. On *Magical mystery tour* [LP] [Recorded by The Beatles]. United States: Capitol Records.

Lerner, A. J. (Lyrics), & Lowe, F. (Music). (1998). Wouldn't it be loverly. On *My fair lady* [DVD]. United States: Warner Studios. (Broadway premiere 1956. Movie 1964)

Loggins, K. (2000). Always, in all ways. On *More songs from Pooh Corner* [CD]. United States: Sony.

Lorber, S., Harris, S., & Colucci, J. (1992) No one else on earth [Recorded by Wynona Judd]. On *Wynona* [CD]. Universal City, CA: Curb Music Company / MCA Records.

Lowry, R. (Words & Music). (1990). Shall we gather at the river. In *The worshiping church: A hymnal.* Carol Stream, IL: Hope Publishing. (Original words & music written 1864)

Lullabies for a Small World. (2003). [CD]. Various artists. United States: Ellipsis Arts.

Luther, B., Mayo, A., & Lindsey, C. (1999). There will come a day [Recorded by Faith Hill]. On *Breathe* [CD]. Nashville: Warner Bros.

Martin, C. D. (Words), & Gabriel, C. H. (Music). (1981). His eye is on the sparrow. In *Songs of Zion*, W. B. McClain (Ed.). Nashville, TN: Abingdon Press. (Original words written 1906)

Mathers, M. [aka Eminem]. (2002). Lose yourself [Recorded by Eminem]. On *8 mile* [CD]. United States: Interscope Records.

McCarthy-Miller, B., & Gallen, J. [Directors]. (2001). *America: A tribute to heroes* [Telethon Broadcast DVD]. United States: Wea/Warner Brothers.

McCartney, P., & Lennon, J. (1970). Let it be [Recorded by The Beatles]. On *Let it be* [LP]. United States: Capitol Records.

McEntire, R. (1991). *For my broken heart*. Nashville, TN: MCA Nashville.

McGraw, T. Official Page at GACTV.com. (2004, Sept.) *Tim McGraw live like you were dying*. Retrieved December 18, 2005 from http://www.gactv.com/artists/tim.html

McKennitt, L. (2004). *To drive the cold winter away* [CD & DVD]. United States: Quinlan Road Limited.

Mendelssohn, L. [Collector & Ed.]. (n.d.). *Lullabies of the world*, disc 1 & 2 [CDs]. Washington, D.C.: Smithsonian Folkways Recordings. (Original recording 1963 [Tape])

Mitchell, J. (2000). Both sides now. On *Both sides now* [CD]. United States: Warner Brothers. (Original recording 1968)

Moyers, B. (2002). *Amazing grace with Bill Moyers* [DVD]. United States: Films for the Humanities. (Original PBS TV 1992. Original VHS 1994)

Music from the Oklahoma City memorial service: A time of healing [CD] (1995). Various artists. United States: Warner Brothers.

Music of the Civil Rights Movement. (2005). Music of the civil rights movement. In *Silver Burdett Making Music*. Referenced December 18, 2005, from www.sbgmusic.com/html/teacher/reference/historical/civilrights.html

NBC's Today Show. (2004, June 4). *Dance, dance, dance revolution ultramix*. Retrieved December 18, 2005 from http://www.ddrgame.com

Newman, R. (Music & Words). (1974). "Louisiana 1927." Los Angeles, CA: WB Music Corp.

Nichols, T., & Wiseman, C. (2004). *Live like you were dying* [Book with CD]. Recorded by Tim McGraw. Nashville, TN: Rutledge Hill Press [book] and Curb Records [CD single].

Pulse: A stomp odyssey. (2002). Various artists [IMAX Theaters]. International: Giant Screen Films, Stern Productions, and Leve Productions, Walden Media, & Yes/No Productions.

Reagon, B. J. (1993). *We who believe in freedom will not rest — Sweet honey in the rock — Still on the journey* [Book & CD]. New York: Anchor Books, Doubleday.

Rodgers, R., & Hammerstein, O. (1999). Getting to know you. On *The king and I* [DVD]. United States: 20th Century Fox.

Sanders, M. T., & Silers, T. (2000). I hope you dance. Recorded by Lee Ann Womack on *I hope you dance* [CD and Book]. United States: Rutledge Hill Press.

Schumann, R. (Music) & Hinson, M. (Ed.) (1990). Träumerei (Dreaming), Op. 15, No. 7. In *World's Greatest Melodies for Piano*. Van Nuys, CA: Alfred Publishing Co., Inc. (Original work 1838)

Shamblin, A., & Nelson, B. (1992). It's never easy to say goodbye. Recorded by Wynona Judd on *Wynona* [CD]. Nashville, TN: Curb Records.

Simon, L. (Music), Schulman, S. H. (Director), Norman, M. (Lyrics), & Landesman, H. (Producer). (1991). *The secret garden (1991 original Broadway cast recording)* [CD]. New York: Sony.

Simon, P. (1964). The sound of silence. On *Simon and Garfunkel — Greatest hits* [LP], United States: Sony.

Simone, N. (1997). *Saga of the good life and hard times* [CD]. Indianapolis, IN: BMG Music.

Sing for freedom: The story of the civil rights movement through its songs. [CD]. (1992). Washington, D.C.: Smithsonian Folkways. Various Artists.

Sondheim, S. (2005). Putting it together. On *Sunday in the park with George: 1984 original Broadway cast* [CD]. United States: RCA. (Original recording 1984. Sung by Mandy Patinkin)

Springsteen, B. (1990). My father's house. On *Nebraska* [CD]. United States: Sony.

Springsteen, B. (2002). My city of ruin. On *The rising* [CD]. United States: Sony.

Strouse, C., & Charnin. M. (1998). Tomorrow. On *Annie* (1977; Original Broadway Cast) [CD]. [Recorded by Andrea McArdle]. United States: Sony. (Original recording 1977)

Taylor-Good, K. (2003). On angel's wings. On *On angel's wings* [CD & book]. Nashville: Insight Publications.

Taylor-Good, K., & Collins, B. (1993). How can I help you say goodbye? [Recorded by Patty Lovelace]. On *Only what I feel* [CD/cassette]. Nashville, TN: Epic.

Titon, J. T., Cornett, E., & Wallhausser, J. (1997). *Songs of the old regular baptists: Lined-out hymnody from South Eastern Kentucky.* Washington, D.C.: Smithsonian Folkways.

Washington, D.C.: Smithsonian Folkways. Various Artists.

Webber, A. L. [Music], Hart, C., & Stilgo, R. [Lyrics]. (1986). The music of the night [Recorded by Michael Crawford]. On *Phantom of the Opera* [CD]. London: Decca.

West, K. (2004). Jesus walks. On *College Dropout* [CD]. United States: Roc-a-Fella.

Websites

AARP Grief and Loss, Funeral Arrangements, End of Life, Community Resources
http://www.aarp.org/families/grief_loss

African Music Encyclopedia
http://www.africanmusic.org/glossary.html

ALS Association (Amyotrophic Lateral Sclerosis)
http://www.alsa.org

Alzheimer's Association
http://www.alz.org

American Music Therapy Association (AMTA)
http://www.musictherapy.org

American Orff Schülwerk Association (AOSA)
http://www.aosa.org

Association for Clinical Pastoral Education, Inc. (ACPE)
http://www.acpe.edu

Association for Death Education and Counseling (ADEC)
http://www.adec.org

Association of Professional Chaplains (APC)
http://www.professionalchaplains.org

Before Their Time
http://www.beforetheirtime.org

Caring Info: It's About How You Live
http://www.caringinfo.org

Centering Corporation – Your Grief Resource Center
http://www.centeringcorp.com

Certification Board for Music Therapists (CBMT)
http://www.cbmt.org

Children's Hospice International
http://www.chionline.org

Computer-Assisted Information Retrieval Service System
http://imr.utsa.edu/CAIRSS.html

Copyright Licensing and Compliance Solutions from Copyright Clearance Center
http://www.copyright.com

Dolmetsch Online Music Dictionary
http://www.dolmetsch.com/musictheorydefs.htm

EDELE Search Tool (Epidemiology of Dying and End-of-Life Experience)
http://www.edeledata.org

Emotional Intelligence Consortium: Research on Emotions and Emotional Intelligence
http://www.eiconsortium.org

Ethnomusicology, Folk Music, and World Music Contents, from University Libraries
http://www.lib.washington.edu/music/world.html

Growthhouse.org —Guide to Death, Dying, Grief, Bereavement, and End of Life Resources
http://www.growthhouse.org

Health Journeys: The Guided Imagery Resource Center
http://www.healthjourneys.com

Journal of Loss and Trauma
http://www.tandf.co.uk/journals/titles/15325024.asp

Lyric Search Net
http://www.lyricsearch.net

MMB Music, Inc.
http://www.mmbmusic.com

Multicultural Media: World Music Dance CD's and Videos
http://www.multiculturalmedia.com

MusicNotes.Com — Downloadable Music Scores
http://www.musicnotes.com

Music of the Soul — Joy S. Berger
http://www.musicofthesoul.com

National Hospice and Palliative Care Organization (NHPCO)
http://www.nhpco.org

NOJO — The Official Website of the New Orleans Jazz Orchestra
http://www.thenojo.com

Nordic Journal of Music Therapy
http://www.hisf.no/njmt/index.ssi

Peace Through World Music
http://www.rhythmweb.com/peace/index.html

Popular Song Lyrics Search Engine
http://www.lyricsfreak.com

Pulse: A Stomp Odyssey
http://www.pulsethemovie.com.

U. S. Copyright Office — Copyright Catalog: Books, Music, etc.
http://www.copyright.gov/records/cohm.html

Voices: A World Forum for Music Therapy
http://www.voices.no

Young People's Chorus of New York City
http://www.ypc.org.

INDEX

Y